WELCOMING THE

outsider

Homilies for the year of Luke

GEOFFREY PLANT

Published by
Garratt Publishing
32 Glenvale Crescent
Mulgrave, Vic. 3170
www.garrattpublishing.com.au

Copyright ©2009 Geoffrey Plant
Reprinted 2022

All rights reserved. Except as provided by the Australian copyright law, no part of this book may be reproduced in any way without permission in writing from the publisher.

Design and typesetting: JGD Graphic+Web www.jgd.com.au
Text editing: Cathy Oliver

National Library of Australia Cataloguing-in-Publication entry

Author: Plant, Geoffrey.

Title: Welcoming the outsider / Geoff Plant.

ISBN: 9781920682019 (pbk.)

Subjects: Preaching.

Dewey Number: 251

In memory of my parents,

Frank and Ruby,

whose lives were the finest homily.

Acknowledgements

The author and the publisher are grateful for permission from the following people and sources to reproduce copyright material : Michael Leuing ; 10 lines from Chapter One, from Care of the Soul by Thomas Moore, © 1992 Thomas Moore. Reprinted by permission of HarperCollins Publishers ; *Forgotton Among the Lilies* by Ronald Rolheiser (Doubleday, 2005) ; *Necessary Losses* by Judith Viorst
(N.Y. :Simon &Schuster, 1986).

Excerpts from THE JERUSALEM BIBLE, copyright (c) 1966 by Darton, Longman & Todd, Ltd. and Doubleday, a division of Random House, Inc. Reprinted by Permission.

Excerpts from THE NEW JERUSALEM BIBLE, copyright (c) 1985 by Darton, Longman & Todd, Ltd. and Doubleday, a division of Random House, Inc. Reprinted by Permission.

Every attempt has been made to contact holders of copyright. The author and publisher welcome inquiry from those where this was not possible.

CONTENTS

Introduction 7
First Sunday of Advent 10
Second Sunday of Advent 13
Third Sunday of Advent 17
Fourth Sunday of Advent 21
Christmas Day 24
Holy Family 28
Epiphany 31
First Sunday of Lent 35
Second Sunday of Lent 38
Third Sunday of Lent 42
Fourth Sunday of Lent 45
Fifth Sunday of Lent 49
Passion Sunday 52
Holy Thursday 54
Good Friday 56
Easter Sunday 58
Second Sunday of Easter 61
Third Sunday of Easter 64
Fourth Sunday of Easter 67
Fifth Sunday of Easter 70
Sixth Sunday of Easter 73
Seventh Sunday of Easter 76
Ascension of the Lord 79
Pentecost 82
Most Holy Trinity 86
Body and Blood of Christ 89
Assumption of the Blessed Virgin Mary 92
All Saints 94
Baptism of the Lord 97

Second Sunday in Ordinary Time 100
Third Sunday in Ordinary Time 103
Fourth Sunday in Ordinary Time 106
Fifth Sunday in Ordinary Time 109
Sixth Sunday in Ordinary Time 112
Seventh Sunday in Ordinary Time 115
Eighth Sunday in Ordinary Time 118
Ninth Sunday in Ordinary Time 121
Tenth Sunday in Ordinary Time 124
Eleventh Sunday in Ordinary Time 127
Twelfth Sunday in Ordinary Time 131
Thirteenth Sunday in Ordinary Time 135
Fourteenth Sunday in Ordinary Time 139
Fifteenth Sunday in Ordinary Time 142
Sixteenth Sunday in Ordinary Time 145
Seventeenth Sunday in Ordinary Time 148
Eighteenth Sunday in Ordinary Time 151
Nineteenth Sunday in Ordinary Time 154
Twentieth Sunday in Ordinary Time 158
Twenty-First Sunday in Ordinary Time 162
Twenty-Second Sunday in Ordinary Time 165
Twenty-third Sunday in Ordinary Time 168
Twenty-fourth Sunday in Ordinary Time 171
Twenty-fifth Sunday in Ordinary Time 174
Twenty-sixth Sunday in Ordinary Time 177
Twenty-seventh Sunday in Ordinary Time 181
Twenty-eighth Sunday in Ordinary Time 185
Twenty-ninth Sunday in Ordinary Time 188
Thirtieth Sunday in Ordinary Time 191
Thirty-first Sunday in Ordinary Time 193
Thirty-second Sunday in Ordinary Time 197
Thirty-third Sunday in Ordinary Time 201
Christ the King 204

INTRODUCTION

This book is a collection of homilies for Year C of the liturgical cycle, the year of St Luke. I have called it *Welcoming the outsider*, thereby sounding a note that resonates throughout Luke's gospel, and which is particularly evident in the stories unique to Luke. In Luke's infancy narrative, which functions as an overture to the gospel, the good news about the birth of Jesus is first announced to shepherds – people regarded as outsiders because they were unable to observe the full rigors of the Jewish Law (homily for the feast of the Epiphany). At the beginning of his public ministry Jesus returned to Nazareth and preached in the local synagogue. What an uproar he caused by reminding the locals of God's graciousness to two outsiders – Naaman the Syrian and a widow living in the town of Zarephath (fourth Sunday in Ordinary Time). And when asked, 'Who is my neighbour?' Jesus tells a story in which the hero is an outsider, a despised Samaritan (homily for the fifteenth Sunday in Ordinary Time). Luke alone tells the story of another Samaritan, one of ten lepers healed by Jesus, but the only one who returns to give thanks. The story that we know as the Prodigal Son is about two brothers who are both outside (though in different ways), and a father who goes outside to meet them (homily for the fourth Sunday of Lent). One of the criticisms constantly levelled against Jesus by the Pharisees was that he welcomed sinners and ate with them. Anthropologists point out that you can learn a great deal about a society by looking closely at who eats together. They argue that the dining table is a miniature of society at large. In choosing to eat with 'outsiders' Jesus confronts us with a powerful parable of the kingdom, not in words but in action (homily for the twenty-second Sunday in Ordinary Time). In Luke's gospel, the final words that Jesus spoke from the cross to another human being were addressed to an outsider: 'Today you will be with me in paradise.' Jesus died as he had lived, welcoming the outsider (homily for the feast of Christ the King).

A homily attempts to build a bridge between the word of God and the congregation for whom it is preached. This involves exegesis, a term that means 'to thrash or lead out.' Since there is no text without context, the homilist seeks first to thrash out the meaning of the text for those who first heard it. The second step is hermeneutics, a word related to the name Hermes, messenger and spokesman of the gods in Greek mythology. What message does this passage of scripture have for a congregation over two thousand years later? At the end of the Scripture readings at Mass the lector says: 'This is the Word of the Lord', and the congregation responds: 'Thanks be to God.' But we must keep in mind that this timeless Word of God is expressed in human words, in first century words and images. Like all words, they are limited by the age that produced them. Each subsequent generation of believers, and each culture, must journey beyond those first century words and images and allow the eternal Word of God to become incarnate in their own language and culture.

An earlier version of these homilies appeared in the *Australian Catholic Record,* and I am grateful to Fr Gerard Kelly for permission to reproduce them here. I would also like to express my gratitude to the parishioners of St Luke's Parish, Revesby, for their support and encouragement over the past nine years. I am a priest of the Archdiocese of Sydney, and that is reflected in many of these homilies. Those of you using this book as a resource for your own preaching will have to be creative in substituting local examples if I have been too parochial. In one homily, for example, I used a story that reflects the traditional animosity between two teams in the Australian Rugby League competition. But such animosity exists between teams in all sporting competitions, so nothing is lost by changing the names to reflect local prejudices. The homily for the Seventh Sunday of Easter refers to examples of religious intolerance in Sydney, but I'm sure this city doesn't hold a franchise on bigotry. Once again, preachers will have to substitute local examples if the homily is to ring true.

Creative homilists are literary scavengers, seeking an interesting story, an amusing anecdote, a deft phrase or an offbeat insight that can be dragooned into the service of the gospel. There is little originality in these homilies and I am ever conscious of the observation made by Bernard of Chartres (1080-1130), and recorded in John of Salisbury's *Metalogicon: 'Nos esse quasi nanos, gigantium humeris incidents,'* we are dwarfs, but we stand on the shoulders of giants.[1] So, let me acknowledge some of the shoulders I have stood upon. I have made good use of the Sacra Pagina and Anchor Bible commentaries on the New Testament, and I highly recommend Fr Brendan Byrne's study of Luke's gospel, *The Hospitality of God.* I still draw inspiration from William Barclay's New

---

[1] As quoted by John of Salisbury, *Metalogicon,* IVc, PL CXCIX, p.900.

Testament commentaries, and more recently from those by Bishop Tom Wright. I would also like to acknowledge my debt to the many books by Fr William Bausch, particularly *Storytelling: Imagination and Faith*. Fr Anthony de Mello's collections of stories are always close at hand, and Fr Ronald Rolheiser, the Reverend Alan Jones and Thomas Merton are constant companions on my own spiritual journey.

My thanks to Garry Eastman at John Garratt Publishing for his encouragement and support in publishing these homilies.

FIRST SUNDAY OF ADVENT

(YEAR C)

And then they will see the Son of Man coming in a cloud with power and great glory. (Lk 21:27)

January, the first month in our calendar, is named after the Roman god Janus, a name that derives from the Latin word for doorway. The month of January is therefore a doorway to the New Year. The god Janus was often represented with a double-faced head – one face turned backwards to the past; the other face towards the future. At the beginning of a new year we often look back over the past, and then look ahead to make resolutions for the future.

Advent is the beginning of the Church's liturgical year, and the Scripture readings for this season are also double-faced – looking backwards and forwards. We look backwards to Bethlehem, celebrating the birth of our Saviour, but the Advent readings also invite us to look forward, to the final coming of Christ in glory. Today's gospel directs our attention ahead – to the Son of Man who is coming at an hour we do not expect. The language describing this coming is dramatic. It is a good example of what is called apocalyptic writing. Apocalyptic is a Greek word meaning to reveal, or literally, to remove the veil or curtain. The future is hidden from our eyes, as if by a veil or a curtain. We may have a fairly good idea of what the rest of the day holds for us, but then again we may be in for a surprise. I suspect that most of us don't really want to peep through the curtain, to know what the future holds in store for us, at least not in precise detail. However, we might be consoled to know that in the end, all will be well. Apocalyptic writing is invariably addressed to communities who are being oppressed and it brings a message of hope. It doesn't attempt to predict the future in minute detail, but it does bring an assurance that all will be well.

Apocalyptic writing has its own stock of symbols and images, and today's gospel offers us a typical example: signs in the sun and moon and stars; nations in agony; the clamour of the ocean and its waves; and men dying of fear. Such images or picture language, even if they are not to be taken literally, capture the mood of gloom and foreboding felt by a community facing persecution. But they are not to fear, for the Lord is coming; liberation is near at hand.

As we begin this holy season of Advent we are confronted with an apocalyptic vision of the Son of Man coming in a cloud and great glory. It seems unnecessary to warn us to stay awake when confronted by such terrifying signs announcing his arrival. But will the Lord arrive in such a dramatic fashion?

I've always been fascinated by an amphitheatre that was built overlooking Sydney's Balmoral Beach. In early 1923 a woman by the name of Mary Eleanor Rocke began to purchase land at the northern end of Edwards Bay in Balmoral with the intention of building an amphitheatre on behalf of an organisation called the Order of the Star in the East. The amphitheatre was designed to face North Head and Middle Head, so it was ideally located to view the entrance to Sydney Harbour. The foundation stone was laid on July 28, 1923, and the amphitheatre was completed just over a year later. It towered over twenty metres above the beach and could accommodate more than three thousand people. It cost something in the vicinity of £20 000 to complete.[2]

And why did these people build such an elaborate structure looking out towards the entrance to Sydney harbour? The Order of the Star had as its sole purpose the preparation of the way for an expected World Teacher, or Messiah. They put it this way: 'We believe that a Great Teacher will soon appear in the world, and we wish so to live now that we may be worthy to know Him when He comes.'

It's hard to know whether the Order of the Star actually believed that their Great Teacher would come to Sydney, walking on the water through Sydney Heads. But that was the story that quickly spread about the amphitheatre. People generally believed that members of the Order of the Star had built the amphitheatre so that they would have box seats for the Second Coming. Alas, the Great Teacher failed to arrive and the amphitheatre was finally demolished in 1950. A block of flats now stands on the site. Throughout Christian history there has been no shortage of people who have predicted the time and the place of Christ's coming. We, too, are people waiting for the coming of Christ, but the gospel warns us that the Son of Man is coming

---

[2] For more information on the amphitheatre see P.R. Stephensen, *The History and Description of Sydney Harbour,* Rigby, Adelaide,1966, p.389; Jill Roe, 'Three visions of Sydney Heads from Balmoral Beach', in Jill Roe (ed) *Twentieth Century Sydney,* Hale and Iremonger in association with The Sydney History Group, Sydney, 1980, pp. 89-104; 'Balmoral Amphitheatre', *The Sydney Morning Herald,* (January 15, 1937), 4; Keith Newman, 'Amphitheatre To Become Flats', *The Sydney Morning Herald,* (April 16, 1950), 2. For photographs of the amphitheatre,
see http://image.sl.nsw.gov.au/cgi-bin/ebindshowpl?doc=pxa215/a971;thumbs=1

at an hour we do not expect. The Lord seldom enters our lives in a blaze of glory. More often than not, he speaks to us in and through the tedium of daily life, and so we must remain attentive to the present moment.

The Zen tradition tells of a man fleeing a ferocious tiger. The animal steadily gains ground and the hapless victim can run no further, for he has come to the edge of a cliff. If he stands his ground, the tiger will devour him. To leap from this height means certain death on the rocks below. In desperation he scrambles over the edge of the cliff, clutching a vine sprouting from a crevice in the rock face. But the fragile vine cannot bear his weight and will surely break. He must choose — death from the tiger above or the rocks below. But just at that moment he catches sight of a cluster of wild strawberries growing on a nearby ledge. Reaching out he plucks one and eats it with great delight. Ahh!

And ….? What happened next? Well, that's not the right question to ask. It is easy to be so obsessed with the tiger above or the rocks below that we fail to savour the strawberry of the moment. We're so often elsewhere rather than here, in the present moment. We're inattentive to what is right before our eyes. Consider the parable of the presbytery garden. When I arrived at my present parish I planted roses and gerberas, two of my favourite flowers, in the small garden bed in front of the presbytery. A friend who is a passionate advocate of native Australian plants keeps reminding me that much of the flora brought to Australia by European settlers (including my roses) is not suitable for our harsh and dry climate. It's taken us a long time to appreciate the beauty of Australian native species, and to acknowledge the reality of our dry climate. I've now started planting Grevilleas, and they are thriving, despite the dry soil and lack of rain. Be attentive to where you are!

Jesus criticised his contemporaries for not reading the 'signs of the times.' They looked to the sky and forecast the weather, but they were oblivious to the signs of God's presence in their midst. That can happen when we look in the wrong place, or fail to see what is right before our eyes. The Lord does not come into our lives in a blaze of glory, walking upon the water through Sydney Heads. More often than not, he comes to us, unannounced, unheralded and unexpected, amidst the ordinary tedium of our daily lives.

SECOND SUNDAY OF ADVENT

(YEAR C)

A voice cries in the wilderness,
' Prepare a way for the Lord, make his paths straight'. (Lk 3:4)

John the Baptist emerges from the desert with a message of repentance. The desert may be understood on several different levels. The desert from which John emerged was an actual place, but 'the desert may also be understood as an inner geography of desolation and abandonment ... It is the valley of our deepest solitude.' [3] The desert is not primarily a place; it is an experience. It is not a setting; it is a state of soul. There's been a revival of interest throughout much of this century in the story and the spirituality of the desert. The story of the desert is associated with the Desert Fathers and Mothers who fled into the deserts of Egypt, Palestine, Arabia and Persia in the fourth and fifth centuries. They fled into the desert to find both God and themselves. But the desert tradition finds its origins much earlier than the fourth and fifth centuries. The origins of the desert tradition are to be found in the Old Testament, especially in that epic story we call the Exodus, the great story of liberation from slavery in Egypt.

The long years of the Exodus were a period of testing and discovery. It was in the wilderness the children of Israel found their identity as a people. It was in the wilderness they received the Law; it was there they received their vocation. Nothing would ever be the same again. It was a defining moment, and all of the subsequent history of the Jewish people must be interpreted in the light of that experience.

The desert is both a place and an experience, but it is never an end in itself. So, what happens in the desert? Firstly, the desert is a place of solitude. Solitude must never be confused with loneliness or isolation. The German Protestant theologian Dietrich Bonhoeffer (1906-1945) who was murdered by the Nazis in 1945, wrote a book called *Life Together.* It grew out of his experience of teaching people preparing for the ministry. One chapter he calls 'The Day with Others'; another chapter he calls 'The Day Alone.' In 'The Day Alone', he observes: 'Let him who cannot be alone beware of community. He will only do harm to himself

---

[3] John Chryssavgis, *In the Heart of the Desert*, World Wisdom, Bloomington, Indiana, 2003, p.xi.

and to the community.'[4] He explains that many people are driven to seek the company of others because they cannot endure being alone. They use others as a means of running away from themselves.

Solitude does not necessarily imply an abandonment of the world. Theophan the Recluse said: 'Do not forget that you can be alone amid the noise of the world; and equally you can be surrounded by the hubbub of the world whilst withdrawn in the wilderness.'[5] In chapter six of St Matthew's gospel, we hear the words of Jesus: 'When you pray, go into your room and shut the door and pray to your Father who is in secret, and your Father who sees all that is done in secret will reward you (6:6).' The room, the solitary place, the inner hermitage, is the arena for engagement and encounter. Pope John Paul II once observed 'No movement in religious life has any value unless it is also a movement inwards to the 'still centre' of your existence, where Christ is.'[6]

The solitude of the desert teaches the necessity of waiting upon God. It teaches lessons of patience, attentiveness, learning to be unhurried, waiting in silence, and perseverance. The spiritual writer Alessandro Pronzato says this:

Never be in a hurry. Do not expect to hear God's word immediately on your arrival in the desert. You must wait in silence. Your whole being should be in an attitude of listening. All other activities should be subordinated to the act of waiting for God. And God may speak through His word or through His silence.[7]

Secondly, the wilderness or the desert is a place of testing. The desert exposes our vulnerabilities. It brings to the surface the fears that are buried deep within ourselves. Brother Ivan has this to say: 'Each one of us has to confront the terrible demons which we carry inside: demons of aggression, resentment, pride, sadness, despair.'[8] Pronzato says:

If you therefore go to the desert to be rid of all the dreadful people and all the awful problems in your life, you will be wasting your time. You should go to the desert for a total confrontation with yourself. For one goes to the desert to see more and to see better. One goes to the desert especially to take a closer took at the things and people one would rather not see, to face situations one would rather avoid, to answer questions one would rather forget.[9]

The life of the American Trappist monk Thomas Merton was a journey into the

---

[4] Dietrich Bonhoeffer, *Life Together*, SCM Press, London, Seventh Impression, 1968, p.57.
[5] John Moses, *The Desert, An Anthology for Lent*, Canterbury Press, Norwich, 1997, p. 39.
[6] Adrian B. Smith, *'The Spiritual Value of Transcendental Meditation'*, in Spirituality, Vol 3, Sept-Oct, 1977, No. 14, p.306.
[7] John Moses, op. cit., p.42.
[8] Ibid, p.55.

desert. He was born in France on January 31, 1915. His mother was an American and his father a New Zealander, but the family moved to the United States to avoid the war. His mother died when he was six years of age, and Merton and his younger brother John Paul accompanied their father firstly to Bermuda and then back to France. After completing his primary schooling in France Merton was sent to board at Oakham Public School in England. His father Owen died a few days before Tom turned 16.

Merton won a scholarship to Clare College, Cambridge, but he behaved badly at university. His guardian, Tom Bennett, told him to amend his ways, but to no avail. At the end of his first academic year he set sail for America, and his guardian strongly advised him not to return to Cambridge. Merton took his advice and enrolled at Columbia University in New York City, where he successfully completed a Master of Arts degree. Tom became increasingly interested in religion, specifically Catholicism, and was eventually baptized on November 16, 1938 at the age of 23.

After making a retreat at the Cistercian Abbey, Our Lady of Gethsemani, near Louisville, Kentucky, Merton wrote to the Abbot asking if there was any prospect of his being received as novice. The Cistercians accepted him and he was formally received into the monastery on December 13, 1941, at the age of 26. The monastery of Our Lady of Gethsemani followed a rule of life that went back to the sixth century: the rule of St Benedict. The Cistercians (named after their mother house Citeaux) were an eleventh century reform movement, interpreting the rule more strictly than other Benedictines. The Trappists were a reform of the Cistercian movement, named after the Abbey of La Trappe. They lived the monastic life even more strictly than the eleventh century Cistercians, and hence they became known as the Cistercians of the Strict Observance or, more informally, as Trappists.

When Merton joined the monastery, some 20 years before the changes inaugurated by the Second Vatican Council, life at Gethsemani was strict. The monks used horses instead of tractors to plough their fields. They slept in dormitories with little privacy and no central heating. All the monks slept fully clothed on straw mattresses, supported by four planks. The meals were meagre: no meat, fish or eggs. Nor did the monks speak to one another. They communicated through sign language. Despite the austerities of Cistercian life, Merton longed for solitude, and in August 1965 at the age of 50 he received permission to take

[9] Ibid, p.57.

up full-time residence in a small dwelling on the monastic property. And what did life in the hermitage teach him?

The world of men, he wrote, has forgotten the joys of silence, the peace of solitude which is necessary, to some extent, for the fullness of human living. Not all men are called to be hermits, but all men need enough silence and solitude in their lives to enable the deep inner voice of their own true self to be heard at least occasionally. When that inner voice is not heard, when man cannot attain to the spiritual peace that comes from being perfectly at one with his own true self, his life is always miserable and exhausting. For he cannot go on happily for long unless he is in contact with the springs of spiritual life which are hidden in the depths of his own soul.[10]

Merton was emphatic on the need for solitude. 'Without solitude of some sort there is and can be no maturity. Unless one becomes empty and alone, he cannot give himself in love because he does not possess the deep self which is the only gift worthy of love.'[11]

---

[10] Thomas Merton, *The Silent Life*, Farrar Straus & Giroux, New York, 1957/1991, p.166.
[11] Thomas Merton, *Disputed Questions*, A Harvest Book, San Diego, 1960, p.207.

THIRD SUNDAY OF ADVENT

(YEAR C)

'What must we do?' (Lk 3: 10)

You'll notice that the third of our Advent candles is rose-coloured. This Sunday in Advent was once known as *Gaudete* Sunday because the theme of rejoicing pervades the liturgy (*Gaudete*, the Latin for 'rejoice', being the opening word of the old Introit antiphon, taken from St Paul's letter to the Philippians, and now today's second reading). The liturgy invites us to rejoice because of the proximity of salvation, and the rose-coloured candle symbolises that joy.

Three groups of people come to John the Baptist asking, 'What must we do?' John doesn't encourage them to give away all their possessions and follow him, nor does he counsel the soldiers and tax collectors to abandon their jobs and take up a more genteel profession. He simply exhorts them to be people of integrity and compassion in what they are already doing. Tax collectors are to be honest; soldiers must be content with their pay and not abuse their authority; and people in general must reach out to the poor.

The congregation founded by Mother Teresa, the Missionaries of Charity, established a refuge for destitute men in the Melbourne suburb of Fitzroy. During one of her visits to Melbourne Mother Teresa was approached by a young man who volunteered to accompany her back to Calcutta. 'I want to love and serve Jesus by working with you among the poorest of the poor in the slums of Calcutta.' Mother Teresa looked kindly at the young man but replied, 'If you wish to love and serve Jesus you don't have to travel any further than Melbourne.' There is always a temptation to think that God is calling us to work for the kingdom in exotic and faraway places, and for a handful of people that may be true. But for most of us the call to fidelity is to be lived out right where we are.

In his book *Care of the Soul* the American psychotherapist Thomas Moore writes about a patient who was depressed and completely bored with his job. For over ten years he'd been employed in a manufacturing shop, and during all that time he was planning his escape. He would go back to school to gain the necessary qualifications to enter a profession that he liked. But he was so preoccupied with his plan of escape that his work suffered. Years went by, and he became increasingly dissatisfied. He hated his job. If only he could realise his ambitions. 'Have you ever thought,' Moore asked him one day, 'of being where you are, of entering fully this job that you're putting your time and energy into?'

'It's not worth it,' he said. 'It's beneath me. A robot could do it better.'

'But you do it every day,' Moore observed. 'And you do it badly, and you feel bad about yourself for doing it badly.'

'You're saying,' he said incredulously, 'that I should go to this stupid job as if my heart were in it?'

'You're in it, aren't you?'

He came back in a week to say that something had changed in him as he began to take his 'stupid' job more seriously.[12]

Eckhart Tolle, author of the best seller The Power of Now, asks a question of his reader: 'Are you resisting your here and now?' He points out that 'Some people would always rather be somewhere else. Their 'here' is never good enough.'[13] He uses a parable to make his point:

A beggar had been sitting by the side of a road for over thirty years. One day a stranger walked by. 'Spare some change?' mumbled the beggar, mechanically holding out his old baseball cap. 'I have nothing to give you,' said the stranger. Then he asked: 'What's that you are sitting on?' 'Nothing,' replied the beggar. 'Just an old box. I have been sitting on it for as long as I can remember.' 'Ever looked inside?' asked the stranger. 'No,' said the beggar. 'What's the point? There's nothing in there.' 'Have a look inside,' insisted the stranger. The beggar managed to pry open the lid. With astonishment, disbelief, and elation, he saw that the box was filled with gold.[14]

Fr John S. Dunne, Professor of Theology at the University of Notre Dame, tells of early Spanish sailors who reached the continent of South America after an arduous voyage. As they approached the mouth of the Amazon River, an expanse of water over 325 kilometres wide, the sailors assumed it was a continuation of the Atlantic Ocean. The Amazon River contains over 20 percent of the earth's fresh water, and during the rainy season it discharges over 300 000 cubic metres per second into the ocean. Fresh water can be detected over 320 kilometres out to sea, and the water is drinkable well beyond sight of the coastline. Sailing upon

---

[12] Thomas Moore, *Care of the Soul*, HarperPerennial, New York , 1994, p.8.
[13] Eckhart Tolle, *The Power of Now*, Hodder, Sydney, 2004, p.82.
[14] Ibid, p.11.

the world's largest source of fresh water, some of the sailors died of thirst.[15] Be alert to the present moment.

The Peanuts character Lucy is sitting at her booth offering psychiatric help for five cents. Charlie Brown seeks her counsel: 'What can you do when life seems to be passing you by?' Lucy invites Charlie to follow her to the top of a small hill and she points to the horizon. 'See the horizon over there? See how big this world is? See how much room there is for everybody?' She then asks, 'Have you seen any other worlds?' To which Charlie replies, 'No.' Lucy continues: 'As far as you know this is the only world there is ... right?' Charlie agrees, 'Right.' She pushes on: 'There are no other worlds for you to live in ... Right?' Again, Charlie agrees, 'Right.' 'Well,' shouts Lucy, 'live in it then!' [16]

John Shea tells of Andrea Kulin's experience of being attentive to the present moment:

I've had the experience, while teaching, of sitting with a distressed child and being uncertain how to help. Sometimes, rather than going into my own reaction of distress, I was able to be there quietly, openly, just 'taking in' the child, and from somewhere, something came that was the right thing, the thing the child needed. I don't know where that came from but it felt like a different form of intelligence.[17]

'Age quod agis', says John the Baptist, do well what you do. Be good tax collectors; be good soldiers. Fr Ronald Rolheiser makes a pertinent observation: Rarely is life enough for us. *Rarely are we able to live restfully the spirit of our own lives. Most often what, where, and how we are living seem small, insignificant, petty and depressingly domestic ... Rarely do we taste the coffee we drink. Instead we go through our days too preoccupied, too compulsive, too driven and too dissatisfied to really be able to be present to and celebrate our own lives. Always, it seems, we are somehow missing out on life.* [18]

It is a perennial temptation to think that I could find God if only I were *there* rather than *here*; if I were employed doing *that* rather than *this*. John the Baptist's message finds an echo in the advice that Martin Luther King offered to a group of students six months before he was assassinated:

If it falls to your lot to be a street sweeper, sweep streets like Michelangelo

---

[15] cf. Philip Yancey, *Finding God in Unexpected Places*, Hodder & Stoughton, London, 2002, pp.xii-xiii.
[16] Charles Schulz, *The Complete Peanuts*, 1963 to 1964, Fantagraphics Books, Seattle, 2007, p.114.
[17] John Shea, *Eating With the Bridegroom*, Liturgical Press, Collegeville, 2005, pp.22-3.
[18] Ronald Rolheiser, *Forgotten Among the Lilies*, Doubleday, New York, 2005, p. ix.

painted, sweep streets like Beethoven composed music, sweep streets like Leontyne Price sings before the Metropolitan Opera. Sweep streets like Shakespeare wrote poetry. Sweep streets so well that all the hosts of heaven and earth will pause to say: Here lived a great street sweeper who did his job well.[19]

---

[19] From a talk to a group of students at Barratt Junior High School, Philadelphia, October 26, 1967. For the full text of the speech see http://seattletimes.nwsource.com/mlk/king/words/blueprint.html.

FOURTH SUNDAY OF ADVENT

(YEAR C)

Yes, blessed is she who believed that the promise made her by the Lord would be fulfilled. (Lk 1:45)

Mary set out to visit her cousin Elizabeth in the hill country of Judah, a journey of about one hundred kilometres to the south. Mary would have been about twelve, the traditional age at which a girl was betrothed in first century Palestine. It was an arduous journey, but Elizabeth was delighted and greatly honoured to receive a visit from her cousin. Mary supported her elderly relative during the final stages of pregnancy, and was undoubtedly present for the birth of Elizabeth's son, John, whom we know as the Baptist. In welcoming Mary, Elizabeth also welcomed her Lord, for Mary herself was pregnant at the time of her visit. Catholics know this scene as the second joyful mystery of the rosary, the Visitation.

Artists have painted the scene of the Visitation many times, often portraying the meeting between Elizabeth and Mary embracing, in royal robes, with a retinue of servants to care for the messy details of life. In reality, of course, they were two peasant women who journeyed on foot, and certainly without servants or ladies-in-waiting.

As you know, both Mary and Elizabeth conceived in unusual circumstances. The angel Gabriel greeted Mary with the news that she was to conceive and bear a son. 'How can this come about' Mary asks, 'since I am a virgin?' The Holy Spirit will come upon you and the power of the Most High will cover you with its shadow. And so, this teenager gave her fiat: 'Let what you have said be done to me.' Denise Levertov's poem Annunciation reflects Mary's courage. 'She did not cry, 'I cannot, I am not worthy,' / nor 'I have not the strength.' / She did not submit with gritted teeth, / raging, coerced. / …. Courage unparalleled, / opened her utterly.' [20]

The circumstances surrounding Elizabeth's pregnancy were also mysterious. While Zechariah her husband was serving in the temple the angel Gabriel

---

[20] For a copy of the poem, go to
http://www.chriscorrigan.com/parkinglot/levertov.htm#_Toc23572792

appeared to him with the news that Elizabeth, although well beyond the age of child-bearing, would bear a son. Zechariah doubted, and was rendered dumb until the birth of the child.

Catholics have always revered Mary and called her blessed, but not primarily because she is the biological mother of Jesus. There is a scene in the gospels in which Jesus was surrounded by a crowd, and Mary and the family of Jesus were seeking him. Unable to make their way through the crowd they passed on a message to him. When Jesus was told, 'Your mother and brothers and sisters are outside asking for you', he replied, 'Who are my mother and my brothers?' And looking round at those sitting in a circle about him, he said, 'Here are my mother and my brothers. Anyone who does the will of God, that person is my brother and sister and mother (Mk 3:34-35).'

Mary and Elizabeth are therefore truly related to Jesus because they said a resounding 'Yes' to the will of God in their lives. They stepped out in faith. And what is faith? Faith is a word that has many shades of meaning. A few days ago a student asked me the difference between an agnostic and an atheist. He wasn't sure which of the two he was. I explained that an agnostic is a person who doesn't have absolute certitude about the existence of God. The word comes from the Latin *agnoscere,* meaning to be uncertain. An atheist on the other hand is a person who states categorically that God does not exist. I would love to have the certitude of the atheist! I think I startled the student when I admitted that I was an agnostic. I went on to explain that our human journey is peppered with doubt and belief and unbelief are inextricably woven into the fabric of every believer's soul. Italy's greatest poet, Dante Alighieri, commenced his epic masterpiece, *La Commedia,* with the words 'In the middle of the road of my life I awoke in a dark wood where the true way was wholly lost.' Lost within the 'labyrinth of life', we must wind the golden string into a ball and find our way out. [21] The Cistertian monk, Thomas Merton once prayed, 'My Lord God, I have no idea where I am going. I do not see the road ahead of me. I cannot know for certain where it will end.' [22] And Legolas the Elf, a character in J.R.R. Tolkien's The Lord of the Rings, observed that 'Few can foresee whither their road will lead them, till they come to its end.' [23] We are all pilgrims and, in the words of Cardinal Basil Hume, 'A pilgrim wanders through life, often limping,

---

[21] Bede Griffiths, *The Golden String*, Harvill Press, London 1954), 11.
[22] Thomas Merton, *Thoughts in Solitude,* Burns and Oates, Sixth Impression, London, 1991, p.84.
[23] J.R.R. Tolkien, *The Two Towers,* HarperCollins, London, 1997, p.481.

sometimes bewildered, at times quite lost; and the pilgrim is searching, often quite unconsciously, for something or someone to make sense of life, and certainly to make sense of death.' [24]

In the face of doubt and bewilderment, Mary and Elizabeth placed their faith in God's word. A young rock climber became stranded halfway up a cliff face, fearful that he could go no further and unable to return below. He was hanging on for dear life to a vine that was growing in a crevice in the rock face. He began to pray. Then he heard the voice of God asking him, 'Do you really believe in me?' 'I do, I do!' he replied, as his life hung in the balance. 'Do you trust me?' asked the voice of God. 'Yes, yes!' the man answered. Then the voice of God came back: 'then I will see to it that you are saved. Now do what I tell you to do. Now ... Let go!'

---

[24] Basil Hume, *To Be A Pilgrim*, St Paul Publications, London, 1984, p.38.

CHRISTMAS DAY

(DECEMBER 25)

As for Mary, she treasured all these things and pondered them in her heart.
(Lk 2: 19)

A few days before Christmas, 2007, The Sydney Morning Herald carried an article entitled 'One wise man's different spin on things.' The article quoted the Archbishop of Canterbury, Dr Rowan Williams, who referred to the story of the three wise men as nothing but a 'legend'. He is also reported to have said that not all followers must believe in the virgin birth of Jesus. The Australian's coverage of the same story included responses from some local church leaders. Sydney's Catholic archbishop, Cardinal George Pell, was clear and unambiguous. 'What is important is that the Christ child was and is the son of God,' he said. 'For this belief and fact, the virgin birth is essential. Those who doubt or deny this are departing from essential Christian teaching.'[25]

We are understandably curious about what really happened, but ultimately questions about meaning are far more important. In 1941 the German biblical scholar Rudolf Bultmann employed the term 'demythologise' to describe his attempt to express the theological meaning of the bible's mythological language.[26] In other words, he was attempting to discover the meaning that lay behind the narrative. So, rather than asking the question, did the magi (or wise men) really exist?, we might find it more productive to ask what St Matthew sought to tell us when he (and he alone) included the story of the wise men in his gospel. And what were the gospel writers telling us about Jesus through the story of the virgin birth?

We look at life with what John Shelby Spong describes as a 'Western mind-set' that conditions us to demand 'a yes-or-no answer.' In other words, something either happened or it did not; it was either real or it was not.[27] Perhaps that's

---

[25] 'One wise man's different spin on things', *The Sydney Morning Herald*, December 21-23, 2007; Jill Rowbotham, 'Three wise men leading us astray', *The Australian*, December 21, 2007. For a transcript of the Archbishop of Canterbury's BBC interview, check his website: http://www.archbishopofcanterbury.org/

[26] FL Cross and EA Livingstone, *The Oxford Dictionary of the Christian Church*, Oxford University Press, Reprinted 1997, p.468.

[27] John Shelby Spong, *Resurrection: Myth or Reality,* Harper, San Francisco, 1994, pp.9-10.

why the word 'myth' has acquired pejorative connotations in colloquial usage. We use the word to describe a story that may sound plausible at first hearing, but doesn't stand up to closer scrutiny. In the lead up to the 2008 federal election, for example, the Government ran a number of advertisements about the workplace relations system. It is a 'myth', the advertisement told us, that 'nowadays, employers can do practically anything they like.' The 'fact' of the matters is 'No they can't.'[28] Myth in this sense is synonymous with 'misinformation' or 'falsehood'. In a recent Quick Crossword, the clue was 'Falsehood (4)', and the anticipated answer was 'myth'.[29] The word 'myth' in its more technical sense refers to the great stories of humanity that help us to navigate our way through the mystery of human existence. They may or may not be based on historical events. The truth of these epic stories, however, lies beneath the narrative level and we will be unduly distracted if we become overly preoccupied with their historicity. Or to put it another way, viewed from the outside some stories are incomprehensible. One must enter them, for their truth is experienced only from the inside.[30]

Consider an example. The 1200-year-old Anglo-Saxon epic *Beowulf* was recently made into a movie directed by Robert Zemeckis. Is it a true story? The first part of Beowulf tells of how the peaceful seaside community of Heorot is rudely shattered by the arrival of Grendel, a monster of almost supernatural power, who lives in the depths of a nearby lake. The inhabitants of Heorot are terrorised as, night by night, Grendel attacks the hall in which they sleep, seizing one victim after another and tearing them to pieces. Enter the hero Beowulf, who sets out to do battle, first with Grendel, and then with his even more terrible monster mother. There is a tremendous climactic battle, with much severing of limbs and threshing about underwater, until both monsters are slain. The community comes together in great jubilation; the threat has been lifted and normal life can continue again.[31]

If we stripped away the mythical elements of Beowulf, would the story be any less compelling? Well, in the mid-1970s you probably saw a 'demythologised' version of the story. Huge queues formed outside cinemas all over the Western

---

[28] This full page advertisement appeared, for example, in Melbourne's *Herald Sun,* on Friday August 3, 2007.
[29] The *Sydney Morning Herald*, Friday, January 30, 2009.
[30] Cf. Elie Wiesel, *Souls on Fire: Portraits and Legends of Hasidic Masters*, Simon & Schuster Paperbacks, New York, 1972, p.5. Wiesel is referring specifically to tales about the Baal Shem, but his observation has a much wider relevance.
[31] Christopher Booker, *The Seven Basic Plots,* Continuum, New York, 2004, pp.1-2.

world to see one of the most dramatic horror films ever made. Steven Spielberg's *Jaws* told the story about a little Long Island seaside resort, Amity, that was terrorised by presence of a monstrous shark of almost supernatural power. For weeks on end the life of the community is overwhelmed by fear and confusion as the shark savagely attacks one victim after another. Enter the hero, the local police chief Brody, who sets out with two companions to do battle with the monster. There is a tremendous climactic fight, with much severing of limbs and threshing about underwater, until at last the shark is slain.[32] Sounds familiar, doesn't it? Beowulf demythologised! Both stories are variations on one of the seven basic themes of literature identified by Christopher Booker: 'Overcoming the Monster.' The dynamic of such stories is essentially the same, whether they be about historical tyrants such as Hitler or Pol Pot or fictional characters such as Grendel.[33]

Everyone was astonished at what the shepherds had to say, and we, like Mary, are invited ponder these things in our hearts. What is Christmas about, once we get to the core of the story? Let's leave aside, for a moment, aspects of the story that some people may find hard to accept – angelic appearances to shepherds, the star of Bethlehem, the wise men from the east, the virgin birth, the slaughter of the innocents, and the flight into Egypt. What might a contemporary, 'demythologised' version of Christmas look like?

Inspired by the Montreal Homeless Men's Choir and his previous experience with the Sydney Street Choir, Opera Australia tenor Jonathan Welch gathered together a group of homeless people to form *The Choir of Hard Knocks*. There were poor people, many struggling with mental illness, alcohol and drug addiction; some were feeling lost after broken relationships. All of them in one way or another were marginalised from mainstream society. But they could all sing. Some sang well, others not so well.

The whole venture was not without its risks and disappointments. There were personality clashes, the collapse of good resolutions and sundry upheavals. This is not a story about instant transformations, about humpty-dumpty being put back together again once and for all. As Jonathon Welch said on the television program *60 Minutes:*

It's called the revolving door – they come through the door and then they're

---

[32] Ibid, p.1.
[33] Ibid, p.21.

okay for a little bit of time and then they go back (to) the other side through the door and then they come back and then they go around again and that's part of, that part of the demon that they are struggling with and the illnesses that they are struggling with too, but all I try to say is that the door was always open.

There developed a great sense of working together and often for the first time in ages a sense of joy and of seeing themselves as people of worth. I don't know what Jonathan Welch's religious background is but as the story unfolded he appeared to me as a truly Jesus figure: reaching out to people discarded by the rest of society; forming those people into a genuine community; enabling them to forgive themselves and make a new start in life; helping them to recognise their intrinsic worth; teaching them to love one another and put aside their petty differences; challenging them to discover and to realise their true potential; teaching them to love life and to live it to the full.[34]

At its core, is that not the story of the incarnation? Amidst the fragility and brokenness of our humanity, God takes flesh and becomes as we are – forming us into community; enabling us to forgive ourselves and to make a new start in life; helping us to recognise our intrinsic worth; teaching us to love one another and put aside our petty differences; challenging us to discover and realise our true potential as human beings; and teaching us to love life and live it to the full.

---

[34] This reflection on The Choir of Hard Knocks comes from a talk given by Bishop Pat Power at Chevalier College, Bowral, 10 November, 2007. Peter Harvey's interview with Jonathan Welch was part of the *60 Minutes* program, broadcast on GTV9 on July 15, 2007.

THE HOLY FAMILY OF JESUS, MARY AND JOSEPH

(YEAR C)

He went down with them then and came to Nazareth and lived under their authority. (Lk 2: 51).

It is the Christmas story that sets the Christian faith apart from all other religions. Christianity makes the claim that in the person of Jesus, God assumes our humanity and becomes as we are. He lived under the authority of Mary and Joseph, and grew in wisdom, stature, and favour with God as a member of a family.

As with Jesus, so with all of us: the family is the most important school of holiness in our society. Most of us first heard the Christmas story from our parents. I learnt how to pray within my family. I first experienced love, compassion and forgiveness within my family. I first heard the gospel, not as spoken words, but as a lived reality, within my family. For that reason, I found it strange that when I entered the seminary in 1965 my family was held at arms length. Parents were permitted four brief visits during the year, and we were allowed to write home only once a month. All letters had to be submitted unsealed to the Master of Students, and on more than one occasion I had to rewrite letters to my family, either because of spelling mistakes, or because I had said something that was deemed to be inappropriate.

I still have a copy of the rule book. The first year of seminary life didn't really encourage visitors, but if they came, we had to make their visit short and snappy. Rule number 69 says: 'All shall avoid conversation with seculars, not only with women, but also with men, as being harmful to the spirit of devotion.' Rule number 72 said that we should avoid kissing even our own relations. It was as if the family that had nurtured my vocation might suddenly become an agent of subversion. Fortunately, the situation has changed in the years following the Second Vatican Council. But if one looks closely at the windows in most Catholic churches, and if one consults the list of saints canonised in recent years, the conclusion is overwhelming. If you want to be a canonised saint, then become a priest or a member of a religious order. Or failing that, try martyrdom! Almost anything but living in a family! Just look around at the sacred images in most churches. Most of the other people presented to us as heroes of the faith are members of the clergy or religious orders. By any objective standard, that is an extremely jaundiced view of sanctity.

In the fourth and fifth centuries, many Christians sought to become saints by fleeing into the desert. They are known to us as the desert fathers and mothers, and we have record of their quest for holiness.[35] They sought sanctity in the solitude of the desert because they felt that a saintly life was difficult or impossible amidst the evil and corruption of the city.

And so it was that over 1700 hundred years ago, a young man decided to become a saint. He left his home, family and possessions. He said goodbye to relatives and friends, sold all he owned, gave the money to the poor, and walked off into the desert to find God. He walked through the desert sands until he found a dark cave. In the solitude of his cave, he thought: 'Here I will be alone with God. Here nothing can distract me from God.

He prayed day and night in the dark cave. But God sent him great temptations. He began to imagine all of the good things of life that he had left behind, and he wanted them desperately. But he was determined to give up everything in order to have God alone. After many months the temptations stopped. And so this young man, whom the Church now knows as St Antony of Egypt, was at peace, having nothing but God.

But according to legend, God spoke to him during prayer. 'Antony, leave your cave for a few days and go off to a distant town. Look for the town shoemaker. Knock on his door and stay with him for a while.' The holy hermit was puzzled by God's command, but he did as the voice of God commanded, and left the next morning. He walked all day across the desert sands, and by nightfall he came at last to a small village. Finding the small dwelling of the shoemaker, he knocked on the door and was greeted by a smiling face. 'Come in and join us for a meal', said the shoemaker. 'You look tired and hungry, and you need a bed for the night.' The shoemaker called his wife, and they prepared a fine meal for the hermit and gave him a good bed to

---

[35] The collection of their sayings is known as the *Verba Seniorum* (literally, the words of the elders). For an English translation see Benedicta Ward, *The Desert Fathers: Sayings of the Early Christian Monks*, Penguin Books, London, p.2003). See also, Thomas Merton, *The Wisdom of the Desert*, Sheldon Press, London, 1974.

sleep on. The hermit stayed with the shoemaker and his family for three days.

He was deeply touched by the love he experienced within that family, although his cave seemed more and more attractive when the baby cried during the night, and the young children jumped all over him to greet him each morning. The hermit asked many questions about their lives, but he didn't tell them much about himself, even though the couple was very curious about his life in the desert. They talked a lot and became good friends. Then the hermit said his goodbye to the shoemaker and his family. He walked back to his cave wondering why God had sent him to visit this family. It was when he had settled down again in his cave that he again heard the voice of God, asking him: 'What was the shoemaker like?' The hermit answered:

He is a simple man. He has a wife and children. They seem to love each other very much. He has a small shop where he makes shoes. He works very hard. They have a simple house. They give money and food to those who have less then they have. And they have a strong faith in you and pray often. They have many friends. And the shoemaker enjoys telling jokes.

God listened carefully, then said: 'You are a great saint, Antony. And the shoemaker and his wife, they, too, are great saints'.[36]

Herein lies a simple yet profound truth. The Lord calls us into his kingdom by many different paths. Some, like Antony, are called to serve God in religious life; others like the shoemaker and his wife serve God through family life. Antony was called to holiness through the solitude of the desert; most Christians, though, are called to holiness by quite a different path, a path you'll recognise in this poem by Fay Inchfawn:

I wrestle - how I wrestle!- through the hours. Nay, not with principalities and powers - Dark spiritual foes of God's and man's - But with antagonistic pots and pans; With footmarks on the hall, With smears upon the wall, With doubtful ears and small unwashed hands, And with a babe's innumerable demands.[37]

---

[36] Adapted from Brian Cavanaugh, *The Sower's Seeds*, Paulist Press, New York, 1990, pp.58-59.
[37] Quoted in William Barclay, *The Gospel of Luke*, The Saint Andrew Press, Edinburgh, Reprinted 1971, p.312.

THE EPIPHANY OF THE LORD

(YEAR B)

After Jesus had been born at Bethlehem in Judaea during the reign of King Herod, some wise men came to Jerusalem from the east. (Mt 2:1).

The shepherds bid you farewell. They departed earlier today, returning to their flocks. The magi, the wise men from the East, greet you. On the feast of the Epiphany we celebrate their arrival, bearing gifts of gold, frankincense and myrrh.

Consider, though, how different this episode might have been had there been wise women instead of wise men. They would have asked for directions and therefore arrived in time to help deliver the baby. They would have cleaned the stable, made a casserole, and brought practical gifts instead of gold, frankincense and myrrh.

We are entirely dependent upon the gospels of Luke and Matthew for the scene represented in the traditional Christmas crib. Luke tells us about the shepherds, but doesn't mention the magi; Matthew tells us about the visit of the magi, but doesn't mention the shepherds. But the gospels of Luke and Matthew agree about this – the first people to visit the newly-born Messiah were outsiders.

Shepherds were despised by the religiously orthodox people of Jesus' time. The nature of the shepherd's job meant that he remained with his sheep day and night. It was quite literally a full-time job. Shepherds were therefore unable to observe the full rigours of the Jewish law. To put it in contemporary jargon, they didn't keep a kosher kitchen. Nor were they free to travel to the temple in Jerusalem for the great religious festivals. They were 'often considered as dishonest, outside the Law.'[38] Shepherds were beyond the bounds of religious respectability – ritually and literally unclean or, in the words of one author, 'mangy, stinking (and) bathless.'[39]

The Magi were also outsiders. They didn't belong. They were not Jews. They

---

[38] Raymond E. Brown, *The Birth of the Messiah,* Doubleday, New York, 1979, p.420.
[39] F. W. Danker, *Jesus and the New Age According to St Luke,* St Louis, 1972, p. 27, quoted in Robert J. Karris, "The Gospel According to Luke", in Raymond E. Brown, Joseph A. Fitzmyer, Roland E. Murphy (eds) *The New Jerome Biblical Commentary,* Geoffrey Chapman, London, 1989, p. 683.

came from 'the East', possibly Persia (now Iran), and some scholars suggest that they may have been Zoroastrians.[40] So, the only two gospels which tell us anything at all about the birth of Jesus agree on this one fundamental point: the infant King of the Jews was revealed first to outsiders. Matthew and Luke thereby sound a note that resonates throughout their gospels: Jesus constantly reaches out to the marginalised – to tax collectors and sinners, to lepers and the lame, to the blind and deaf, to the poor and downtrodden. And that is indeed a magnificent epiphany – a manifestation of God's compassion.

'Epiphany' comes from two Greek words meaning a 'shining forth', or manifestation. There are many manifestations or epiphanies in the gospels – occasions on which something is manifested or revealed about Jesus. The visit of the magi is the first such manifestation: the wise men from the East recognise in Jesus 'the infant King of the Jews' and come to do him homage.

Although Christian tradition speaks of 'three kings', our source for this story – Matthew's gospel – is vague about their number, and they are described as wise men, not kings. At some stage, however, Psalm 71 contributed to the Epiphany scene. Psalm 71, the responsorial psalm chosen for today's feast, was originally written as a coronation hymn for one of Israel's kings. It speaks of the 'kings of Tarshish and the seacoasts' paying tribute, and 'the kings of Sheba and Seba' bringing gifts for the newly crowned king. The Christian imagination began to interpret this psalm in the light of Matthew's gospel, and the wise men are transformed into kings bearing gifts

Although the gospel of Matthew doesn't tell us how many wise men (or magi) there were, Christian tradition eventually settled on the number three, probably suggested by the three gifts of gold, frankincense and myrrh. A tradition dating back to the sixth century has even given them the delightful names of Gaspar, Melchior and Balthazar. [41]

Matthew's gospel mentions two sets of wise men,[42] and there is a lesson to be learnt from both. We read of the wise men from the East who had set out on a quest to find the infant king of the Jews – Gaspar, Melchior and Balthazar.But as soon as Herod heard of an infant king of the Jews he consulted his own wise men, the chief priests and scribes.

---

[40] Raymond E. Brown, *The Birth of the Messiah*, p.168.
[41] Cf "Magi" in FL Cross and EA Livingstone (Eds) *The Oxford Dictionary of the Christian Church*, p.1020.
[42] An insight from William J. Bausch, *Telling Stories, Compelling Stories,* Twenty-Third Publications, Mystic, CT,1991, p.60.

A word about Herod. The Romans appointed Herod king of the Jews in 40 BC, and he ruled from 37 BC until his death in 4 BC.[43] He was called Herod the Great, and in many ways he deserved the title, but he had one fatal flaw – he was insanely suspicious, and ruthlessly eliminated potential rivals, including three of his sons. The Roman emperor Augustus once wryly observed that it was better to be Herod's pig than his son – a pun in the original Greek text, *hus* being the Greek word for pig and *huios* the word for son.[44]

You can imagine Herod's state of mind when he heard talk of a rival king of the Jews. He immediately summoned the chief priests and scribes and asked them where the child was to be born. Without batting an eyelid, Herod's own wise men respond immediately – 'at Bethlehem in Judea'. And they even quoted chapter and verse from the prophet Micah (5:1). But we never hear of Herod's wise men again. They knew exactly where the child was to be born, but they didn't budge. They didn't do a thing. They refused to become involved. They avoided taking any risks. And there was a risk. Suppose they had set out on the journey? Suppose they had found the 'infant king of the Jews'? What changes might they have to make in their lives?

The magi, those wise men who followed a star, did take the risk. They embarked upon a journey into the unknown, not knowing where it might lead; not knowing what they might find; not knowing how it might change their lives. They have a lesson to teach us. If we truly seek God's will, we must take the same risk and step out into the unknown, not knowing where it might lead us, or how it might challenge us.

There is also a lesson to be learnt from Herod's wise men. In thinking about them I'm reminded of Paulo Coelho's novel *The Alchemist*. It has been translated into 61 languages, a Guinness world record, and it has sold more than sixty-five million copies in more than 150 countries, becoming one of the best-selling books in history. The story begins with Santiago, a young shepherd, arriving with his flock at an abandoned and derelict church and deciding to stay the night. The roof of the church had long fallen in, and an enormous sycamore tree has grown on the spot where the sacristy once stood. He has been haunted by a dream in which a young child transports him to the Egyptian pyramids and says to him, 'If you

---

[43] This means that Jesus must have been born before 4 BC. David Ewing Duncan notes that "Other Gospels and historical sources suggest dates ranging from 6 or 7 BC to AD 7, though most historians lean towards 4 or 5 BC." *The Calendar,* Fourth Estate, London, 1998, p.101.
[44] William Barclay, *Gospel of Matthew*, Volume 1, The Saint Andrew Press, Edinburgh, Eighth Impression, 1969, pp.19-20.

come here, you will find a hidden treasure.' But Santiago wakes up just as the child is about to show him the exact location of the treasure. He travels many roads, far and wide, seeking the hidden treasure, but returns at last to the small, abandoned church where the story began, because, he now realises, that is where the treasure is buried.[45]

Herod's wise men didn't need to follow a star or travel to faraway and exotic lands. The infant king of the Jews was already present in their midst. The lesson is clear, even if they failed to profit by it. We may travel far and wide, but that which we seek is so often already present in our midst.

---

[45] Paulo Coelho, *The Alchemist*, Harper, San Francisco, 1998, p.14.

FIRST SUNDAY OF LENT

(YEAR C)

Filled with the Holy Spirit, Jesus left the Jordan and was led by the Spirit through the wilderness, being tempted there by the devil for forty days.
(Lk 4:1-2)

Easter always falls on a Sunday between March 22 and April 25, corresponding roughly to early spring in the Northern Hemisphere. Ash Wednesday therefore falls anywhere between February 4 and March 10. The season of Lent formally ends with the celebration of the Lord's Supper on Holy Thursday night, the beginning of the three holy days we call the Triduum. And, incidentally, Sundays are never counted as part of the 40 days of Lent. Our English word Lent comes from *lencten*, an Old English word meaning 'springtime.' While we in the Southern Hemisphere are moving towards autumn, the Northern Hemisphere is approaching spring.

During these 40 days of Lent we are called into the desert. The desert is both a place and an experience. Ultimately, though, it is not a setting but a state of soul. Few Christians are called to be hermits (literally a 'desert-dweller', coming from the Greek for desert, *eremos*), but the desert experience should be familiar to every disciple of Jesus. The essential elements of desert spirituality are distilled into the three Latin imperatives: *tace, fuge, quiesce* (be silent, flee to solitude, rest in contemplation). Henri Nouwen offers this insight: 'A life without a lonely place, that is, without a quiet centre, easily becomes destructive.'[46] So, what happens in the desert? The desert asks a simple question: What is in your heart? In what do you believe? Ultimately the desert summons us to journey within.

The desert is the *arena* (which is the Latin word for 'sandy place') where God chooses to met us. It is a place of discernment; what is real and what is fantasy? The Cistercian monk Thomas Merton (1915–1968), writing in the early 1950s, said that 'there is no greater disaster in the spiritual life than to be immersed in unreality.' Our life is maintained and nourished 'by our vital relation with realities

---

[46] Henri Nouwen, *Reaching Out: Three Meditations on the Christian Life*, Ave Maria, Notre Dame, IN, 1974, p.21.

outside and above us. When our life feeds on unreality, it must starve.'[47] Arthur Miller's play *Death of a Salesman* is about Willy Loman, a tragic figure whose life of self-delusion ends in suicide. Willy's son Biff says of his father, 'He never knew who he was.' Shakespeare's *King Lear* is also about truth-telling. Stripped of all that he possessed, Lear laments, 'Who is it that can tell me who I am?'

Alan Jones, Dean of San Francisco's Grace Cathedral, writes, 'Many of us have been telling a story to ourselves and to the world about what we think is true and real for us so long that we have come to believe it absolutely.'[48] Lent summons us into the desert to be probed. 'About what? About yourself and the story you've been telling yourself about yourself. How far is it a lie?'[49] Merton wrote about the false self:

My false and private self is the one who wants to exist outside the reach of God's will and God's love - outside of reality and outside of life. And such a self cannot help but be an illusion.[50]

Before he began his public ministry Jesus was led by the Spirit into the desert, and there he was tempted. This gospel episode always reminds me of a powerful image from Homer's epic poem *The Odyssey*. *The Odyssey* tells the story of Odysseus' voyage home to Ithaca following the fall of Troy. The return home is a hazardous journey, a Road of Trials, fraught with many obstacles. Odysseus and his men must sail past the island of the sirens, sea nymphs with the head of a woman and the body of a bird who by their sweet singing lured mariners to destruction on the rocks surrounding their island. Odysseus had been forewarned and ordered his men to block their ears with wax, but he wished to hear their seductive call and had himself tied with rope to the mast of the ship. The sirens are an archetypal image of the alluring call that ultimately leads to destruction.

Like all of us, Jesus had to distinguish between the voice that whispers attractive lies and the voice of God. In the desert he had to confront a basic question: What does it mean to be God's anointed one (the *Christos*, or Christ)? What is the true direction of the mission God has entrusted to me? These are essentially the same two questions each of us must face: Who am I, and what am I called to do?

Who am I? A man once found an eagle's egg and placed it in the nest of a backyard hen. The eaglet hatched with the brood of chicks, and grew up with them. All his life the eagle did what the backyard chickens did, thinking that

---

[47] Thomas Merton, *Thoughts in Solitude,* Burns & Oates, London, 1958, p.19.
[48] Alan Jones, *Living the Truth*, Cowley Publications, Boston, 2000, p.117.
[49] Ibid, p.118.
[50] Thomas Merton, *New Seeds of Contemplation*, Burns & Oates, London, 1961, p.33.

he was a backyard chicken. He scratched the earth for worms and insects. He clucked and cackled. And he would thrash his wings and fly a few feet into the air. Years passed and the eagle grew very old. One day he saw a magnificent bird far above him in the cloudless sky. It glided in graceful majesty among the powerful wind currents, with scarcely a beat of its strong golden wings. The old eagle looked up in awe. 'Who's that?' he asked. 'That's the eagle, the king of the birds,' said his neighbour. 'He belongs to the sky. We belong to the earth – we're chickens.' So the eagle lived and died a chicken, for that's what he thought he was.[51] How many of us fail to discover the eagle within and spend our lives scratching the earth for worms and insects? Conversely, how many of us devote our lives to tasks that might superficially seem important but are utterly futile? Nasrudin, the wise fool, often taught his disciples through acted-out parables. On one occasion he was in his garden sprinkling bread crumbs around the flower beds. A neighbour came by and asked, 'Why are you doing that?' Nasrudin answered, 'Oh, I do it to keep the tigers away.' Somewhat puzzled the neighbour replied, 'But there aren't any tigers within thousands of miles of here.' Nasrudin replied, 'Effective, isn't it?'[52]

Lent summons us to listen to those questions: Who am I, and what am I called to do? In *The Tibetan Book of Living and Dying*, there is an interesting discussion about laziness. The author contrasts Eastern and Western types of laziness, and argues that Western laziness is quite different. 'It consists of cramming our lives with compulsive activity, so that there is no time at all to confront the real issues.'[53] As Nasrudin was trying to teach us, we can be so busy sprinkling bread crumbs that we never stop to ask if it's truly necessary.

'Every one of us,' wrote Thomas Merton, 'is shadowed by an illusory person: a false self.'[54] This holy season of Lent summons us into the desert, into the solitude that rips off all masks and disguises; into the solitude that confronts us with the shadowy areas of our life, the false and illusory self. The desert summons us to discover the true self, the authentic self. Who am I, and what am I called to do?

---

[51] Christina Feldman and Jack Kornfield (Eds), *Stories of the Spirit, Stories of the Heart*, (HarperSan Francisco, 1991), 265.
[52] Ibid, 241.
[53] Sogyal Rinpoche, *The Tibetan Book of Living and Dying*, Rider, London, 1992, p.19.
[54] Thomas Merton, *New Seeds of Contemplation*, p.33.

SECOND SUNDAY OF LENT

(YEAR C)

Jesus took with him Peter and John and James and went up the mountain to pray. (Lk 9:28)

Jesus, together with Peter, James and John, went up a mountain to pray. Mountains have traditionally been places of encounter between God and humanity, what Celtic Christianity would call 'thin places.' George MacLeod, founder of the Iona Community, referred to the island of Iona as a 'thin place - only a tissue paper separating earth from heaven.'[55] In the words of Thomas Merton:

We are living in a world that is absolutely transparent, and God is shining through it all the time. This is not just a fable or a nice story. It is true. ... It becomes very obvious that God is everywhere and in everything and we cannot be without Him. It's impossible. The only thing is that we don't see it.[56]

But Peter, James and John, like Moses and Elijah before them, did 'see it' on Tabor and Sinai, paper thin places where the veil momentarily lifted and their hearts were opened. Marcus Borg describes a thin place as a 'sacrament of the sacred, a mediator of the sacred, a means whereby the sacred becomes present to us. A thin place is a means of grace.'[57]

Moses and Elijah had both encountered God on a mountain. The first Book of Kings tells of a strange encounter between God and the prophet Elijah that occurred on Mount Horeb sometime in the ninth century BC. There are striking parallels and contrasts between Elijah's meeting the Lord on Mt Horeb and Moses' encounter with God on Mt Sinai. And, by the way, Mt Horeb and Mt Sinai are different names for the same mountain.

What is the background to Elijah's night in a cave on Mt Horeb? This episode occurred during the reign of King Ahab, a weak man dominated by his powerful wife, Jezebel. Jezebel was a foreigner, a Sidonian, and worse still, she worshipped Baal. Elijah couldn't tolerate the worship of false gods, and he challenged the

---

[55] Ronald Ferguson, *George MacLeod: Founder of the Iona Community,* HarperCollins, London, 1990, p.144.
[56] From an audiotope of Merton made in 1965, quoted in Marcus J. Borg, *The Heart of Christianity,* HarperSan Francisco, 2003, p.155.
[57] Marcus Borg, *The Heart of Christianity*, p.156.

prophets of Baal to a showdown on Mt Carmel. The account of this contest is to be found in Chapter 18 of the First book of Kings. The prophets of Baal, 450 of them, were to dismember a bull, but not set fire to it, and then call upon the name of their god to consume the offering with fire. Elijah would also prepare a bull and call upon the name of the Lord. The contest was simple: whichever god devoured the offering with fire was God indeed. The prophets of Baal began by dancing around their makeshift altar, calling upon the name of Baal. They shouted all the louder and gashed themselves until blood flowed from the wounds. In a frenzy they ranted and raged, but Baal remained silent. Elijah taunted them, suggesting that Baal was preoccupied or busy or gone on a journey, or maybe asleep and needed to be woken up! But there was no voice, no answer, no sign of attention.

Then it was Elijah's turn. To increase the degree of difficulty, he ordered water to be poured over his offering. No sooner had Elijah completed his prayer than fire fell from the heavens and consumed his offering. That was proof enough for the crowd that had gathered to witness the contest. They seized the prophets of Baal and slaughtered them all. Needless to say, Queen Jezebel was not impressed, and uttered dire threats against Elijah: 'May the gods bring unspeakable ills upon me if by this time tomorrow I haven't done away with you.'

Elijah fled for his life, or as Monsignor Knox's quaint translation has it, he 'took fright and set out upon a journey of his own devising.' He fled into the wilderness where he grew tired, weary and hungry. While he slept, the Lord sent an angel with tea and scones. He continued his journey, finally reaching Mt Horeb after wandering in the wilderness for 40 days and 40 nights. This is where today's first reading begins. Elijah seeks God's presence. A mighty hurricane splits the mountain and shatters the rocks, then an earthquake shakes the mountain, and then a fire. But God was not to be found in the hurricane, nor in the earthquake, nor in the fire. Elijah then feels the whisper of a gentle breeze, and he covers his face, for in this almost imperceptible whisper he recognises the Divine Presence.

I believe that the author of the book of Kings has told this story as a deliberate parallel to the story of Moses' encounter with God on Mt Sinai. Here's how the parallel works: Moses and Elijah both flee from a hostile power: Moses flees from Pharaoh; Elijah flees from Queen Jezebel. They both wandered in the wilderness: Moses for 40 years; Elijah for 40 days. They both grow hungry and are fed by God: Moses and the people with manna from heaven; Elijah with scones and water brought by an angel.

Moses and Elijah then ascend the mountain of the Lord, but here the two stories differ significantly. Moses' meeting with God was orchestrated by Cecil B. de Mille or George Lucas. Listen to that meeting, as recorded in the book of Exodus:

Now at day break ... there were peals of thunder and flashes of lightning, dense cloud on the mountain and a very loud trumpet blast; and, in the camp, all the people trembled. Then Moses led the people out of the camp to meet God; and they took their stand at the bottom of the mountain. Mount Sinai was entirely wrapped in smoke, because Yahweh had descended on it in the form of fire. The smoke rose like smoke from a furnace and the whole mountain shook violently. Louder and louder grew the trumpeting. Moses spoke, and God answered him in the thunder. (Ex 19:16-19).

God descended in the form of fire, and spoke to Moses in the thunder; it was indeed a mountain full of terrors and fury.

Elijah's experience of God was quite different. God was not in the fire; God was not in the hurricane; God was not in the earthquake. The Lord's presence was the sound of a gentle breeze.[58] Herein lies a lesson. If cataclysms of nature such as thunder, lightning and earthquakes once heralded the divine presence, it is not so now. The Lord is present in stillness and silence; the divine word is a subtle whisper. In other words:

the small and insignificant events of life are the stage upon which the revelation of God is enacted. It is so easy to be awed by the spectacular and overlook the ordinary. Yet most lives are made up of the ordinary, and it is there the 'tiny whispering voice' of God will be heard, if we are attuned to it.[59]

Our Lenten journey so far: Last week into the desert and today onto the holy mountain, leading us into a thin place where our hearts are opened. In 1954 Fr Michel Quoist published a collection of prayers that proved enormously popular.[60] Many of Quoist's prayers took as their starting point things constantly before our eyes and so familiar that we invariably take them for granted: the telephone, green blackboards, a wire-fence, a brick, a bald head, the underground, a swing, a five pound note, even a pornographic magazine. But for those who have ears to hear and eyes to see, all life becomes a sign revealing the love of God. The whole

---

[58] Translated variously as a 'still small voice' (*Revised Standard Version*); a 'sound of sheer silence' (*New Revised Standard Version*), a 'light murmuring sound' (*New Jerusalem Bible*), a "low murmuring sound" (*New English Bible*), a 'tiny whispering sound' (*New American Bible*).

[59] Dianne Bergant, *Preaching the New Lectionary, Year A*, The Liturgical Press, Collegeville, MN, 2001, p.317.

[60] The English translation of *Prayers of Life* was published in 1963 by Gill and Macmillan.

world is paper thin. Next week we'll hear the story of Moses encountering God in the burning bush. From the middle of the bush God speaks: 'Come no nearer. Take off your shoes, for the place on which you stand is holy ground.' And yet the Jesuit poet Gerard Manley Hopkins affirms a fundamental truth when he writes 'The world is charged with the grandeur of God.'[61] And Elizabeth Barrett Browning reminds us that 'Earth is crammed with heaven / And every bush aflame with God / But only those who see take off their shoes.'[62]

---

[61] Gerard Manley Hopkins, 'God's Grandeur', in Richard Ellmann and Robert O'Clair (Eds), *The Norton Anthology of Modern Poetry*, W.W. Norton & Company, New York, 1973, p.80.
[62] Quoted in Philip Yancey, *Finding God in Unexpected Places*, p.27.

THIRD SUNDAY OF LENT

(YEAR C)

A man had a fig tree planted in his vineyard and he came looking for fruit on it but found none. (Lk 13:6).

There is a story from the Middle Ages about a young woman who was expelled from heaven. As she left, she was told that if she could bring back the gift that is most valued by God, she would be welcomed back. Having travelled the world, she first brought back some drops of a martyr's blood, but no – that did not gain her re-entry into heaven. Then she brought back the coins that a destitute widow had given to the poor. No luck! The gates of heaven remained firmly closed. Then she brought back a bible that had been used by a great preacher. No luck! Then the dust from the shoes of a missionary labouring in a remote wasteland. No luck! One thing after another was rejected. One day she sat in a village square and watched a small boy playing by the local fountain. A man rode up on horseback and dismounted to take a drink. As the man stooped down to drink he saw the child, and suddenly remembered his boyhood innocence. Then, looking in the fountain and seeing the reflection of his hardened face, he realised what he had done with his life, and tears of repentance welled up in his eyes and began to trickle down his cheeks. The young woman took one of these tears of repentance back to heaven and was received with joy.[63]

The symbols of our Lenten journey so far: the desert, the mountain, and today the fig tree, a symbol of the key word in today's gospel, repentance. There are times when all of us can identify with the barren fig tree because we have failed to bear fruit. Like the Prodigal Son we have squandered our inheritance; we are salt that has lost its tang; we have hidden our light under a basket. But the Lord, the owner of the vineyard, graciously gives us time to look anew at our lives. Repentance is not about wearing sackcloth and ashes – either literally or metaphorically!! It is about seeing our life in a new way. When the man in our story saw his face reflected in the waters of the

---

[63] Adapted from William Bausch, *A World of Stories*, Twenty-third publications, Mystic, CT, 1998), pp.314 -5.

fountain, he realised with great sadness and dismay what he had made of his life.

Repentance is a translation of *metanoia*, a Greek word that means literally 'a change of mind', a new way of thinking or seeing. Writing to the Christians of Rome, St Paul exhorted them, 'Do not model your behaviour on the contemporary world, but let the renewing of your minds transform you...' (Romans 12:2). Metanoia, therefore, is about a change in consciousness, and unless that happens our beliefs are just toys.

Jesus is told about two violent incidents in which misfortune falls upon seemingly innocent people. The first is an atrocity brought about through human cruelty. Some Galileans on a pilgrimage to the Temple in Jerusalem were slaughtered at Pilate's behest. The second incident was due to natural causes; 18 people killed by the sudden collapse of a tower in Siloam. The implication seems to be that these people must surely have been guilty of grave sin if they met such violent and untimely deaths. It was a deeply engrained attitude of the time that there was a direct link between your behaviour and the circumstances of your life.

Such attitudes are by no means confined to antiquity. Some years ago when I was chaplain to a women's hospital I recall talking with a woman after a stillborn delivery. Both she and her husband were deeply distressed, but the mother's own feelings of grief were compounded by a profound sense of guilt. Some years beforehand she'd had an abortion, and she concluded that this stillbirth was God's punishment.

The American Jewish rabbi Harold Kushner stood by helplessly while his son, Aaron, died from a rare disease at the age of 14. This rare disease, progeria, causes rapid ageing. When Aaron died as a young teenager, he looked like an old man. Kushner's attempts to come to terms with his son's death resulted in a book entitled *When Bad Things Happen to Good People*.[64] In the course of writing this book he found that many people instinctively linked misfortune with divine punishment. As a young rabbi he was called on to assist a family through the tragic and unexpected death of their 19-year-old daughter from a burst blood vessel in her brain. As he entered the family home Kushner had braced himself for anger, shock and grief, but he was totally unprepared when he heard their first words, 'You know, Rabbi, we didn't fast last Yom Kippur.'[65] On a lighter note, Kushner tells the story of an 11-year-old boy who was

---

[64] Harold S. Kushner, *When Bad Things Happen to Good People*, Pan Books, London, 1982.
[65] Ibid, p.16.

prescribed glasses after a routine eye examination. No one was unduly surprised because his parents and his older sister all wore glasses. But the boy himself was devastated and seemed unable to tell anyone why he was so upset. Eventually the truth came out. A week before the eye examination the boy and two older friends had come across some issues of *Playboy* magazine in a neighbour's recycling bin. With a sense of guilt he spent several minutes pouring over pictures of naked women. And now God was striking him with blindness! [66]

Kushner observes, 'One of the ways in which people have tried to make sense of the world's suffering in every generation has been by assuming that we deserve what we get, that somehow our misfortunes come as punishment for our sins.' Against the background of such instinctive and ingrained attitudes, Jesus asserts that the Jews killed by Pilate and those killed by the falling tower were no more deserving of death than anyone else. In other words, don't judge those people, but let these tragic incidents jolt you out of your own complacency and take stock of your own lives. Jesus focuses on the suddenness of these tragedies and the possibilities that the victims may have been unprepared. Jesus makes the point that these disasters should be a warning that death may come unexpectedly, and so repent while you have time.

The fig tree is a symbol of repentance. It would have been perfectly acceptable practice for the owner of a vineyard to cut down an unproductive tree after three years without fruit. But the fig tree is strangely allowed time to produce fruit. Logic and good farming practice suggest that the unproductive tree should be destroyed, but the point of this parable is that Jesus, the Son of a loving God, does not follow such principles. He is aware that many people need time and patience, and he is prepared to give it to them. This holy season of Lent is a time of grace, a time to tend to the unproductive fig tree of our own lives.

---

[66] Ibid, pp.19-20.

FOURTH SUNDAY OF LENT

(YEAR C)

A man had two sons. (Lk 15: 11).

Some time ago the Israeli psychologist George Tamarin invited over a thousand Israeli schoolchildren, aged between eight and fourteen, to listen to the account of the battle of Jericho as recounted in the book of Joshua. It is a bloodthirsty story indeed. After the legendary walls of that city had come tumbling down, Joshua and his men killed all who remained in the city – men and women, young and old. Even the oxen, sheep and asses were put to the edge of the sword. Finally, Joshua and his men burned the city with fire. Tamarin then asked the children a simple question: 'Do you think Joshua and the Israelites acted rightly or not?' The children had to choose between A (total approval), B (partial approval), and C (total disapproval). Sixty-six percent gave total approval, and twenty-six percent total disapproval; eight percent gave partial approval.

Tamarin then presented to a different group of Israeli children the same scenario, with one significant difference. He replaced Joshua's name with General Lin and Israel with 'a Chinese kingdom 3000 years ago.' Seventy-five percent disapproved of General Lin's behaviour and only seven percent approved!

When some of the children who responded to the first scenario – Joshua and the battle of Jericho – were asked to explain the answer they gave, not all who disagreed with Joshua's actions did so because they were horrified by the wholesale slaughter. One child disapproved of Joshua's conquering Jericho because it would have entailed entering impure territory: 'I think it is bad, since the Arabs are impure and if one enters an impure land one will also become impure and share their curse.' One child who totally approved of Joshua's conduct explained why: 'Joshua did good because the people who inhabited the land were of a different religion, and when Joshua killed them he wiped their religion from the earth.' [67]

They were different! They were outsiders; they were unclean. This brings us to the point of today's parable, popularly known as the parable of the prodigal son. Sometimes it is called the parable of the merciful father; the *Jerusalem*

---

[67] Richard Dawkins, *The God Delusion*, Bantam Press, London, 2006, pp.255-7.

Bible calls this parable 'the lost son (the 'prodigal') and the dutiful son.' One wit observed that the most appropriate title should be the parable of the absent mother, arguing that none of this drama would have taken place if there had been a mother present in the home!

Which title best captures the essence of this parable's message? As with all parables, the context offers a significant clue, and the immediate context of this parable is a complaint by the Pharisees and scribes: 'This man welcomes sinners and eats with them.' The parable is therefore a response to that accusation. Jesus is teaching us something very important about God's kingdom.

Pharisees were *perushim*, the separate ones, although they did not geographically separate themselves like the Essene community at Qumran by the shores of the Dead Sea. The Pharisees were not evil or wicked people. Quite the contrary! They were zealous fanatics who arose around the middle of the second century BC as one response to the radical Hellenisation (i.e. the imposition of Greek culture) unleashed by Antiochus IV and his Jewish supporters. Antiochus attempted to stamp out the Jewish religion, even going so far as to erect a statue of Zeus in the Jewish temple. The Pharisees sought to preserve the integrity of their own religious tradition, and therefore refused to have anything to do with people who did not share their own zealous and single-minded devotion to the Torah and the tradition of the elders, and hence their objection to the kind of people whom Jesus chose to welcome. That kind of blinkered existence can warp our minds.

This single-minded devotion to the Law and the traditions of the elders obviously set the Pharisees apart, but one prominent Pharisee, and I'm referring to Saul of Tarsus, underwent a sudden shift in perspective and came to realise that we are not saved by the Law. As Saul says in Anita Mason's novel *The Illusionist:*

People find it much easier to do something rather than to be something, and if they think they can enter the Kingdom by being circumcised and eating the right kind of food, that's all they'll do. ... The Law is a trap. It fools people into thinking it's their salvation, and it can never be. The Law is a labyrinth no human being can ever find his way through. [68]

While today's parable is a lesson in the mercy of God it says much more. If we focus primarily upon the merciful father why clutter up the story with the introduction of the second son? That unnecessarily complicates the plot. It would be a simpler story if there were only one son – a son who sought his inheritance,

---

[68] Anita Mason, *The Illusionist,* Abacus, London, 1983, p.233.

squandered it, and returned home to the great joy of his father. The parable would then logically end with the killing of the fatted calf and the celebrations that follow.

I would suggest that the story is most appropriately named The Father and his two sons. It is easy to see that the Father is God himself, and the younger son represents the sinners whom Jesus welcomes and dines with. But who is the elder brother, that loyal and dutiful son who stayed at home working on the father's estate? He undoubtedly represents the Pharisees whose accusation prompts the telling of this parable.

The Pharisees' dedicated commitment to duty is embodied in the elder brother of the parable. The elder brother who has done the right thing all his life comes in from the fields. We can share his righteous indignation as he hears the sounds of celebration for his wayward brother who has been fully welcomed back into the family – despite his abuse of the freedom and responsibility which was given to him.

So what is this parable saying? It reminds us that God's graciousness, God's forgiveness, God's love, is not something that can be earned through an earnest dedication to duty. It is a gift, bestowed as God wishes. And if, like the elder brother, we think that's unfair, then so be it! God is unfair.

But the question that unlocks the central message of the parable is this: 'Where is the Father located in the parable?' At the two most interesting moments in the parable the father is *outside*. He is *outside,* watching, waiting and hoping for a lost son to return. While the boy is outside, the father embraces him and kisses him tenderly.

The father also goes *outside* to meet his elder son. The elder son is out in the fields, and when he hears the music he asks one of the servants what is happening. We are told that he refused to go inside, and so the father comes *outside* to plead with him. The father does not sit comfortably inside, waiting for his sons to come to him. He is to be found outside, seeking his sons – each of them lost in his own way.

In Luke's gospel, from beginning to end, the outsider is welcomed. The news of the birth of Jesus was announced first to shepherds as they watched over their flocks. Shepherds were often considered to be dishonest and outside the Law. The final words that Jesus spoke from the cross to another human being were addressed to an outsider: 'Today you will be with me in paradise.'

Each of the two sons in today's parable is 'outside.' The younger son squanders his inheritance in a foreign land far from home and is reduced to utter degradation tending unclean animals. He is certainly outside the Law. As Henri Nouwen observes:

What he did was wrong; not only his family and friends knew it, but he himself as well. He rebelled against morality and allowed himself to be swept away by his own lust and greed. There is something very clear-cut about his misbehaviour. [69]

When at last he comes to his senses he begins the homeward journey, having rehearsed the appeal he would make to his father. While he was still a long way off, his father saw him and ran out to embrace him. He puts a ring on his finger and shoes on his feet, symbols that he has been welcomed back not as an outsider but as a member of the family.

The elder brother is also outside. Coming in from the fields he refuses to go in, so the father again goes outside to urge him to join the activities inside. There is a great deal of the Pharisee in the elder brother. He has done his duty faithfully, a model son who has never once disobeyed his father's orders. Quite understandably he considers himself hardly done by and taken for granted when he learns of the welcome lavished upon his brother. This self-righteous and self-pitying son was, in Mark Twain's phrase, 'good in the worst sense of the word.' We see a dark power erupt in him and boil to the surface. He becomes a resentful, proud, unkind, selfish person.

What, then, is this saying to us? Inside it is comfortable and secure; outside it is dark and uncertain. Inside it is light and warm; outside it is dark and cold. Inside there are people like me, family; outside there are strangers. Inside it is peaceful; outside it is hostile. I have no doubt that the father had shared many moments of love and intimacy with his sons inside; but the greatest expressions of his love occur *outside*.

Ever since the man and the woman whom we know as Adam and Eve were exiled from the Garden, we have been dwelling outside, alienated from God and our authentic selves, fractured and dislocated. Today's parable is about coming home, about returning inside to the warmth and love of home.

---

[69] Henri J. M. Nouwen, *The Return of the Prodigal Son*, Darton, Longman & Todd, London, 1992, p. 66.

FIFTH SUNDAY OF LENT

(YEAR C)

The scribes and Pharisees brought a woman along who had been caught committing adultery. (Jn 8: 3)

In 1989 Iran's Ayatollah Khomeini called for the execution of the Anglo-Indian novelist Salman Rushdie. Khomeini denounced Rushdie's novel *The Satanic Verses* as blasphemous. There was an immediate outcry and vehement protests at what was considered to be a barbaric sentence imposed by a religious fanatic. Even though many people thought that Rushdie's book was in bad taste, that it deliberately offended many Muslims, that it derided one of the great world religions and violated the Koran, they were horrified at the Ayatollah's decree. A year earlier some Christians attempted to burn down a cinema in Paris that was showing Martin Scorcese's film *The Last Temptation of Christ*, a film adaptation of the controversial 1951 novel of the same name by Nikos Kazantzakis. More recently, in July 2001, a man walked into the reception area of a Melbourne abortion clinic, pulled a rifle out of a bag and shot dead a security guard.

Just on a hundred years ago a statue was erected in the *Campo dei Fiori* in Rome, a mere stone's throw from the Vatican. The statue was erected to the memory of Giordano Bruno, a great philosopher and a Dominican friar. On February 17, 1600 Bruno was burned alive in the *Campo dei Fiori*, on the spot where his statue now stands. He was sentenced to death by Pope Clement VIII as an 'impenitent and pertinacious heretic.' Giordano Bruno's ideas were unorthodox for the time, and offensive to both the Catholic and Protestant Churches. Today historians would regard Bruno as an important figure in the history of Western thought.

Like Ayatollah Khomeini and Pope Clement VIII, the scribes and Pharisees had an uncompromising view of religion. They were the officially accredited experts in the interpretation and application of God's word. But like so many accredited experts they were interested only in preserving and maintaining their own world view and not seriously examining another outlook that may embody a more profound truth. The truth embodied in the teachings of Jesus was obviously a threat to scribes and Pharisees we meet in today's gospel, and so they attempted to embarrass and discredit him with a woman caught in adultery.

What does the Jewish Law (the Torah) say about this situation? The Law is very clear. In the Book of Leviticus (20:10) we read 'The man who commits adultery with his neighbour's wife will be put to death, he and the woman.' This is repeated in the Book of Deuteronomy (22: 22): 'If a man is caught having sexual intercourse with another man's wife, both must be put to death: the man who has slept with her and the woman herself. You must banish this evil from Israel.' The Law is clear and unequivocal.

Well, you've heard how Jesus deals with the situation. He writes on the ground, and when they persist with their questions, he replies, 'If there is one of you who has not sinned, let him be the first to throw a stone at her.' Then he continued writing on the ground. We're told that the men began to leave, one by one, leaving Jesus alone with the woman. Jesus neither condemns nor condones what the woman has done. He simply says, 'Go away, and don't sin any more.'

On April 12, 1961, Yuri Gagarin became the first human being to travel into space. When the Russian first astronaut returned to earth after spending one hour and forty-eight minutes in space he was triumphantly paraded around Red Square. Nikita Khrushchev, premier of the Soviet Union, asked to see the astronaut privately. 'Comrade', Khrushchev said. 'I want to ask you a very delicate question! When you were up there in outer space, did you see God? Does God exist?' The astronaut was unequivocal in his reply, 'Yes, Comrade President, I did see God, and yes, he does exist.' To which Khrushchev replied, 'Ah, I always thought so, but for the sake of the USSR, and for the sake of the Communist Party, promise me you'll never mention it to anyone as long as you live.' Being a person of integrity, the astronaut gave his solemn promise.

Some time later the astronaut went on a world tour, and when visiting Rome he was granted an audience with the Pope. When the astronaut and the Pope were alone, his holiness whispered in the astronaut's ear. 'Tell me, when you were up there in outer space, did you see God? Does God exist?' But the astronaut felt bound by his earlier promise to Khrushchev, and so he replied: 'No, I didn't see God. And, no, God doesn't exist.' The Pope nodded his head and said: 'Just as I thought. Just as I always thought! But, please, Comrade Astronaut, so you won't disillusion countless millions of people around the world, promise me you will never mention a word of this to anyone as long as you live!' The bewildered astronaut then made a solemn promise for the second time.

What do the fictional Krushchev and Pope have in common with the scribes and the Pharisees of today's gospel? What do they have in common with the Ayatollah Khomeini and Pope Clement VIII? They both share an overwhelming desire to preserve their own world view in the face of all opposition. I'm reminded of George Orwell's novel *Nineteen Eighty-Four,* written in 1949, the year before he died. *Nineteen Eighty-Four* is a caustic attack on the totalitarian state, but it is also a satire on the human capacity to filter out any view of reality that threatens the status quo. The inhabitants of Nineteen Eighty-Four resort to what Orwell calls Newspeak. Newspeak is a use of language with certain interesting affinities to what today is called 'political correctness.' Newspeak is a way of maintaining loyal adherence to party policy, even when it appears to be severely challenged by reality. Here the devices of Blackwhite and Doublethink come into play.

Blackwhite means a loyal willingness to say that black is white when Party discipline demands it. But it means also the ability to *believe* that black is white, and more, to know that black is white, and to forget that one has ever believed the contrary. This demands a continuous alteration of the past, but that is made possible by what Newspeak calls *doublethink*. 'Doublethink' is defined as 'the power of holding two contradictory beliefs in one's mind simultaneously, and accepting both of them.'[70]

Today's gospel reminds us that our ultimate allegiance is not to the 'party', whatever the 'party' may mean in our own situation. Our ultimate allegiance is to the truth. And as unnerving and annoying as it may be, the truth cannot always be domesticated within the comfortable confines of our culture or creed. Before issuing death sentences, before burning heretics at the stake, before burning down cinemas, before bombing abortion clinics, before stoning the adulterer, we would do well to be as sparing in our condemnations as our Master. The truth will not shatter our world. The truth, Jesus said, will set us free.

---

[70] George Orwell, *Nineteen Eighty-Four*, Chancellor Press, London, 1949, p.226.

PASSION (PALM SUNDAY)

(YEAR C)

Blessings on the King who comes, in the name of the Lord! (Lk 19: 38)

Two men were talking about their wives. One complained that whenever he had a fight with his wife she became historical. His friend, thinking that he'd used the wrong word, corrects him: 'You don't mean historical, you mean hysterical.' But the other replied, 'No, I mean exactly what I said. The minute we have an argument, she remembers everything wrong I ever did from the minute I met her!'

Well, sometimes we can dwell too much on the past, but for the Jewish people, 'memory is the key to survival – and history is the greatest teacher.' In the Jewish tradition three major festivals are known as *sholosh r'golim*, literally 'three feet' because they commemorated three major moments of Jewish history.[71] The greatest of the three pilgrimage festivals was Passover. Passover starts on the fifteenth day of the Jewish month of Nissan. Because the Jewish calendar is based upon a lunar year, the date of Passover according to the Gregorian calendar varies from year to year. In a nutshell, though, Passover is celebrated on the first full moon following the vernal or spring equinox (of the northern hemisphere).

Passover was the most popular of the three great Jewish pilgrimage feasts, a time when a great multitude of pilgrims travelled to Jerusalem. EP Saunders estimates that between 300 000 and 500 000 people attended the festivals in Jerusalem, especially Passover.[72] It must therefore have been a time of heightened security, and the Roman garrison permanently stationed in the Fortress Antonia was augmented by additional troops from Caesarea Maritima, a huge all-weather port constructed by Herod on Judea's Mediterranean coast, and the seat of the Roman governor.

Along with thousands of others, Jesus had made the pilgrimage to Jerusalem for the great festival. On Palm Sunday we commemorate his entry into the holy city. The meaning of this entry into Jerusalem is clear, for it uses symbolism from the prophet

---

[71] Benjamin Blech, *The Complete Idiot's Guide to Understanding Judaism,* Alpha Books, New York, 1999, p.159.
[72] EP Saunders, *Judaism: Practice & Belief 63BCE – 66C*, SCM Press, London, 1992, p.128.

Zechariah. The coming king, according to Zechariah, will be humble and mounted on a donkey; he will banish war from the land – no more chariots, war-horses, or bows. He will be a king of peace (cf Zech 9:9-10).

As Jesus entered the holy city from the east, Pontius Pilate and his legions entered the city from the west. Imagine the Roman procession: 'cavalry on horses, foot soldiers, leather armour, helmets, weapons, banners, golden eagles mounted on poles, sun glinting on metal and gold.' And the sounds: 'the marching of feet, the creaking of leather, the clinking of bridles, the beating of drums.'[73] This procession was intended to intimidate: rise up against us at your own peril!

At the beginning of Holy Week we prepare to celebrate once again the archetypal pattern as the centre of Christian life: death and resurrection; crucifixion and vindication. Without resurrection – God's decisive reversal of the authorities' verdict on Jesus – the cross is simply pain, agony, and horror. Easter without Good Friday risks sentimentality. Easter as the reversal of Good Friday is God's 'no' to the powers who killed him, powers still very much active in our world.[74]

One procession entering the city on what we now call Palm Sunday proclaimed the kingdom of God, the other the power of empire. One procession entered the city led by a column of imperial cavalry; the other a sole figure riding a donkey, followed by enthusiastic followers and sympathisers.

Pilate's procession 'embodied the power, glory, and violence of the empire that ruled the world.'[75] Jesus' procession embodied an alternative vision, a kingdom of non-violence and peace. Which procession are we in?

---

[73] Marcus J. Borg & John Dominic Crossan, *The Last Week*, HarperSan Francisco, 2006, p.3.
[74] Ibid, pp.209-210.
[75] Ibid, pp.2-4.

HOLY THURSDAY

'I have given you an example so that you may copy what I have done to you.'
(Jn 13: 15)

I've been fascinated by the prospect of cloning the now extinct Tasmanian Tiger. The last known Tasmanian Tiger died in Hobart Zoo in 1936, but the Australian Museum has the remains of a very young tiger, collected in 1866 and perfectly preserved since then in a bottle of alcohol. DNA has been extracted from the tiger pup, the first step in bringing the extinct marsupial back to life. But cloning a tiger is only part of the problem. The tiger became extinct because it could not survive in a hostile environment. Dingos, for example, were one of the reasons for the tiger's extinction on the mainland. I mention the Tasmanian tiger because it raises the question of ecological systems. We all need our own ecosystem to survive. A rare frog, for example, needs its own ecosystem if it is to survive the hazardous journey from spawn to tadpole to frog. It requires its own environment, with food, ponds and climate if it is to thrive. If cloned, the Tasmanian tiger will become extinct yet again unless we can provide the right ecosystem.

Tonight's liturgy singles out four essentials ingredients of the Christian ecosystem. Firstly, we gather together as members of the Body of Christ. Christ is the head and we, each one of us, part of that body. Needless to say, my body functions well when all of my limbs and organs are healthy. I will not die were I to lose a finger or a toe, but I am certainly affected by the loss. The sad reality we are faced with today is that only about twenty percent of Catholics attend Mass regularly. The Body of Christ is severely handicapped by their absence and the loss of their gifts. A Christian is also likened to a branch, drawing life from the vine. Cut off from that vine we wither and die. We also form part of the fabric of a spiritual building that rests upon Jesus as the cornerstone and the apostles and prophets as foundation stones.

Secondly, we gather to hear God's Word, as we do at every celebration of the Eucharist. We are a people formed, informed and reformed by the Word of God. The prophet Isaiah likens God's word to the falling rain and snow: The Lord says:

For, as the rain and the snow come down from the sky and do not return before having watered the earth, fertilising it and making it germinate to provide seed for the sower and food to eat, so it is with the word that goes from my mouth: it will not return to me unfulfilled or before having carried out my good pleasure and having achieved what it was sent to do. (Is 55:10-11).

We are formed, informed and reformed by the Word of God. A regular and prayerful reading of the Scriptures is an essential element in every Christian's spiritual ecosystem.

Thirdly, on this one night of the year we enact the washing of feet. This episode is recorded only in John's gospel, and it's interesting to note that even though this gospel contains a lengthy discourse on the Bread of Life, it does not include an institution narrative. Was John subtly telling his community that we gather in vain to celebrate the Eucharist if we do not also wash each other's feet?

Finally, having been nourished at the table of the Word, we now turn to the table of the Eucharist. Consider for a moment the story of the two disciples walking to Emmaus after the death of Jesus. The mysterious stranger who joins them is the risen Lord, but they fail to recognise him. Nor do they recognise him when he explains how all that has just happened in Jerusalem is the unfolding of God's plan. It is only when they sit down for a meal that the disciples suddenly recognise Jesus, and they recognise him in the breaking of the bread. Each time we gather around the table of the Lord, we encounter him in the breaking of the bread, as did the disciples on the road to Emmaus.

Tonight's liturgy tells us who we are as disciples of Jesus; it defines our ecosystem. We are a community called to love one another in humble service, a community of disciples nourished and sustained on our pilgrimage by the Word and Bread of Life.

GOOD FRIDAY

And bowing his head, he gave up the spirit. (Jn 19:30)

The novels of the Jewish Rabbi, Chaim Potok, are set amidst a community of hasidic Jews known as Ladovers, named after the town of Ladov in Russia where the founder of their sect was born. It is a very observant community, devoted to fulfilling the Jewish law in every detail.

In one of his novels, *My Name is Asher Lev*, Potok tells the story of a young boy who has a gift not highly regarded in the Hasidic community. It is the gift of painting.[76] The young Asher Lev is told by his father that his drawings are foolishness. 'Have you nothing better to do with your time.' Such a talent comes from the *sitra achra* – the dark side. But the boy is not deterred by his father's disapproval, and continues to draw.

His mother wants to support her son's great gift, even though she does not understand it. But she does not wish to offend her husband who is adamant that his son must give up his drawing and devote himself more seriously to the study of the Torah.

The aged rabbi who leads the community is not so dogmatic, and makes arrangements for a Jewish painter to take the young Asher Lev under his wing. In time, Asher Lev becomes a highly acclaimed painter, but his father's attitude remains unchanged. He is wasting his life, says the father. He has betrayed me.

When he sees some of his son's paintings, particularly those of the naked human body, he dismisses such painting as at best a frivolity and at worst a desecration. Asher Lev's artistic career reaches a crisis point when he attempts to portray the anguish of his mother's experience – torn between the love of husband and son.

It was Picasso who said: 'Art is a lie which makes us realise the truth.'[77] And so to portray the anguish of his mother artistically, he borrows a form unique to Christian iconography: the scene of the crucifixion. In one sense, he tells a lie to portray a truth that transcended words. What evolved became an artistic masterpiece, titled Brooklyn Crucifixion. It was a canvas portraying his mother crucified, and her husband and son standing at the foot of the cross.

---

[76] Chaim Potok, *My Name is Asher Lev*, Penguin Books, Harmondsworth, Middlesex, 1972.
[77] Quoted in Chaim Potok, p.5.

The critical response was initially hostile: Jews labelled him a traitor, an apostate, someone who inflicted shame upon his family and upon the Jewish people. Some Christians denounced him as a mocker of ideas sacred to Christians, a blasphemous manipulator of forms revered by Christians for two thousand years. His father, upon seeing the painting, was struck with rage, bewilderment and sadness.

And why did he choose the image of crucifixion, and risk being reviled? Asher Lev explained that there was no image from his own Jewish tradition that he could borrow to portray his mother's lonely torment. No image which captured her agony, her anguish and her suffering. 'I wanted an image that immediately said: 'Body and soul in protracted solitary torment.' I wanted an image of long and lonely suffering.' And so he was drawn to the image of the crucified one.

EASTER SUNDAY

'Why look among the dead for someone who is alive?' (Lk 24: 5)

A tribe of American Indians known as the Hopi people live in the Navajo reservation in north-eastern Arizona. The children of the Hopi people undergo an interesting initiation rite at an early age. The initiation rite is a deliberately structured process of disenchantment to mark their entry into adulthood. The rite centres around the kachinas. Kachinas are masked spirits who visit the village.[78] During the rite of initiation the kachinas tell the children secret stories. They frighten the children with their grotesque masks, and they dance to entertain them. But the climax of the ceremony holds a surprise. The children are taken into a *kiva*, an underground ceremonial chamber, and there they wait for the *kachinas* to dance for them one last time. The children are waiting. They can hear the *kachinas* call out as they approach the ladder at the opening of the *kiva*.

But to the children's amazement, the *kachinas* enter the *kiva* without their masks. For the first time in their lives, the young children discover that the *kachinas* are actually members of their own village impersonating the spirits. It is a profound experience of disenchantment for the children.

During the rite the children naively believe that the masked dancers really are the spirits of the Hopi tribe. Up until this moment they have identified the symbols of the sacred – the masked dancers – with the sacred itself. The unmasking shatters this childish faith. Looking back on the experience, one Hopi said:

I cried and cried into my sheepskin that night, feeling I had been made a fool of. How could I ever watch the Kachinas dance again? I hated my parents and thought I could never believe the old folks again ... I know now it was best and the only way to teach the children, but it took me a long time to know that.[79]

Disenchantment initiates the children into a more profound sense of the sacred. It is a maturing process. The kachinas must be appropriated in a new way. The sacred is infinitely more than the masked dancers.[80] At first, the experience of disenchantment

---

[78] Frank Waters, *Book of the Hopi,* Penguin Books, New York ,1977, p.167
[79] Dorothy Eggan, *'The General Problem of Hopi Adjustment'*, American Anthropologist 45 (1943), p.372.
[80] Sam Gill, 'Disenchantment' in *Parabola*, Summer, 1976, Vol.I, No.3, pp.6-13.

appears negative; it shatters our world. Things aren't as we thought they were. Disenchantment is always a challenge to rediscover and reappropriate the truth at a deeper, at a more profound level. The great Dominican theologian and preacher, Meister Eckhart, put it this way: 'Do not cling to the symbols but get to the inner truth.'[81]

Disenchantment is a summons to venture deeper into the mystery that lies at the heart of all reality. It is an experience of death and rebirth; it is often painful and traumatic. Some time ago, I was preaching on the theme of disenchantment, and after Mass a woman asked if she could talk to me about the homily. Many years ago her daughter had been sexually abused by a priest. The priest subsequently faced trial and was jailed, but the mother's faith was left in tatters. She had been brought up in a traditional Catholic family that placed the priest on a pedestal. The priest was *alter Christus*, another Christ; he was the focus of Catholic life. This betrayal had shattered her childhood image, and she who was once a devout Catholic now seldom attends Mass. There was no quick fix for this woman's anguish, but in our conversation she admitted that her experience had been similar to the removal of the *kachinas'* masks. Just as the young children were led to understand that the masked dancers were not spirits, she had to accept that this priest was not the church. She was summoned through this trauma to deepen her understanding of God and the church.

The same could be said of those Catholics who have struggled to come to terms with changes in the Catholic Church since the Second Vatican Council. The Tridentine Mass had remained virtually unchanged for over four hundred years. There was a rich devotional life in local parishes, and seminaries and religious orders were blessed with many vocations. Liturgical changes were introduced rapidly and without sufficient preparation. Latin gave way to the vernacular liturgy, and many people felt that the sense of mystique they experienced at Mass had evaporated. Once again, the kachinas' masks have been removed.

When the masks of the *kachinas* are removed, we undergo a death experience. The secure world that we once knew is shattered; firm foundations crumble; certitude dissolves into doubt. The disciples of Jesus knew the feeling well. Their Master had been executed as a criminal, his dead body laid to rest in a borrowed tomb. They, meanwhile, all fled in fear.

Disenchanted disciples, enduring the pain of loss, perhaps even the pain of

---

[81] Meister Eckhart, '*Good Hinders the Best*', in R. Blakney, *Meister Eckhart*, (Harper Torch-books, 1941), quoted in Michael Whelan, *Without God All Things Are Lawful*, St Pauls, Sydney, 1994, p.101.

deception. Was this man really the Messiah, or were we deceived? But as the disciples are soon to discover, disenchantment is more an experience of discovery than of loss. He whose lifeless body was laid to rest in the tomb has shattered the bars and burst the gates of death. He who is risen from the dead remains with his disciples forever.

If the *kachinas* do not remove their masks, the children remain in a world of illusion. If the seed is not buried in the earth, it remains but a single seed. Why look among the dead for someone who is alive? (Lk 24:5).

SECOND SUNDAY OF EASTER

(YEAR C)

Thomas, called the Twin, who was one of the Twelve, was not with them when Jesus came. (Jn 20: 24)

'**There were many other signs that Jesus worked and the disciples saw**, but they are not recorded in this book.' Aren't these some of the most exasperating words in the whole of the New Testament? John quite unashamedly tells us that he knew much more about the life and teachings of Jesus, but he chose not to tell us. As disappointing as that may be, it does give us an insight into why he wrote the gospel. He had no intention of writing a biography – the life and times of Jesus Christ! His wrote what he did to invite a response of faith. 'These are recorded so that you may believe that Jesus is the Christ, the Son of God, and that believing this you may have life through his name.'

Having said that, though, I've always been fascinated by one detail included in today's gospel that is seemingly irrelevant to the story. We're told that Thomas is the twin. We're never told who the twin is, nor is this fact mentioned again in the gospel. If John is going to be economical with information about Jesus' life, why does he bother to tell us a seemingly irrelevant detail about one of his disciples? Well, the simple answer is, we don't know. But of all the explanations I've read in various gospel commentaries, the answer that I like best is this: We're told that Thomas is 'the twin' because we're supposed to ask the question, 'Who is Thomas' twin?' And the answer is – me! I am Thomas' twin. Like Thomas, I also want to touch, to feel, to see with my own eyes. As a Christian, I'm asked to accept a great deal on faith. A few facts that I could test or verify empirically wouldn't go astray.

The French philosopher Gabriel Marcel (1889–1973) made a useful distinction between 'problem' and 'mystery'. 'Whenever a problem is found,' Marcel wrote, 'I am working upon data placed before me...'[82] Problems can be subjected to empirical verification and scientific testing. A mechanic repairing an engine, a computer programmer tracking down an error in the system, a student grappling with

---

[82] Gabriel Marcel, *Being and Having*, Collins: Fontana Library, London, 1965, p. 185

a mathematical equation, a scientist studying the AIDS virus, a person challenged by a crossword puzzle, or someone absorbed in a whodunit, are all immersed in a 'problem'. Time and experience will eventually yield an answer to these kinds of problems. They may totally absorb us, at least for a while, but we are capable of divorcing ourselves from them and getting on with something else.[83]

'Mystery', as Marcel defines the term, is not a puzzle to be solved as Sherlock Holmes would do. Mystery describes those problems that engage us at a more profound level of our being. A mystery is a problem that encroaches upon and invades its own data.[84] It involves those questions in which we ourselves are immersed, questions that we cannot put to one side. We are actors, not detached spectators, in the theatre of mystery. Does my life have any ultimate meaning? Is there a divine being? If there is, has that being ever communicated with humanity? How does one determine right from wrong, good from evil, and are these ultimately arbitrary terms that vary from age to age, from one culture to another? Does human suffering have any meaning? Is there life after death in some form or another? The answers to 'mystery', if there be any, are not 'in the back of the book.' They may be rationally explained, but unlike 'problem' they are not amenable to empirical verification. In the words of an ancient saying, life is not a problem to be solved, but a mystery to be lived.

'Mystery' is a source of uneasiness in a society where 'truth' for many people is synonymous with 'fact', which can be demonstrated, confirmed and proved by scientific methods. Science has debunked many self-evident truths held passionately in past ages, not the least of which was the commonly held belief that the earth was at the centre of the universe. The scientific and philosophical revolutions that gave birth to the modern world view confidently affirmed the autonomy and self-sufficiency of human reason. The legacy of the Enlightenment dismissed metaphysical speculation as 'idle intellectual fantasy' that was a 'disservice to humanity'.[85] Science, reason and empirical data were to be the Enlightenment's lethal weapons in the battle against dogmatic religion and popular superstition.[86] However, such weapons may have scaled the battlements of 'problem', but 'mystery' remains an inviolable fortress. That's not to say that what we hold in faith is irrational. It simply means that our beliefs cannot be verified empirically or scientifically tested. For example, when I die one of two

---

[83] cf. Kenneth T. Gallagher, *The Philosophy of Gabriel Marcel*, Fordham University Press, New York, 1962, pp.31-2.
[84] Gabriel Marcel, op. cit., p.186.
[85] Richard Tarnas, *The Passion of the Western Mind*, Ballantine Books, New York, 1991, p.310.
[86] Ibid, p.312.

things happens: I become dust and ashes and no more, or, in some way or another I live on. I believe, in faith, that physical death will not be the end of me, but I can't prove that scientifically.

In his *Introduction to Christianity,* the theologian Joseph Ratzinger (now Pope Benedict XVI) explored what it means to be a Christian, and particularly the nature of faith and doubt. To make an important point he used a story included in an anthology compiled by the Jewish philosopher Martin Buber (1878–1965) entitled *Tales of the Hasidim.* Buber tells a story about a self-assured adherent of the Enlightenment, a very learned man who had heard of the saintly Rabbi of Berditchev. He intended to visit the rabbi in order to argue with him, to shatter his religious beliefs. When he entered the rabbi's room, he found him walking up and down with a book in his hand, wrapped in thought. The rabbi paid no attention to the new arrival. Suddenly the rabbi stopped, looked at the visitor fleetingly, and said, 'But perhaps it is true after all'. The visitor was taken aback. His knees trembled, so terrible was the rabbi to behold and so terrible his simple utterance to hear. But Rabbi Levi Jizchak now turned to face him and spoke quite calmly:

My son, the great scholars of the Torah with whom you have argued wasted their words on you; you laughed at them. They were unable to lay God and his Kingdom on the table before you, and nor can I. But think, my son, perhaps it is true.

The exponent of the Enlightenment opposed him with all his strength; but this single word 'perhaps' ate at him long after he had left the rabbi, and it finally broke his resistance. [87]

Ratzinger points out that the word 'perhaps' unites the believer and the unbeliever. I believe, 'perhaps' I am wrong; I do not believe, 'perhaps' I am wrong. Only fundamentalists and fanatics are uncomfortable with a journey peppered with 'perhaps'. The rabbi was able to confront his own doubts and insecurities; the adherent of the Enlightenment was so secure and smug in his own world view that he was unable to entertain the possibility that he might be wrong. If we are honest we will admit that faith is a cocktail of belief and doubt, with variable quantities of each ingredient. Ultimately, we arrive at the truth, not by asking the right question, but by setting out on a quest, and that requires tremendous courage. As much as we might like to see and touch like Thomas, the words of the Lord in today's gospel are directed to us: 'Blessed are those who have not seen and yet believe.'

---

[87] Martin Buber, *Tales of the Hasidim*, Shocken Books, New York, 1947, pp.228-229.

THIRD SUNDAY OF EASTER

(YEAR C)

Jesus called out, 'Have you caught anything, friends?' (Jn 21: 5)

Jesus asks two questions in today's gospel, addressed not only to the disciples and to Peter, but to each of us as well. The first question is, 'Have you caught anything, friends?' The disciples reply, 'No.' There is a sense of emptiness in their reply. They have followed Jesus for almost three years and his execution has brought their lives to a standstill. The sense of loss is numbing and with heavy hearts they return to the lake they know so well and resume their former occupation. It is difficult to come to terms with loss – the loss of a friend or spouse, the end of a marriage, the loss of employment, even the loss of our children growing up and leaving home.

Loss is an encompassing theme in life. Only recently I was speaking with a friend who is confronting a profound loss in her own life. After more than fifteen years of marriage she has not fallen pregnant. Several operations that initially offered hope have not helped, so she and her husband opted for the IVF program, but after several attempts that has not proved successful either. Just prior to Easter they tried the IVF program yet again, at a cost of almost $8000, but to no avail. Given the fact that she is almost 40 years old, the odds are against her falling pregnant. However sad and depressing that may be, there comes a time to let go.

This is a lesson that the disciples of Jesus had to learn. Their time with him had not turned out as they had expected. The anointed one of God (the Christ) was not supposed to die as a common criminal upon a cross. But as they are soon to discover, they are on the threshold of a future far more glorious than they could ever have imagined. These seasoned fishermen have laboured fruitlessly throughout the night. A stranger on the shore encourages them to throw out their net one more time. They do, and their catch is amazingly bountiful.

The second question in today's gospel is addressed to Peter. 'Do you love me?' When the disciples came ashore they saw some bread there, and a *charcoal fire* with fish cooking on it. Why is it important that we know that it was a *charcoal* fire? Here John is making a link with an earlier episode in the gospel. Do you recall when Jesus was arrested he was taken to the high priest's palace for interrogation. As Peter entered the palace he is challenged by the girl on duty at the door: 'Aren't you another of that man's disciples?' He answered, 'I am not.' We're told that it was cold, and the servants and guards had lit a charcoal fire (18:18). The charcoal fire is the symbolic link between Peter's denial and the second question in today's gospel.

Earlier in the gospel Peter had insisted, 'loudly and emphatically, that he at least will remain loyal to Jesus. He's not going to let him down. He wants to follow him wherever he goes: to prison, to death, wherever. In fact, he is prepared to lay down his own life on Jesus' behalf (13:36-37).'[88] Peter's bravado is soon tested, and it all goes horribly wrong, not once, but three times.

This second question, 'Do you love me?' is about forgiveness and healing. Two of the disciples betrayed Jesus – Judas and Peter. *The Gospel According to Judas*, written by the novelist Jeffrey Archer in collaboration with the Australian biblical scholar Fr Francis Moloney, is the fictional story of Judas told by his (fictional) son, Benjamin. Although this 'gospel' incorporates a good deal of material from the canonical gospels, it puts an interesting spin on the betrayal of Judas. According to the scenario presented by Archer and Moloney, Judas is fearful of what might happen to Jesus in Jerusalem, so he betrays him to a scribe on the understanding that Jesus will be led away to safety. The scribe reneges on the deal and becomes part of the plot to have Jesus killed. Judas in this scenario is the betrayed rather than the betrayer. Judas doesn't hang himself, but rather lives out the remainder of his life as a member of the Essene community, an ascetic Jewish sect living at Qumran by the shore of the Dead Sea. Nothing is said about the death of Judas in the gospels of Mark, Luke or John, but Matthew's gospel tells us that Judas commits suicide. Fr Francis Moloney thinks it 'most likely' that Matthew included this detail to further blacken Judas' name. Fr Moloney, an internationally acclaimed biblical scholar, said that he helped Jeffrey Archer write this novel because he wanted 'to encourage Christians to see Judas as fallible but redeemable like all humankind.' [89] I have a great deal of sympathy with Moloney's sentiments.

We so often burden our conscience unnecessarily by allowing past sins and failures to weigh us down and cripple our journey of faith. In saying that, I have

---

[88] Tom Wright, *John for Everyone, Part 2, Chapters 11-21*, SPCK, London, 2002, p.159.
[89] Elena Curti, 'Judas the obscure', *The Tablet*, 31 March 2007, p.9.

in mind a graphic image from the 1986 film, The Mission, set in South America in the middle of the eighteenth century. Two of the central characters in the film are the Jesuit missionary, Fr Gabriel (played by Jeremy Irons) and a ruthless slave trader, Rodrigo Mendoza (Robert De Niro). The unsuspecting Mendoza finds his fiancée in bed with his younger brother, Felipe, and erupts in a passionate rage. In the ensuing duel, Mendoza kills his brother, but avoids punishment because he's an aristocrat. However, he cannot calm his troubled conscience and decides to undertake a severe penance. To this end, Mendoza consults Fr Gabriel, who suggests that he might return with him to the mission of San Carlos. It was a fitting penance, for it was in that region that Mendoza had captured local Indians for the slave trade.

Fr Gabriel and the contrite Mendoza embark upon the long and arduous journey to San Carlos, through breathtakingly beautiful country. Mendoza is weighed down by guilt and remorse. He is also burdened by a heavy rope net that he drags along behind him. The net that he had once used to ensnare Indians for the slave trade now contains the armour and weapons of his former life, including the sword that had killed his brother. In such hazardous terrain, progress is slow and difficult. One of the Jesuit missionaries, exasperated at Mendoza's self-imposed penance, cuts the bundle loose. But Mendoza is not to be absolved so easily; he recovers the bundle and continues the journey, burdened as before. Some time later the rope is again cut, this time by a local tribesman, and the net plunges into the ravine below, impossible to recover. Mendoza is at last free to continue unencumbered.

So often the bundles we drag behind us are more subtle than Mendoza's, but no less of a burden. Our fidelity to the Kingdom of God must lie in our resolve to be faithful despite all our infidelities, to press ahead and not look back, despite the weight of past sinfulness. Both Judas and Peter had betrayed their Lord, but one looked back in despair and hanged himself; the other looked forward in hope and became the rock upon which Jesus built his church.

FOURTH SUNDAY OF EASTER

(Y E A R   C)

'The sheep that belong to me listen to my voice.' (Jn 10: 27)

Behind today's gospel lies the image of the first century Palestinian shepherd. In Palestine at the time of Jesus, sheep were kept mainly for wool and milk, not to be slaughtered for food. The shepherd therefore knew his flock well, giving names to each of the sheep. They recognised his voice and followed him alone. The author HV Morton, writing in the 1930s, describes the way in which a Palestinian shepherd talks to his sheep. In his fascinating book In the Steps of the Master, Morton writes:

Sometimes the shepherd talks to the sheep in a loud sing-song voice, using a weird language unlike anything I have ever heard in my life. ... Early one morning I saw an extraordinary sight not far from Bethlehem. Two shepherds had evidently spent the night with their flocks in a cave. The sheep were all mixed together and the time had come for the shepherds to go in different directions. One of the shepherds stood some distance from the sheep and began to call. First one, then another, then four or five animals ran towards him; and so on until he had counted his whole flock. [90]

It would seem that little has changed over the centuries. It was a scene that Jesus was undoubtedly familiar with when he said: 'The sheep that belong to me listen to my voice; I know them and they follow me.'

In many parts of the Catholic Church today is designated Vocation Sunday. 'Vocation', as you're often reminded, comes from the Latin word *vocare*, meaning 'to call'. We are called, but for various reasons we may choose not to listen, to be selectively deaf. A woman whose husband had become violently ill wasted no time in driving him to the casualty ward of the local hospital. After the doctor had examined the man thoroughly he asked if he could speak with the wife in private.

'Your husband's heart,' the doctor explained, 'is in a very bad condition. Here's what you must do: Firstly, remove all stress from his life. He

---

[90] HV Morton, *In the Steps of the Master*, Methuen & Co, London, Seventeenth edition, 1945, p.154.

can continue working, but when he gets home, keep the kids quiet and have them ready for bed. Make sure you're always looking attractive and ready for romance should he be in the mood. Let him relax with a drink in front of the television and watch whatever program he wishes. Always cook his favourite meals, and keep the house spotlessly clean. Make sure his clothes are washed and ironed immaculately. Don't ever argue with him, and never nag; always do what he wants without question. Unless you fulfil my instructions to the letter, your husband will be dead within the month.

The wife was badly shaken by the prognosis and rejoined her husband. 'What did the doctor have to say?' asked the husband. 'The doctor said that you'll be dead within a month!'

We are called, but who or what are we called to be? When Rabbi Zusya grew old and knew that his time on earth was nearing a close, his students gathered around him. One of them asked him if he was afraid of dying. 'I am afraid of what God will ask me,' the Rabbi said. 'What will he ask you?' 'He will not ask me, 'Zusya, why were you not like Moses?' He will ask me, 'Zusya, why were you not Zusya?'

We are not all called to follow the same spiritual path, an insight expressed beautifully in this story from the desert fathers: 'Abbot Mark once said to Abbot Arsenius: 'It is good, is it not, to have nothing in your cell that just gives you pleasure? For example, once I knew a brother who had a little wildflower that came up in his cell, and he pulled it out by the roots.' 'Well', said Abbot Arsenius, 'that is all right. But each man should act according to his own spiritual way. And if one were not able to get along without the flower, he should plant it again.' [91]

Today we are invited to listen to the call God addresses to each of us individually. Each of us has a vocation, although not everyone might appreciate that fundamental truth. That becomes painfully obvious in Woody Allen's 1983 movie Zelig. Leonard Zelig, played by Allen, is a man so starved for acceptance that he literally transforms himself into whoever he is around. He is so eager to fit in, to be accepted, to be liked, that he turns black, Chinese, obese, and Indian chief. Zelig adopts not only their physical but also their mental characteristics. He is a human chameleon, becoming the company he keeps. Zelig baffles medical experts at a Manhattan hospital, but only Dr. Eudora Fletcher, played by Mia Farrow, seems to want to cure her sick patient. Little is known about him, except that he was born to a Jewish immigrant family and that his father, Morris, was a

---

[91] Thomas Merton, *The Wisdom of the Desert*, Sheldon Press, London, 1974, pp.67-8.

Yiddish actor. The theory the experts come up with for his condition, is that his ability to transform himself evolved from a young age as the result of constantly trying to conform. Underneath the comedy is the tragic, poignant story of a man who lacks his own unique personality. 'I'm nobody: I'm nothing,' he tells Dr Fletcher.

But nobody is nobody; nobody is nothing. Cardinal Newman once wrote: 'God has committed some work to me which he has not committed to another.'[92] Rowan Williams, the Archbishop of Canterbury, echoing the sentiments of Rabbi Zusya, once said, 'At the Day of Judgment, as we are often reminded, the question will not be about why we failed to be someone else; I shall not be asked why I wasn't Martin Luther King or Mother Teresa, but why I wasn't Rowan Williams.'

I have called you, the Shepherd says; listen to my voice and trust in the gifts I have given you to be faithful to that call.

---

[92] John Shea, *The Relentless Widow: The Spiritual Wisdom of the Gospels for Christian Preachers and Teachers*, Liturgical Press, Collegeville, MN, 2006, p.134

FIFTH SUNDAY OF EASTER

(YEAR C)

'I give you a new commandment: love one another.' (Jn 13: 34)

Today's gospel tells us that the defining characteristic of the Christian community is love. But what is the nature of that love? Lucy is extremely skeptical when Linus informs her that he intends to become a doctor. And why couldn't he become a doctor? Because, Lucy tells him, he doesn't love mankind. Linus protests: He does love mankind; it's only people that he can't stand.[93]

Pope Benedict reminds us of the vast semantic range of the word 'love.' In the English language it is extremely elastic. We speak of 'love of country, love of one's profession, love between friends, love of work, love between parents and children, love between family members, love of neighbour and love of God.'[94] And we can talk about loving ice cream, or loving our pet dog, or a particular movie that we loved.

What, we may ask, does it mean to love, and to love as Jesus has loved us? Today's gospel confronts us with the 'new commandment', that we love one another. The word most frequently used for 'love' in the New Testament is *agapē* (together with the verb *agapāo* and the adjective a*gapētos*). These three words occur a total of 320 times in the New Testament and almost a third of those occurrences are in gospel and letters of St John (44 in the gospel and 62 in 1-3 John).[95] The use of *agapē* in the Johannine letters is distinguished from the gospel in the fact that God's love and our love for God are in relationship to our love for one another.[96] In other words, we cannot love God if we do not love one another.

Let us clear up what *agapē* is not. It is not 'falling in love.' The American psychiatrist M. Scott Peck in his international best seller *The Road Less Travelled* describes romantic love as 'a trick that our genes pull on our otherwise perceptive mind to hoodwink or trap us into marriage.'[97] In his classic work *The Art of*

---

[93] Charles Schulz, *The Complete Peanuts, 1959 to 1960*, Fantagraphics Books, New York, 2006, p.136.
[94] Pope Benedict XVI, *Deus Caritas* Est, n.2
[95] Horst Balz and Gerhard Schneider (eds), *Exegetical Dictionary of the New Testament, Volume 1*, William B. Eerdmans Publishing Company, Grand Rapids, MI,1990, p.9.
[96] Ibid, p.12.

Loving Erich Fromm draws our attention to the confusion that occurs between *falling* in love and the permanent state of being in love, or as he would say, 'standing' in love. By its very nature falling in love is not lasting. [98] It is not an act of will, nor is it a conscious choice.

If the love that Jesus enjoins upon his disciples has nothing to do with falling in love, neither is it friendship. Friendship is a rare and precious gift, and in the words of Ben Sira 'something beyond price ... the elixir of life' (Si 6:15, 16). It is psychologically and emotionally impossible to be friends with everyone, and there are some people whom we will never include among our friends, despite the best will in the world. *Agapē* is not about friendship, just as it has nothing to do with falling in love. M. Scott Peck defines the kind of love we call *agapē* as 'the *will* to extend oneself for the purpose of nurturing one's own or another's spiritual growth.

That is the insight of that well-known, but hair-raising fairytale, *Rapunzel*. Once upon a time, a little baby named Rapunzel, is kidnapped by an ugly old hag of a witch and taken to a tower in a secluded part of the forest. There Rapunzel grows up to be an exceedingly beautiful person is every way. But the witch, envious of her beauty, continually tells her: 'You're ugly, you're hideous, you're repulsive. In fact, I've done you a favour by locking you away from the sight of other people, because if they saw you they would tell you how ugly you are, and, my dear, your heart would be broken.' Rapunzel is a prisoner, not so much of the stone tower, but rather of the image of herself created by the witch.

Well, fairy tales aren't allowed to end quite like that, and so it happens that a handsome young prince, strolling through the forest, happens perchance to come across this strange tower – strange because it had no doors. As the young prince looked towards an upper window, he happened to see the face of Rapunzel, and immediately falls in love. But how to gain access? The prince, an astute young lad, remained hidden so he could observe how the witch left and returned: 'Rapunzel, Rapunzel, let down your hair, and I shall climb your golden stair.' Thus the witch came and went. Rapunzel, you realise, had not been to the hairdressers for a long time!

And so, when the witch departed to do the shopping, the prince tried his luck. 'Rapunzel, Rapunzel, let down your hair and I shall climb your golden stair.' Rapunzel lowers her hair, and up he climbs. I did warn you that this was

---

[97] M. Scott Peck, *The Road Less Travelled*, Arrow Books, London, Reprinted 1999, p.95.
[98] Erich Fromm, *The Art of Loving*, Unwin Books, London, Tenth Impression, 1971, p.11.

a hair-raising story! And what happened when Rapunzel and her prince met? In meeting her prince Rapunzel perceives an image of herself that she had not thought possible. In the encounter with her beloved, she is recreated. This is true not only in the case of Rapunzel, but with all of us. We desperately need to see in the mirror of another's eyes our own goodness and beauty, if we are to be truly free. Until that moment, we, too, will remain locked inside the towers of ourselves.[99]

Genuine love is volitional rather than emotional.'[100] Erich Fromm calls it 'the active concern for the life and the growth of that which we love.' [101] St Paul's rhapsody to love in 1 Corinthians 13: 4-6 describes *agapē* as :

always patient and kind; ... never jealous; ... not boastful or conceited, it is never rude and never seeks its own advantage, it does not take offence or store up grievances. Love does not rejoice at wrongdoing, but finds its joy in the truth. It is always ready to make allowances, to trust, to hope and to endure whatever comes.

Another important point to make about Christian love is this: it is manifested more often than not in the tedium of daily life, in very little, ordinary things. When Agnes Gonxha Bojaxhiu joined the Institute of the Blessed Virgin she received the name Teresa after St Therese of Lisieux, a young Carmelite nun who had died from tuberculosis at the age of 24 a century earlier in 1897. We know Agnes Gonxha Bojaxhiu as Mother Teresa of Calcutta, and during her lifetime she was acclaimed as a saintly woman. She lived the gospel heroically on the world stage, even winning the Nobel Peace Prize. Her life could not have been more different from that of her namesake. Therese of Lisieux had lived a cloistered life of obscurity in an enclosed convent since she was 15 years old. Just a few weeks before she died, one of her community made this observation: 'She's a sweet little Sister, but what will we be able to say about her after her death? She didn't do anything.' In fact, Therese's sister, Mother Agnes, who knew her best, left the manuscript of her life unnoticed and unread for three months.[102] St Therese's 'little way' is about being salt and light, but she remained truly hidden, forgetting herself in quiet acts of love. 'In my little way,' she wrote, 'are only very ordinary things.'

---

[99] John Powell, *Why Am I Afraid to Love?* Argus Communications, Chicago, IL,p. 29.
[100] M. Scott Peck, *The Road Less Travelled*, p.126.
[101] Erich Fromm, *The Art of Loving*, p.25.
[102] James McCaffery, 'A saint for our season', *The Tablet,* 19 October 1996, p.1351.

SIXTH SUNDAY OF EASTER

(YEAR C)

'Peace I bequeath to you, my own peace I give you.' (Jn 14:27)

The Oxford Dictionary defines peace as freedom from, or cessation of war; freedom from civil disorder. That definition tells us more about what peace is not, rather than what peace is. If peace is simply freedom from war or civil disorder, then we have enjoyed very few days of peace during this century. The French Commission, Justice and Peace, noted that between 1945 and 1980 there have been only sixty days in which no military conflict was recorded anywhere in the world.[103] Nor has the situation improved since 1980. Every day the evening news gives us the latest update on the situation in Iraq or Afghanistan, and the latest fatalities in the ongoing conflict between the Israelis and the Palestinians.

Peace is surely much more than 'freedom from' – freedom from war, freedom from aggression, freedom from hostility. In fact, the New Testament scholar Raymond Brown writes that the peace that Jesus bequeaths to his disciples has nothing to do with the absence of warfare, nor with an end of psychological tension, nor with a sentimental feeling of well-being.[104] The peace which Jesus offers – *Shalom* – is a peace that no experience in life can ever take from us. It is a peace that no sorrow, no danger, no suffering can ever diminish. It is a peace that is independent of outward circumstances.

Shalom is not 'a vague wish for inner calm and outer harmony.' [105] The root meaning of shalom is to be whole or complete.[106] But the peace that comes from wholeness or completeness is elusive because inside of us, it would seem, 'something is at odds with the very rhythm of things and we are forever restless, dissatisfied, frustrated, and aching ... (T)here is within us a fundamental

---

[103] French Commission, Justice et Paix, in Le Monde entre deux Eres – Reflections on War and Peace in the Present Times, 20 February 1980, 2, cited in Michael Whelan, *Without God All Things Are Lawful*, St Pauls, Homebush, NSW, 1994, p.81.
[104] Raymond Brown, *The Gospel According to John XIII-XXI*, Doubleday & Company, New York, 1970, p.653.
[105] John Shea, *The Relentless Widow: The Spiritual Wisdom of the Gospels for Christian Preachers and Teachers*, p.141.
[106] Joseph P. Healey, 'Peace', in David Noel Freedman (Ed), *The Anchor Bible Dictionary, Volume 5* Doubleday, New York, 1992, p.206.

disease, an unquenchable fire that renders us incapable, in this life, of ever coming to full peace.'[107] The German theologian Karl Rahner wrote about the 'torment of the insufficiency of everything attainable.'[108] One response to this restlessness is to fill the void with possessions, but this will not lead to peace. *Shalom* may be likened to a wise man who sat in meditation by the riverbank. A disciple bent down to place two enormous pearls at his feet, a token of reverence and devotion. The wise man opened his eyes, took one of the pearls in his hands, but held it so carelessly that it slipped and rolled down the bank into the river. The horrified disciple plunged into the river in a desperate attempt to find the pearl. He dived into the muddy waters again and again until late in the evening, but he had no luck in finding the pearl. Finally, all wet and exhausted, he roused the wise man from his meditation and said: 'You saw where the pearl fell. Show me the spot so that I can get it back for you.' The wise man took the remaining pearl in his hand, threw it into the river and said, 'Look there.'[109]

Shalom, peace, is a completeness that is immune to addiction, and we so often fall prey to out-of-control addictions. Maybe there is nothing new in this, but in today's affluent world the objects of addiction – sex, alcohol, drugs, gambling, and pornography, especially internet pornography – are more accessible than ever before. Addiction involves a loss of control, the perfect metaphor for which is the sorcerer's apprentice, a tale told by the second-century Roman poet Lucian, and popularized in Walt Disney's 1940 cartoon animation, *Fantasia*. An old sorcerer went on a trip, leaving his apprentice to fetch water from the well. The boy soon tires of this tedious work and recalls that the sorcerer always used a spell to command a magic broomstick to do his work. The apprentice consults the sorcerer's book of spells, and in imitation of his master, sets the broomstick to work. For a while all goes well and he sits back and relaxes. However, it's not long before the broomstick has fetched enough water, in fact more than enough. The boy suddenly realises to his horror that he doesn't know how to stop the broomstick, and very soon the water begins to overflow and flood the room. In desperation he attacks the broomstick with an axe, but all that does is to split it in two. He now has two sticks, totally out of control, carting twice as much water as before. In a frenzy he lashes out with the axe at the two broomsticks, only to double their number yet again. Just as the whole house is to be washed away, the

---

[107] Ronald Rolheiser, *Seeking Spirituality*, Hodder & Stoughton, London, 1998, p.3.
[108] Quoted in Ronald Rolheiser, *The Restless Heart*, Hodder & Stoughton, London , 1979, p.10.
[109] Anthony de Mello, *The Heart of the Enlightened,* Fount Paperbacks, Glasgow, 1989, pp.28-29.

sorcerer returns and orders the broomstick to stop. A sadder but wiser apprentice is saved from himself.[110]

St Augustine once wrote, 'You have made us for yourself, and our heart is restless until it rests in you.'[111] Shalom, peace, is a completeness and wholeness that comes from being filled with the divine presence. People who are not in touch with the divine source of peace will become a source of conflict and dissension wherever they go. An old man was sitting on a park bench at the edge of town when a stranger approached. 'What are the people like in this town?' the stranger asked. 'What were they like in your last town?' replied the old man. 'They were kind, generous, and would do anything for you if you were in trouble.' The old man reassured him, 'You'll find them very much like that here in this town, too.'

Some time passed and a second stranger approached and asked the same question.' 'What are the people like in this town?' And again the old man replied: 'What were they like in the town you have just come from?'

'It was a terrible place,' came the reply. 'I was glad to get out of it. The people there were mean, unkind, and nobody would lift a finger to help you if you were in trouble.' And the old man replied: 'I'm afraid you'll find them much the same in this town.' [112]

People who are not in touch with the divine source of peace will become a source of conflict and dissension wherever they go. A peace the world cannot give, this is my gift to you.

---

[110] Adapted from William J. Bausch, *Touching the Heart,* Twenty-Third Publications, Mystic, CT, 2007, p.31.
[111] St Augustine, *Confessions,* Book I, Chapter 1.
[112] John Shea, *Dynamics of the Spiritual Life* (audiotape), ACTA Publications, 1966.

SEVENTH SUNDAY OF EASTER

(Y E A R C)

'May they all be one. Father, may they be one in us, as you are in me and I am in you, so that the world may believe it was you who sent me.' (Jn 17: 21).

The American author Mark Twain was a person of great wit and charm, popular in not only in America but also in Europe. During one European trip Twain was invited to dine with a head of state, greatly impressing his young daughter. 'Daddy', she said, 'you know every big person there is to know, except God.' Twain's daughter was referring to the fact that her father was not a religious person, at least in the conventional sense. An example of Twain's irreligious wit comes from one of his notebooks: 'If Christ were here now,' he wrote, 'there is one thing he would not be, and that is a Christian.' That is a sad commentary on the kind of Christianity that Mark Twain had observed. It was obviously a Christianity that had failed to reflect the life, the love, and the compassion of its Lord.

Nor is Mark Twain the first person to have made such an observation. A story, set in C17 Rome tells of a Jew named Solomon. Each Friday before sundown he aimed his spy-glass at the horizon to see if the Messiah wasn't coming. This caused much hilarity among the monks in the nieghbourhood. 'Solomon, Solomon', they laughed in scorn, 'You wait for him who is already come!' But if the truth be known, it was Solomon who was quietly making fun of the monks. As he climbed down from the watch tower he whispered to himself: 'If the unity among these Christians is supposed to be the sign that Jesus is indeed the Messiah, then his disciples have surely betrayed him, and therefore his credentials are false, for there are deep and bitter divisions among them.'[113]   Before ascending into heaven, Jesus prayed to the Father for his disciples: 'May they all be one ... so that the world will recognise that it was you who sent me.' It was no doubt this prayer that Solomon had in mind as he observed the bitter divisions among those who called themselves disciples of Jesus.

[113] Adapted from Roger Peyrefitte, *The Jews*, Panther, London, 1969, p.418.

These words of Jesus invite us to reflect upon the deep and bitter divisions that have existed among Christians. In Australia we can be thankful that the divisions between Christian denominations are not as acrimonious as they once were. As recently as 1971 the then Anglican archbishop of Sydney, Marcus Loane, refused to join Pope Paul VI at an ecumenical prayer service held in the Sydney Town Hall. But over thirty years later Sydney's Anglican archbishop Peter Jensen was present in St Mary's Cathedral to celebrate with the Catholic archbishop George Pell on the occasion of his induction into the College of Cardinals.

The reason for the intense hostility in Australia between Catholic and Protestant goes right back to the beginning of white settlement. Almost one quarter of the 160 000 convicts transported to Australia were Irish, and Australia's first Catholics were convicts, almost exclusively Irish. The words Irish and Catholic were virtually synonymous, whereas English and Scots were almost exclusively Protestant. There were 750 Catholic convicts on the First Fleet, and along with all the other prisoners they were forced to attend the first religious service in the Colony on Sunday, February 3, 1788. The service was held under a large tree at what is today the intersection of Hunter, Bligh and Castlereagh Streets. The Anglican minister who led the service was the Reverend Richard Johnson, and with what could only have been unconscious irony he chose as the text of his sermon a verse from Psalm 116: 'What shall I render unto the Lord for all his benefits toward me?'[114]

The C16 Reformation and the politics that followed it created an enormous chasm between English Protestant and Irish Catholic. They viewed each other across this chasm with incomprehension, hatred and fear. There were also cultural factors which further widened the chasm between Catholic and Protestant in Australia. Most of the Irish convicts came from rural areas, while most of the English convicts came from towns. A significant number of the Irish convicts spoke only Gaelic, and many of them were driven to crime as the direct result of being forced off their own land. In 1641 Catholics owned 59 percent of the land in Ireland; by 1788 they owned only about five percent of the land. These memories were transplanted to Australia, and the division between Catholic and Protestant influenced the patterns of power in Australia for at least the first 150 years of white settlement.

Before ascending to the Father the Lord commissioned his disciples to be witnesses 'not only in Jerusalem but throughout Judaea and Samaria, and indeed

---

[114] Cf. Edmund Campion, *Australian Catholics*, Penguin Books, Maryborough, Victoria, 1988, p.3.

to the ends of the earth.' All Christians are called to pray together for courage and determination to cast aside burdens inherited from the past and to heal ancient and weeping wounds in the Body of Christ.

THE ASCENSION OF THE LORD

(YEAR C)

Now as he blessed them, he withdrew from them and was carried up to heaven. (Lk 24: 51)

A reporter for a suburban newspaper in Sydney's Canterbury district was sitting on a park bench when he noticed a dog attack a young mother pushing her pram. Almost out of nowhere a lad wearing a Canterbury Rugby League football jersey appeared and beat the dog off with a stick. The reporter, a fanatical Canterbury follower, began penning the headline of his next article: 'Canterbury supporter saves young mother from savage dog attack.' He rushed over to congratulate the lad. 'Son, you make an old Canterbury supporter like me stand proud. Congratulations!' But the lad explained that he wasn't a Canterbury supporter at all. He barracked for Parramatta Rugby League club. He'd just borrowed the Canterbury jersey from a friend. With a scowl on his face the reporter took out his notepad and altered the headline he'd just written: 'Parramatta supporter cowardly attacks family pet.'

How quickly perceptions change! Christy Brown was born into a poor, working-class family in Crumlin, Dublin, in 1932. One of thirteen surviving children, he suffered from cerebral palsy and was considered mentally disabled. At the age of five he inexplicably grabbed a piece of chalk from his sister's hand with his left foot and, with great difficulty and incredulity, traced the letter A on a piece of slate. For the first time, his family knew for sure that his intellect was intact. And for the first time, he could start to communicate with them. Through the help of his strong-willed mother, a dedicated teacher, and his own courage and determination, Christy not only learnt to grapple with life's simple physical tasks and complex psychological pains, but he also developed into a brilliant painter, poet and author. Christy could control only the toe of his left foot, but with that toe he typed his autobiography, *My Left Foot*, (published in 1954). The book was subsequently made into a movie starring Daniel Day-Lewis and Brenda Fricker as Christy and his mother.

Before Christy had become well-known he saw a photograph of the English novelist Margaret Forster on the cover of one of her books and he was smitten. He wrote to her and she replied, thus beginning a warm friendship between the two of them. When Christy died in 1981 Margaret Forster said: 'He wrote me some very moving letters. It was clear to me, even then, that he had a great talent. However, though we corresponded for a long time, we never met.' That was not true. Margaret Forster did not want to meet Christy because she had learnt that he was severely physically handicapped. She had built up in her mind a beautiful image of him that was based on the letters he wrote. She feared that this image would be shattered if they met.

On one occasion after Christy had become a published author he visited London and contacted Forster's husband, coaxing him into arranging a meeting with his wife. The meeting was a disaster. The crippled body before her could not possibly be the author of letters filled with such charm and wit. They continued to correspond for some time, but eventually she stopped answering his letters and their friendship ended. Sadly, she burnt almost all of his letters. The sight of Christy's deformed and twisted body had shattered her illusion.[115]

There comes a time in every human life when our experience of reality can be rejected or repressed because it is too painful, or because it fails to measure up to our preconceptions. The disciples of Jesus shared the popular expectations of their time and awaited a David-like Messiah. The idea of a suffering and defeated messiah was abhorrent. When Jesus was arrested and shamefully crucified, the disciples were devastated. The gospel of Mark contains very unflattering portraits of his followers. Fearful for his own life Peter denied even knowing Jesus. The rest fled for their lives. Ascension and Pentecost are the two festivals that bring the Easter cycle of celebrations to a conclusion. They also mark the beginning of the disciples' integration.

The Australian psychologist Peter O'Connor describes a process that applies to individuals and organisations, and it is certainly relevant to the disciples' experience of Jesus. O'Connor describes the typical pattern of idealisation, followed by denigration, followed by integration. Idealisation refers to our tendency 'to desire a perfect, flawless partner or situation – in short, to seek paradise.' The new partner becomes a person 'in whom we see nothing but good, without the merest

---

[115] I am indebted to Flor McCarthy for the story of Christy Brown and Margaret Foster. Cf. *Sunday & Holy Day Liturgies, Year A*, Dominican Publications, Dublin, Reprinted 1992, p.67.

glimpse of any negative.' Sooner or later, however, 'the bubble bursts, reality begins to impinge and we declare that 'the honeymoon is over."' What we often fail to realise is that 'reality is a mixture of positives and negatives, of good and bad, dark and light, and inevitably the dark and imperfect aspects of the idealised partner become apparent. For instance, when reality begins to set in, the once warm, gregarious partner can start to seem over-talkative and dominating, or the decisive and purposeful partner, rigid and uncompromising.' Disillusionment sets in at this stage, and we can opt to bail out of the relationship or organisation. 'Suddenly, the previously all-perfect person becomes all bad, and there is no glimmer of anything positive.' O'Connor calls this the denigration phase, and some relationships never get beyond it. The truth is that 'we cannot achieve paradise and that reality is a lot messier than we'd like.' If we do not give up at this stage we increase our chances of moving into the third stage of the process – integration. The outcome is that we gradually accept the other person as different from us and less than perfect.[116]

Alan Jones, dean of San Francisco's Grace Cathedral, speaks of this same rhythm using slightly different words: enchantment, disenchantment and re-enchantment.[117] It works something like this. When you first meet him you think he's as gorgeous as Brad Pitt, as committed to humanity as Nelson Mandela, as funny as Rowan Atkinson, as athletic as Lleyton Hewitt and as smart as Albert Einstein. That's the stage of enchantment or idealisation. But as time passes you reach the stage of disenchantment or denigration. You come to realise that he's not a bit like these in any category whatsoever. But if you reach the final stage of integration or re-enchantment, you decide that you'll take him anyway.

Ascension and Pentecost record a fundamental shift in the disciples' perception. Having been through a period of profound disenchantment they now understand and experience the reality they had fled from. Their crucified Lord has cast off the shackles of death and promises to be with them always. The power of his presence transforms their lives.

---

[116] Peter A. O'Connor, *Looking Inwards*, Penguin Books, Camberwell, Victoria, 2003, pp.75-77.
[117] Alan Jones, *Living the Truth*, p.77.

PENTECOST SUNDAY

(YEAR C)

'I have said these things to you while still with you; but the Advocate, the Holy Spirit, whom the Father will send in my name, will teach you everything and remind you of all I have said to you.' (Jn 14: 25-26)

The book of Genesis, the first book in the Bible, the book of beginnings, poetically describes God's creation of the world. We read: 'Now the earth was a formless void, there was darkness over the deep, with a divine wind sweeping over the waters.' Creation began with the divine wind sweeping over the waters. Today's first reading from the *Acts of the Apostles* tells of another beginning – the beginning of the Church, and again we read of a wind: 'When Pentecost day came round, they had all met together, when suddenly there came from heaven a sound as of a violent wind which filled the entire house in which they were sitting.' In both Hebrew, the language in which the book of Genesis was written, and in Greek, the language in which Luke wrote the *Acts of the Apostles*, the same word is used for 'wind' and 'Spirit'. Luke, the author of the Acts of the Apostles, invites his readers to see Pentecost as a new creation, or to be more precise, a renewal of creation. As we pray in today's Responsorial Psalm: 'You send forth your Spirit ... and you renew the face of the earth.' Pentecost is a story of renewal and of profound change. God's all-powerful Spirit transforms the hearts of the timid disciples, gathered together out of fear in the upper room.

In today's gospel Jesus refers to the Spirit as the Advocate. 'Advocate' is a translation of the Greek *parakletos*. *Parakletos* is a difficult word to translate precisely into English. The *Jerusalem Bible,* the *New Revised Standard Version* and the *New American Bible* prefer 'Advocate', but it is also rendered into English as Comforter (*King James*), Helper (*New Century* and the *New King James Version*), Counsellor (*Revised Standard Version, New Living Translation*), and Paraclete (*New Jerusalem Bible*). It's interesting to note that the 1966 *Jerusalem Bible* translation opted for 'Advocate', but the *New Jerusalem Bible*, published in 1985, adopted the more obscure word 'Paraclete'. To appreciate the meaning of any word we need to see how it was used in its original context. What would a first century Greek speaker have made of John's gospel calling the Holy Spirit a *paraklētos*? In secular Greek the most characteristic usage of both *paraklein* (the verb) and *paraklētos* refers to help given during a legal trial. The *paraklētos* was a friend of the accused, called in to give a favourable character reference, and also a legal adviser or helper in the relevant court.[118] The Jewish philosopher Philo (c.20BC-c.AD 50) tells how the Jews of Alexandria wished to plead a case before the Roman Emperor Caligula. To obtain a favourable outcome they needed someone with influence and clout at the imperial court. They referred to such a person as a *paraklētos*.[119] A *paraklētos* is therefore an intercessor, a mediator, a spokesman,[120] a term used 'used in a court of justice to denote a legal assistant, counsel for the defence, an advocate; then, generally, one who pleads another's cause, an intercessor, advocate.' [121]

How all of this works out in reality is, I believe, reflected in the story of *The Monastery*, a reality-television show with a difference, broadcast by the BBC in May 2005 as three one-hour episodes. In August 2004, five men from different walks of life came to live at Worth Abbey, a Benedictine abbey in Sussex, for forty days and forty nights while television cameras tracked their progress. Two hundred and fifty people had responded to advertisements inviting them to spend six weeks in a monastery, living alongside the monks. The five men who were ultimately chosen had little or no experience of Catholicism or monastic life. They were challenged by the experience. In the words of the abbot of Worth, Fr Christopher Jamison, they were asked 'to listen continuously and deeply to themselves, to other people and to God. Forty days later, this profound listening had reshaped their hearts and minds as it has reshaped the hearts and minds of many generations of monks and nuns. These men left 'The Monastery' more in touch with life than when they had arrived.' [122]

Who were the five men finally chosen? Tony Burke, 29, is single and lives in London. He'd worked in advertising but when he came to Worth Abbey he was producing trailers for a sex chat line. Gary McCormick, 36, is a painter and decorator from Cornwall. Nick Buxton is single, 37, and studying for a PhD

---

[118] William Barclay, *New Testament Words*, SCM Press, London, 1964, p.218.
[119] In Flaccum 4, 22-23, FH Colson (Tr), *Philo*, Vol IX, Harvard University Press, 1985, p.315.
[120] Raymond E. Brown, *The Gospel According to John, XIII – XXI*, Doubleday & Company, New York, 1970, p.1136.
[121] W E Vine, M F Unger, & W White, *Vine's Complete Expository Dictionary of Old and New Testament Words* T Nelson, Nashville, 1996, on Nelson's Ultimate Bible Reference CD-ROM, Thomas Nelson p. 2003.
[122] Christopher Jamison, *Finding Sanctuary*, Phoenix, London, 2007, p.1.

in Buddhism at Cambridge University. He has been on a spiritual search for the last ten years. Anthoney Wright, 32, is a high-earning, high-energy bachelor from London who works for a legal publishing company. Peter Gruffydd, 70, is married, a published poet and a retired teacher living in Bristol.

Fr Christopher said that the five men found silence the hardest aspect of monastic life to handle and found that being truly silent was something that took time to achieve:

Their first instinct was to fill the silence with something: conversation or music were the common ways of drowning out the silence. After ten days, however, they achieved a breakthrough in their understanding: they started to see that the silence was offering them something they now wanted to receive. So in a moment of drama combined with comedy, they spontaneously handed over their mobile phones and their Walkmans. I had purposely not 'confiscated' these items when they had arrived because I wanted them to be free adults who could learn to make new choices. I wanted them to gain a new perspective and to learn for themselves how to use the silence. One of them, Tony, saw that this also extended to reading novels; this too can be a distraction from what the silence offers because it fills our inner world with distraction. So he handed in his novels along with his phone and Walkman. [123]

Tony's story is a contemporary example of the power of Pentecost. When he came to Worth Abbey he said he arrived 'without a clue. That's to say, without a clue as to what I was expecting. Later on, it became obvious that I was without a clue in other areas of my life up to this very significant point.' Speaking about his own religious background he said, 'My religious background is simple. I haven't got one.'[124] In an address to the students at Worth School in November, 2005, Tony spoke frankly of his life prior to his forty days at Worth Abbey, and the effect it had upon his life:

I'm 30 now, which probably sounds ancient to you, but in my early-twenties I started a career in advertising which was going to give me access to everything I'd ever dreamt of. Money, freedom, women, drugs and loads of booze. Working in Soho, in central London, I saw it all. And did it all. And tried to drink it all. And sometimes it was fun. But most of the time it wasn't. But drinking did make me aware of my spirituality, because there was always a voice telling me not to do it. And I knew that one day I would have to obey that voice. And that I would stop drinking soon, either through death or abstinence. But as I got older my career progressed and I earned more money and commanded more respect

[123] Ibid, p.37.
[124] Tony's story can be found at the Worth Abbey site: http://www.worthabbey.net/bbc/tony.htm

professionally, I began to drink more. And do more. I never went home or ate vegetables. And in Soho, there's always a party to go to. And that's when I started taking cocaine. And that's when I started to lose my battle. Booze and drugs stopped being a want, and started becoming a very definite need. To the point where I was drinking and taking cocaine before I left the house in the morning. I kept Jack Daniels and vodka under my desk at work. And on a number of occasions, I was caught taking drugs at work. But they didn't seem to mind too much. I was fired six months later. But by then I had lost everything. My job, my life, my friends, my self respect and my sanity. Not long after that I was admitted into a rehab unit where I was treated for addiction and depression. ... Within two months of leaving Rehab, I received an email from Tiger Aspect Television, looking for people to go and live in a monastery for six weeks. And I replied without even thinking about it. I personally believe I was singled out for it. And I believe I was brought here by God. However, there is a twist to this tale. I was then offered a job producing soft-porn for small cable TV channel. And that's what I was doing when I left London and arrived at Worth.

When Benedict wrote his rule, 1500 years ago, I doubt very much he expected me to read it. ... But 1500 years later I found myself in this strange and wonderful place – with four strangers and twenty-two monks, with a copy of this little red book (the Rule of St Benedict) in my hand. And this is where I started living. Because I realised that up to that point, by giving in to greed, addiction, consumerism, arrogance, ego, and by being completely irresponsible with people's feelings and emotions – I'd had no life at all. [125]

Tony reached a crisis point towards the end of his stay at the Abbey:

He had taken his stay in the sanctuary of the monastery to heart. His job at that time was making videos to promote a sex chat-line and the thought of returning to his old way of life was worrying him. On his last night he had a profound experience of the presence of God and he knew his life would have to change. Among the several effects of this experience, one was that he gave up his job. He now works for a regular advertising agency and spends time each day in meditation. [126]

Pentecost is about transformation and recreation, and just as God's all-powerful Spirit breathed new life into the disciples gathered together in the upper room, the Spirit continues in our day to renew the face of the earth, and all who dwell upon it.

---

[125] http://www.worthabbey.net/bbc/tony7.htm. The full text of Tony's talk can be downloaded as a PDF file from http://www.worthabbey.net/images/pdf/tony_talk_nov_2005.pdf

[126] Christopher Jamison, op. cit., p.24.

THE MOST HOLY TRINITY

(YEAR C)

Through our Lord Jesus Christ, by faith we are judged righteous and at peace with God. (Rm 5:1)

On the eve of All Saints Day, 31 October 1517, a 34-year-old Augustinian friar named Martin Luther (1483-1546) fastened 95 theses to the door of the castle church at Wittenberg. These 95 theses concerned the scandalous sale of indulgences and other abuses of papal and clerical power, and Father Luther announced that he was ready to defend his position at a public disputation. An indulgence was a remission by the Church of the punishment in purgatory due to forgiven sin, and indulgences could be applied to the living or the dead. In other words, those who had sincerely repented of their sins and received absolution in the sacrament of penance may still have to make up for the harm they had caused. The church offered full (plenary) or partial remission of this punishment.

There was nothing dramatic about Luther's action, for this was the customary procedure for advertising such disputes, which were a regular feature of university life.[127] The background to Luther's writing the 95 theses goes back to the financial difficulties of Archbishop Albert of Mainz. Albert was bishop of three dioceses, but to hold several sees concurrently he needed dispensations from Rome, and they were not cheap. He intended to finance these dispensations by proclaiming throughout Germany the indulgence that Pope Leo X had recently declared for the building of St Peter's in Rome. To put it crudely, some of the money from the sale of this indulgence went to Rome, and part of it paid off Albert's debt.

Luther's objection to indulgences grew out of his reading of St Paul's letter to the Romans, and today's second reading takes us to the heart of Luther's argument. Salvation is not the result of human effort, but rather of God's grace. 'By faith we are judged righteous,' Paul tells the Romans. According to popular preachers of the indulgence, 'Another soul to heaven springs when in the box a shilling rings.' Luther argued that no one can buy the grace freely given by God, what he called the doctrine of justification by faith. And at that time he truly believed that 'if the

---

[127] Henry Bettenson, *Documents of the Christian Church*, 185 ff; Owen Chadwick, *The Reformation*, Penguin Books, Harmondsworth, Middlesex, reprinted 1973, p.43.

pope knew the exactions of the preachers of indulgences he would rather have St Peter's basilica reduced to ashes than built with the skin, flesh and bones of his sheep' (Thesis 50). Taking his cue from the letter to the Romans, Luther argued that we are justified through divine grace alone (*sola gratia*), by faith alone (*sola fide*), and not by good works. He also accepted the Bible as the only authoritative rule of faith (sola scriptura), rejecting what he saw as human traditions.[128]

The impact that Paul's letter to the Romans has had on the history of the Christian church is incalculable.[129] It is 'widely acknowledged as the single most influential document in Christian history' and it has fuelled endless debates on the meaning of righteousness by faith and 'the interplay of faith and works in Christian life.'[130] Is salvation about what we do or about what God does? The British monk Pelagius (c.400AD) represents one extreme. Human beings are responsible for their own actions, he taught, and, if only they have the courage to will it, there is no height of sanctity that they may not attain. According to Pelagius, God gave each of us existence, and it is our responsibility to sanctify ourselves.[131] At the other extreme of the theological spectrum is the doctrine of predestination, expressed in its more rigorous form by John Calvin in the C16. Calvin's view was that 'Christ died on the cross not for all mankind, but only for the elect; that God does not will all men to be saved; that men were created by God whom he decreed from all eternity to be consigned to an eternal destruction.'[132] Predestination in this sense eliminates human freedom and responsibility; Pelagius on the other hand said that salvation was determined solely by human freedom and responsibility.

Paul's letter to the Romans deals with the Law, which refers to 'that set of regulations which were to guide Israel in its covenant with God.'[133] The Jewish people had therefore lived out of a 'works righteousness.'[134] In other words, they were made right before God by faithfully observing the Law. But Paul argues that in reality the law was powerless to achieve this because it was weakened by the flesh. What the law was powerless to do, God has freely done: 'the love of

---

[128] Gerald O'Collins and Mario Farrugia, *Catholicism: The Story of Catholic Christianity*, Oxford University Press, 2003, p.84.
[129] Joseph A Fitzmyer, *Romans,* Doubleday, New York, 1992, p.xiii.
[130] Brendan Byrne, *Romans*, The Liturgical Press, Collegeville, MN 1996, p.1.
[131] Henri Rondet, 'Pelagianism' in Karl Rahner, Cornelius Ernst and Kevin Smyth (Eds), *Sacramentum Mundi: An Encyclopedia of Theology*, Volume 4, Burns & Oates, London, 1969, p.383.
[132] Henry Chadwick, op.cit., p.95.
[133] Joseph A. Fitzmyer, *Romans,* p.132.
[134] Ibid, p.134

God has been poured into our hearts by the Holy Spirit which has been given us' (Rom 5:5).

There is something in all of us that makes us wary of 'free gifts.' What's the catch? What is demanded in return? Some time ago a friend gave me a number of complementary cinema tickets. I was slow to make use of them, and on the day prior to their expiry date I still had a number left, so I stood in the foyer of a theatre offering my unused tickets to anyone who wanted them. People, perhaps quite rightly, were suspicious of my offer of free tickets and reluctant to accept them. From our earliest years we are taught that we succeed in life by hard work. No pain, no gain. There is no such thing as a free lunch. Fr John Powell recalls his time as a student in Germany trying to master the language. While studying he served as a chaplain in a remote Bavarian convent. An 84-year-old nun was assigned to care for his room. Every time he left the room, even for a moment, she cleaned it, and not just superficially. She waxed the floors, polished the furniture, and so forth. On one occasion when he came back from a walk a little earlier than anticipated he found sister in his room, on her knees, putting a final sheen on her waxing job. Fr Powell teased her: 'Sister, you work too much!' The dear and devoted nun straightened up, still kneeling, and looked at him with a seriousness that bordered on severity. She said, '*Der Himmel is nicht billig!*' – Heaven isn't cheap![135] Undoubtedly, this nun had lived a life dedicated to the Lord, and she had worked for the kingdom of God with great fidelity and earnestness. But ultimately, God's love cannot be earned. It is a pure gift, poured into our hearts by the Holy Spirit.

---

[135] John Powell SJ, *Unconditional Love*, Argus Communications, Allen, TX, 1978, p.9.

THE BODY AND BLOOD OF CHRIST

(YEAR C)

Then he took the five loaves and the two fish, raised his eyes to heaven, and said the blessing over them; then he broke them and handed them to his disciples to distribute among the crowd. (Lk 9: 15-16)

The feeding of the multitude is the only miracle story included in all four gospels. Mark's gospel includes two separate accounts of the miracle, and Matthew, who relied significantly upon Mark, included both of Mark's stories into his gospel. So the gospels contain six accounts of a miracle in which Jesus fed a multitude. The gospel writers obviously considered that this story was saying something important about Jesus and his ministry.

What happened on that hillside close by the Sea of Galilee? Did Jesus really feed five thousand men (and presumably many more women and children) from five loaves and two fish? Some commentators, wary of miracles, have offered other imaginative explanations. They suggest, for example, that the crowd of people who followed Jesus would surely not have set off on such a long journey without making some provision beforehand. When it came time to eat, so this explanation goes, people were reluctant to share their food with others for fear that they may not have enough for themselves. But then, Jesus took what little food he and the disciples had, and began to share it among the people. Such a lovely gesture of generosity and compassion touched people's hearts and prompted them to share their food with those around them. As it turns out, there was enough, and more than enough. Such a scenario avoids a supernatural explanation for the feeding of the multitude, although such a change of heart may in its own way be just as much of a miracle! As William Barclay observes of this explanation, 'It may be that this is a miracle in which the presence of Jesus and His loveliness turned a crowd of selfish men and women into a fellowship of sharers.' [136]

Other commentators, also wary of miracles, suggest that Jesus and the disciples

---

[136] William Barclay, *The Gospel of John, Volume 1*, The Saint Andrew Press, Edinburgh, Second Edition, 1972, p.206.

fed the crowd from supplies they had hidden in a cave nearby. The German Protestant theologian Albert Schweitzer suggested that Jesus gave everyone in the crowd a morsel of bread, not to satisfy their physical hunger but as a symbol and foretaste of the heavenly banquet to which we are all invited. The meal was, therefore, 'the antitype of the messianic feast ... a sacrament of redemption.'[137]

What really happened? The simple answer is, we'll never know. Whether or not we believe in miracles depends upon our worldview, and there are no metaphysically neutral scales on which to weigh the evidence. As John P. Meier observes, 'the modern scientific worldview we automatically take with us is light-years away from the worldview of Jesus and the evangelists.'[138] However, Raymond Brown finds no reason to dismiss the miraculous from the ministry of Jesus. 'Indeed, one of the oldest memories of (Jesus) may have been that he did wondrous things – a memory that could have circulated not only among believers but among nonbelievers.'[139]

So rather than being overly obsessed with what really happened, a better question to ask is, 'What were the evangelists trying to tell us about Jesus through this story?' Let us keep in mind that the gospel writers never once use the word 'miracle.' Writing in Greek, they use words such as *dynameis* (mighty deeds), *semeion* (sign), *teras* (wonder), *paradoxa* (astounding deeds) and *thaumasia* (wondrous deeds). There is no doubt that the gospel writers would have considered the feeding of the multitude a miracle, but that is not the word they chose to describe it.

The feeding of thousands of people satisfied their hunger for the moment. There is, though, within the human person a deeper 'hunger' that cannot be satisfied with food. In fact, we 'hunger' and crave for many things in life – for food and shelter, for love and friendship, for a just and compassionate world, for a sense of purpose and meaning in life. Primo Levi, an Italian Jew, was deported to Auschwitz in 1944. In two autobiographical works (*If This Is a Man* and *The Truce*) he writes of his experience in the concentration camp, and then of his long journey home following liberation. In such Nazi camps, where the mortality mounted to between 90 and 98 percent, life was a constant struggle with hunger and cold. However, once the Soviet Red Army had liberated the camp, prisoners

---

[137] Quoted in John P. Meier, *A Marginal Jew, Volume Two: Mentor, Message, and Miracles*, Doubleday, New York, 1994, p.966.
[138] Ibid, p.647.
[139] Raymond E. Brown, *Responses to 101 Questions on the Bible*, Paulist Press, Mahwah, NJ, 1990, p. 66.

were at last free to satisfy their most basic needs for food and warmth. But Levi makes an interesting observation:

As always happens, the end of our hunger laid bare and perceptible in us a much deeper hunger. Not only the desire for our homes, which in a sense was discounted and projected into the future; but a more immediate and urgent need for human contacts, for mental and physical work, for novelty and variety.[140]

But even beyond the hunger for home, human contacts, mental and physical work, and novelty and variety, there is something else, a quest for meaning. In Levi's words, 'The conviction that life has a purpose is rooted in every fibre of man, it is a property of the human substance.'[141] Today's gospel points us towards the one source that can truly satisfy our insatiable hunger for meaning and purpose.

---

[140] Primo Levi, *If this is a Man* and *The Truce*, Abacus, London, Reprinted 1997, p.328.
[141] Ibid, p.77.

THE ASSUMPTION OF THE BLESSED VIRGIN MARY

(YEAR C)

'My soul proclaims the greatness of the Lord.' (Lk 1:46)

Alan Jones, dean of Grace (Episcopal) Cathedral in San Francisco, makes the observation that 'the Church has never known how to treat Mary. She is either adored (often inappropriately) or ignored altogether. ... Many Protestants think of her as a distinguished but dead Roman Catholic!' Today's feast of the Assumption is therefore celebrated with a great deal of enthusiasm in some parts of the Christian church, while other parts are either 'nervous or severely critical of the celebration.' Jones believes that the Assumption is a 'feast worth examining because it can tell us something about ourselves, about our pilgrimage and our destiny.' [142]

Although the dogma of the Assumption was only formally proclaimed by Pope Pius XII on November 1, 1950 in the Bull *Munificentissimus Deus*, it is an ancient feast in the Church's liturgical calendar. [143] The emperor Mauritius introduced the fixed date of August 15 towards the end of the sixth century. In the churches of the East the feast is known as the Dormition (the Falling Asleep) of the Blessed Virgin Mary and is accounted one of the Twelve Great Feasts of the liturgical year.

In the words of Pius XII, 'the Immaculate Mother of God, the ever Virgin Mary having completed the course of her earthly life, was assumed body and soul to heavenly glory.' The Second Vatican Council affirmed the tradition in the Dogmatic Constitution *Lumen Gentium*: 'the Immaculate Virgin, preserved free from all stain of original sin, was taken up body and soul into heavenly glory, when her earthly life was over, and exalted by the Lord as Queen over all things.' [144] In other words, Mary was bodily assumed into heaven, but what does that mean? 'If we are devoid of poetic imagination,' Alan Jones writes, 'we think that the dogma states that Mary rose like a rocket to a place somewhere beyond

---

[142] Alan Jones, *Passion for Pilgrimage*, Morehouse Publishing, Harrisburg, PA, 1989, p.169.
[143] Michel V. Esbroeck, 'Assumption of the Virgin', in David Noel Freedman, {Editor}, *The Anchor Bible Dictionary, Volume 6*, Doubleday, New York, 1992,p.856.
[144] *Lumen Gentium*, n.59.

the solar system.' What Jones calls our 'commitment to literalism' often gets in the way of meaning. Heaven 'isn't like any other place. You don't 'go' there in the same way that you go to New York or Los Angeles.' But the dogma's use of the word *bodily* 'presumes not only that there's a place to go but that there is a 'someone' who is going. ... The dogma means that who Mary was in her fullness of person (in all her glory), recognisable and particular, is with God forever.'[145]

The Assumption is a sign of hope that allows us to live in the world with faith and optimism. In his homily for the feast of the Assumption in 2001, John Paul II said:

In looking to her, carried up amid the rejoicing of the angelic hosts, the whole of human life, marked by lights and shadows, is opened to the perspective of eternal happiness. If our experience of daily life allows us to feel tangibly that our earthly pilgrimage is under the sign of uncertainty and strife, the Virgin assumed into heavenly glory assures us that we will never lack divine help.

The Assumption reminds us that we are all pilgrims. In the C19 a tourist from the United States of America visited the famous Polish rabbi Hafez Hayyim. The tourist was astonished to see that the rabbi's house was only a simple room filled with books. The only furniture was a table and a bench. 'Rabbi, where is your furniture?' asked the tourist. 'Where is yours?' replied Hafez. 'Mine? But I'm only a visitor here, I'm just passing through.' To which the rabbi replied, 'So am I.'[146]

This world, beautiful as it is, is not all that there is. There is a rather macabre reminder of this inescapable truth in the Capuchin church of *Santa Maria della Concezione* on the *Via Veneto* in Rome. The crypt contains the bones of thousands of Capuchin friars interred there between 1528 and 1870. At one point the visitor is confronted by a skeleton wearing the Capuchin habit. Around the neck of the skeleton is a sign bearing a message for the onlooker: 'As you are, I was; and as I am, you will be!' Such also is Our Lady's message to us on this festival day: 'As you are, I was; and as I am, you will be.' That is the assurance St Paul offers us in today's liturgy: 'Just as all men die in Adam, so all men will be brought to life in Christ.' John Paul II reminds us that 'Christ's definitive victory over death, which came into the world because of Adam's sin, shines out in Mary, assumed into Heaven at the end of her earthly life.'[147]

---

[145] Alan Jones, *Passion for Pilgrimage*, p.170.
[146] Christina Feldman and Jack Kornfield (Eds), op. cit., p.347.
[147] Pope John Paul II, Homily for the Solemnity of the Assumption of Mary, August 15, 2001.

ALL SAINTS

'Rejoice and be glad, for your reward will be great in heaven.' (Mt 5:12)

Just as the tomb of the Unknown Soldier symbolises the final resting place of all soldiers who lie in unmarked graves in distant lands, the festival of All Saints originally commemorated those martyrs who died bravely for the faith but whose names were unknown and therefore not included in the canon of the saints. The feast was celebrated at various times throughout the Christian world, but its observance on November 1 dates from the time of Pope Gregory III (d.741). Pope Gregory IV made All Saints a feast for the universal Church, and from the C15 it was celebrated with an Octave (suppressed in 1955).[148]

Although we tend to reserve the word 'saint' for someone who has been formally canonised, the New Testament calls all baptized Christians 'saints' (hagioi). Perhaps today we should turn to the people alongside us at Mass and wish them a happy feast day! All believers are *hagioi* in the sense that they have been called out of the world about them into the presence of God as a holy people. 'Holy,' as used here, does not refer to 'a state or a quality of believers, but to Christ's setting them apart for God, thus removing them from this world (Col 1:12f.).'[149] The feast of All Saints, therefore, could be celebrated as a commemoration of all the faithful departed, but the Church reserves today's liturgy for those 'in whom grace had its most signal triumph, for those who had achieved the Pauline imperative, 'become what you are'.'[150]

Who, then, are saints? The Lutheran sociologist Peter Berger speaks of 'signals of transcendence', a term that he uses to describe phenomena that are part of our ordinary everyday existence, but that somehow point beyond themselves.[151] They are not 'extraordinary spiritual experiences, like the raptures and torments of great mystics. They emerge from the common, everyday realities of life.'[152]

---

[148] Adrian Nocent, *The Liturgical Year: Sundays in Ordinary Time*, The Liturgical Press, Collegeville, MN, 1977, p. 403; FL Cross and EA Livingstone, The Oxford Dictionary of the Christian Church, pp. 41-2.
[149] Horst Balz & Gerhard Schneider (Eds), *Exegetical Dictionary of the New Testament, Volume 1*, p.19
[150] Reginald H Fuller, 'Scripture Readings for November 1971' *Worship*, Vol.45, No.8, October 1971, p.488.
[151] Peter L Berger, *A Rumour of Angels*, Penguin Press, Middlesex, 1970, p.70.
[152] George Weigel, *The Truth of Catholicism*, Perennial, New York, 2001, p.24.

Berger entitled one of his books *A Rumour of Angels*, a title that seeks to describe his experience of meeting a remarkable priest who had chosen to work among the down and outs in a large city, at great personal expense. Why would anyone choose to sacrifice a life of comfort to work among such people? When asked by his friends, the man replied quite simply, 'So that the rumour of God may not disappear completely.'[153]

Today's second reading from the first letter of St John offers a precious insight into what it means to be holy. This letter is part of a polemic against dissidents and false teachers who 'claimed that they were already perfected, and therefore had no need to make any moral effort. Against this our author insists on the element of the 'not yet' in the Christian life. It does *not yet* appear what it shall be.'[154] Abba Macarius, one of the greatest of the desert fathers, was once asked by a young man, 'Abba, tell us about being a monk.' This wisest of monks replied, 'Ah! I'm not a monk myself, but I have seen them.'[155] We, too, looking to those heroes of the faith who have been 'signals of transcendence' could echo St Macarius, 'I am not *yet* a Christian, but I have seen them.'

Who are saints? Perhaps St Macarius can help us, and the clue is to be found in his name. Today's gospel, the beatitudes, tells us that certain people are 'happy.' The Greek word is *makarios*, and the beatitudes are often called macarisms. The English word 'happy' may not be the most appropriate translation of *makarios* because it has the implication of luck or chance. The meaning of *makarios* can be seen from one particular use of the word. According to William Barclay:

The Greeks always called Cyprus hē makaria (the feminine form of the adjective), which means The Happy Isle, and they did so because they believed that Cyprus was so lovely, so rich, and so fertile an island that a man would never need to go beyond its coastline to find the perfectly happy life. It had such a climate, such flowers and fruits and trees, such minerals, such natural resources that it contained within itself all the materials for perfect happiness.

Makarios, therefore, describes 'that joy which is serene and untouchable, and self-contained, that joy which is completely independent of all the chances and the changes of life.' It is a joy 'which sorrow and loss, and pain and grief, are powerless to touch, that joy which shines through tears, and which nothing in life or death can take away.'[156] Despite the vicissitudes of life, the blessed, the

---

[153] Ibid, p.119.
[154] Fuller, op. cit., p.490.
[155] Alan Jones, *Soul Making*, HarperSan Francisco, 1985, p.16.

makarioi, possess a serene and untouchable joy.

And who is *makarios*, blessed? Firstly, the poor in spirit and the gentle. These people are blessed because like St Paul they acknowledge their own weakness (1 Cor 2:3) and rely upon the power of God working in them, a power that can achieve 'infinitely more than we can ask or imagine' (Eph 3:20). A second group of blessed are those who seek justice and those who are merciful. We are talking here of compassion, of the ability to get inside another person's skin and feel their pain. St Francis of Assisi and his friars had embarked upon a rigorous fast in preparation for the feast of Easter. They had resolved to fast for the full 40 days of Lent, and it was to be a severe fast. In the middle of the night, some two weeks into the season of Lent, Francis was awoken by some cries of anguish coming from a friar who was sleeping nearby. The fast had proved too much for this brother, and he was in severe pain. Francis could have exhorted the brother to get a grip on himself. The fast was, after all, a solemn prayer to God that wasn't meant to be easy. Or Francis could have gone to the kitchen and cooked the brother a meal to relieve his intense hunger, which was bordering on starvation. The brother would then have surely felt himself something of a failure, lacking in moral courage, a spiritual pygmy. Francis did indeed go to the kitchen and cook a meal, and came back to the dormitory with two bowls of wholesome food – one for the ailing brother, and one for himself. And together they enjoyed a meal at midnight. Francis had intuitively grasped a fundamental truth. The fast, intended to be an expression of his love for God, would have meant little indeed if it had hardened his heart to the needs of a suffering brother.[157]

---

[156] Ibid.
[157] *Mirror of Perfection*, 27, in Marion A. Habig (ed), *St Francis of Assisi: Writings and Early Biographies*, Franciscan Herald Press, Chicago, 1983, p.1154; 2 *Celano*, 22, in Habig, pp.380-381; *The Legend of Perugia*, 1, in Habig, p.977; St Bonaventure, *Major Life*, vol.V, no.7, in Habig, p.667.

THE BAPTISM OF THE LORD

(YEAR C)

Now when all the people had been baptised and while Jesus after his own baptism was at prayer, heaven opened and the Holy Spirit descended on him in bodily shape, like a dove. (Lk 3: 21-22)

Why was Jesus, the sinless one, baptized by John in the Jordan? At the very beginning of his public ministry Jesus dramatically foretells its glorious conclusion. In the beginning is the end. Going down into the waters of the Jordan, Jesus symbolically enacted his future death and burial; emerging from the waters, he ritually proclaimed his rising from the tomb. St Paul dwells upon the symbolism of baptism when he writes to the Christians living in Rome:

You have been taught that when we were baptized in Christ Jesus we were baptized in his death; in other words, when we were baptized we went into the tomb with him and joined him in death, so that as Christ was raised from the dead by the Father's glory, we too might live a new life. If in union with Christ we have imitated his death, we shall also imitate him in his resurrection. (Rm 6: 3-6.)

The symbolism of our baptismal ritual is compromised because in most parishes we pour a few drops of water upon the head rather than immersing the catechumen (child or adult) into the waters of the font. We have minimised the sacramental action for reasons of time and convenience, even though the general introduction to the ritual of baptism speaks of immersion as 'more suitable as a symbol of participation in the death and resurrection of Christ'. [158] One priest has likened this sacramental downsizing to reducing an intricate piece of music played by a symphony orchestra to someone sitting at a piano and tapping out the main 'tune' with one finger. Maybe a bystander could recognise the basic 'tune' but the richness of the whole is lost. How different when we hear the same piece of music played by an orchestra. Then the tonalities, shades and harmony awaken us to its beauty.[159]

Some years ago I had the opportunity to accompany an English archaeologist

---

[158] Sacred Congregation of Divine Worship, "Christian Initiation, General Introduction", n.22, in International Commission on English in the Liturgy, *Documents on the Liturgy, 1963-1979*, The Liturgical Press, Collegeville, 1982, p.723.

who was visiting ancient Christian sites in Turkey and Cyprus. Although Turkey and Northern Cyprus are now predominantly Muslim countries, there were once vibrant Christian communities in both countries. Some of Paul's letters were addressed to Christians living in Ephesus, Colossae and Galatia – located in what is modern Turkey. St Paul visited Salamis in northern Cyprus together with Barnabas – a native of that city – in 45 AD.

During our travels through Cyprus we visited Salamis and stopped to inspect the ruins of the ancient basilica of St Epiphanius, built in the fourth and fifth centuries. The basilica was destroyed during the Arab attack of 648-9 AD and little remains today. As I walked among the ruins I came across the baptistery. It stood apart from the church, east of the main building. It was a sunken font in the shape of a cross, and baptism was obviously by total immersion. There had been, incidentally, provision for heating the water! As I stood in that font, now desolate and filled with weeds, I thought of the many thousands of catechumens who had walked down the three steps into the water, imitating Jesus going down into the tomb. As they emerged from the font they were beginning a new life, reborn from the womb of the church.

At the very beginning of our Christian life we ritually enact what is the inescapable rhythm of human life – death and resurrection. Jesus once said, 'Unless a wheat grain falls on the ground and dies, it remains only a single grain; but if it dies, it yields a rich harvest.' Life continually summons us to die so that we might live. Ironically, our first 'death' experience is birth. Imagine a child in the womb reflecting upon its situation and thinking, 'Look, I'm cozy here, warm and well nourished, and outside life sounds far too frantic. Mum, if it's all right with you, I'll stay where I am.' I have yet to meet a mother who would be happy to remain pregnant indefinitely because her child in the womb is experiencing stage fright!

Life continually summons us to let something die so that something new might begin. A friend of mine went through the trauma of a marriage break up. His wife had left him to be with someone else, and he refused to accept the fact that his marriage was over. He harboured the illusion that she would soon come to her senses and return to him. He continually phoned his wife, begging her to return, and he made several nasty scenes by turning up unannounced at her workplace and publicly embarrassing her. He dredged up any gossip he could find out about

---

[159] William J. Bausch, *A New Look at the Sacraments*, Twenty-Third Publications, Mystic, CT, Revised edition, 1995, p.7.

his wife's new partner. His obsessive behaviour extinguished whatever embers of affection may still have smouldered amidst the ashes of their relationship. He could talk about little else apart from his failed marriage, re-enacting for anyone who cared to listen the last conversation he'd had with his wife. Friends began to avoid him like the plague because he'd become so fixated. But at last he accepted the reality of his situation; he allowed the past to die and his life was transformed.

The American writer Judith Viorst has written a best seller called *Necessary Losses*. The main thesis of her book is that 'losses are a part of life – universal, unavoidable, inexorable. And these losses are necessary because we grow by losing and leaving and letting go.' She goes on to say:

the road to human development is paved with renunciation. Throughout our life we grow by giving up. We give up some of our deepest attachments to others. We give up certain cherished parts of ourselves. We must confront, in the dreams we dream, as well as in our intimate relationships, all that we never will have and never will be. Passionate investment leaves us vulnerable to loss. And sometimes, no matter how clever we are, we must lose. ... (but) it is only through our losses that we become fully developed human beings. [160]

In these few words Judith Viorst offers a profound insight into baptism. Through our losses we become fully developed human beings. The seed that falls into the ground and dies yields an abundant harvest. Dying with Christ we rise with him to live a new life.

---

[160] Judith Viorst, *Necessary Losses*, Simon & Schuster, New York, 1986, p.17.

SECOND SUNDAY IN ORDINARY TIME

(YEAR C)

There was a wedding at Cana in Galilee. (Jn 2:1)

The water in six stone jars turned into wine. A miracle! It's interesting, though, that the gospel writers never once use the world 'miracle' to describe such marvellous deeds. The changing of water into wine was indeed a miracle, but John prefers to use the word *semeia*, 'sign'. This miracle was, we're told, 'the first of the signs given by Jesus.' In other words, the miracles are much more than acts of compassion or wonderful occurrences that occurred 2000 years ago. They are signs that reveal something important about the person of Jesus. They reveal who he is and what he was sent to do.

Many of the miracle stories included in John's gospel are clearly interpreted for us, and it's not too difficult to understand what they signify about Jesus. The multiplication of the loaves and fishes, for example, clearly points to Jesus as the bread of life. But we can only guess at the significance of the miracle at the wedding feast of Cana. Although it is described as the first of Jesus' signs, we are not told what it signifies. In the Gospels, marriage feasts are often used as metaphors for God's kingdom. In Matthew's gospel, for example, the kingdom of heaven is likened to a king who gave a feast for his son's wedding (Mt 22:1-14; cf. Lk 14:16-24), and the Book of Revelation (chapter 19) tells of great joy in heaven because the time has come for the marriage of the Lamb to his bride. 'Blessed are those who are invited to the wedding feast of the Lamb' (19:9).

Today's first reading from the prophet Isaiah suggests one possible meaning for Jesus' first sign. The context of this reading is the experience of the Jews who returned home to Jerusalem after the Babylonian exile in the C6BC. After languishing by the rivers of Babylon for almost 70 years they are liberated by the Persian king Cyrus. They embark upon the journey home with high hopes; the very desert, they believed, would burst into blossom before them (Isaiah 35). But they returned to little more than rubble and ashes. The city and the Temple lay in ruins about them and the wretched life they now endured bore no relation to what they had imagined. The desolation surrounding them on all sides shattered their dreams and dashed their hopes. They felt forsaken and abandoned.

This reading from Isaiah holds out the hope that all will be well, that God has new things in store for his people. Jerusalem's integrity will shine out like the dawn and all the kings will see its glory. God will make Jerusalem his spouse. 'Like a young man marrying a virgin, so will the one who built you wed you, and as the bridegroom rejoices in his bride, so will your God rejoice in you.' God will vindicate Jerusalem and be as closely united with her as a husband is with his wife. When Jesus provided such an abundance of excellent wine for the wedding feast in Cana it may signify that the day foreseen by Isaiah has at last arrived. In the life and ministry of Jesus the time has now come when God will save his people and enter into a relationship with them so close that it could be compared to marriage.

One of the themes running through the first section of John's Gospel, called by biblical scholars the Book of Signs (chapters 1:19 - 12:50), is the replacement of Jewish institutions and religious views. At Cana the water for Jewish purifications has been replaced by the choicest of wines. John's primary concern is what this reveals about Jesus. Jesus, the one sent by the Father, is the only way to the Father, thereby superseding all previous religious institutions, customs and feasts. The messianic times have been inaugurated with an abundance of wine, and as Jesus says in the synoptic tradition, 'new wine, fresh skins.'

The episode at Cana makes a clear and decisive point. It is a sign pointing to Jesus who is doing something new, but also something in profound continuity with what has gone before. He takes water stored in stone jars that were specially set aside for Jewish rituals of purification, the water that guests would have used to purify themselves before commencing the banquet. (Note that there were six jars, one fewer than seven, the number of perfection.) Jesus turns this water into wine. John's readers would have recognised this as an image associated with the messianic wedding feast, for the image of the bridegroom was often used to describe the longed-for Messiah. Water into wine, the ancient tradition transformed into something far more intoxicating! In both today's first reading (from Isaiah) and in the Gospel, God's decisive intervention gives birth to something new from the womb of the past.

Gerald O'Collins SJ tells of visiting a friend who lived in a 20-story block of flats. A sign hanging on the laundry-room situated in the basement read: 'This laundry-room will close at 6 pm, because that is the way it has always been.'

The friend explained that the janitor always locked everything up at 6 pm, even though most of the tenants didn't get home until much later. Many of the tenants depended on using the laundry because there wasn't a washing machine or dryer in their own apartment. But the janitor had locked himself into a rigid way of doing things, 'because that is the way it had always been.' [161] Many Catholics had difficulty in coming to terms with the changes that were inaugurated with the Second Vatican Council. In this parish one of the acolytes resigned from his ministry when women were permitted to distribute Holy Communion. When the Mass was celebrated in English rather than Latin, our choir master resigned. Be it first century Judaism or Christianity in the twenty-first century, there is always a temptation to oppose change 'because that is the way it has always been.'

Fr Raymond Brown makes the wry observation that 'Jesus would be found guilty by the self-conscious religious majority of any age and background.' It is more than likely, he argues, that 'were Jesus to appear in our time (with his challenge rephrased in terms of contemporary religious stances) and be arrested and tried again, most of those finding him guilty would identify themselves as Christians and think they were rejecting an impostor.' [162]

This is not a summons to jettison the past indiscriminately and invent a new program. As Pope John Paul II wrote at the beginning of the new millennium, 'the new progam already exists: it is the plan found in the Gospel and in the living Tradition, it is the same as ever.'[163] But, in the words of Pope John XXIII, we are here on earth not to guard a museum, but to cultivate a garden flourishing with life and promised to a glorious future.' [164] We are not called upon to sing over and over again melodies from the past. Let us take to heart the words of today's responsorial psalm, 'O sing a new song to the Lord.'

---

[161] Gerald O'Collins SJ, *Experiencing Jesus*, EJ Dwyer, Sydney, 1994, p.100.
[162] Raymond Brown, *The Death of the Messiah*, Volume 1, Doubleday, New York, 1993, p.393.
[163] John Paul II, *Novo Millennio Ineunte*, n.29
[164] Quoted in Henri Fesquet, *Wit and Wisdom of Good Pope John*, The New American Library, New York, 1965, p.103.

THIRD SUNDAY IN ORDINARY TIME

(YEAR C)

'He came to Nazara, where he had been brought up, and went into the synagogue on the sabbath day as he usually did.' (Lk 4: 16).

Each of the evangelists offers us a distinctive insight into the identity and mission of Jesus – who he is and what he is called to do. Like a symphonic overture, their insight is announced through the set piece that each of them places at the outset of Jesus' public ministry. Last week we heard John's set piece: Jesus at the wedding feast of Cana. There he turned water in six stone jars used for Jewish rites of purification into a rich and fruity wine. He takes that which was incomplete (symbolized in Jewish thought by the number six) and transforms it. Today we have Luke's set piece, the inaugural sermon in the Nazareth synagogue.

Jesus lived in Nazareth. Now a city of almost 60 000 people, in the first century it was a small village with a population of between 1600 and 2000 people. Nazareth is never once mentioned in the Old Testament, nor in the writings of the Jewish rabbis. In other words, nothing of any significance ever happened there, and nobody of any importance ever lived there. It was an utterly insignificant village. There Jesus lived and worked as a *tekton*, a carpenter or handy man. At about the age of 30 he began his public ministry, preaching, healing and casting out demons in the surrounding villages. Now he returns to Nazareth.

Modern Nazareth is dominated by the massive basilica of the Annunciation, visible from anywhere in the town. The location of the Nazareth's first century synagogue is lost in antiquity, but there is a small church in modern Nazareth that purports to be built on the site of the synagogue. When Jesus returned to the synagogue of Nazareth he was handed the scroll of the prophet Isaiah. Let's pause for a moment to place Isaiah in context. The prophecy of Isaiah consists of 66 chapters, but it is in fact the work of three distinct people. Chapters 1-39 were written by Isaiah who was called to be a prophet in the year King Uzziah died (742 BC). Chapters 40-55 and 56-66 (called Second and Third Isaiah) were written by unnamed prophets and date from a period about 200 years later – the time of the Babylonian exile, and the years following the return from exile.

The passage that Jesus reads comes from chapter 61 and reflects the situation in Jerusalem following the return from exile. When the exiles returned from Babylon they were confronted with the daunting task of rebuilding their lives from dust and ashes. In this text an unnamed prophet rejoices in the commission that he had received from God: to bring good news to the poor, to proclaim liberty to captives, new sight to the blind, to set the downtrodden free, and to proclaim the Lord's year of favour. With all eyes in the synagogue fixed upon him, Jesus astonished everyone by claiming, 'This text is being fulfilled today even as you listen.' We know this passage as an extract from one of the songs of the suffering servant. It describes the work and suffering of someone who achieved God's work in a totally unexpected way during the Babylonian exile over 500 years earlier. This text had a specific meaning in its original context, but when Jesus spoke in the synagogue at Nazareth he was not giving a history lesson on the Babylonian exile. Rather, he claimed that the words of Isaiah were being fulfilled in his own day, in his own life and ministry, and among his own people. Luke returns to this theme in the final chapter of his gospel when he tells the story of two disciples on the road to Emmaus. They are despondent as they discuss the events that had just taken place in Jerusalem. A mysterious stranger joins them – it is, of course, Jesus explains how Moses and the prophets, written centuries earlier, are the key to understanding the present moment.

Today's first reading also highlights the power of the Scriptures as the people listened attentively to the words of the Law. The word in the Hebrew text of Nehemiah is Torah, inadequately translated into English as 'law'. Torah in its most restrictive meaning refers to the first five books of the Bible – Genesis, Exodus, Leviticus, Numbers and Deuteronomy. It is the heart and soul of God's revelation to Israel, and a copy of the Torah is found in the ark of every synagogue, just as the Blessed Sacrament is reserved in the tabernacle of Catholic churches. The word *Torah* comes from the root *yarah*, meaning 'to shoot' (such as at a target). When you shoot at a target you're trying to hit the bull's eye. So the image behind the word is 'correct direction.' The root of one of the Hebrew words for sin, *chet*, means 'to miss'. *Torah* is therefore liberating and life-giving; it directs our aim to the bull's eye.[165] That is why the psalmist sings the praises

---

[165] cf. Benjamin Blech, *The Complete Idiot's Guide to Understanding Judaism*, Alpha Books, New York, 1999, p.67.

of *Torah*: it revives the soul, gives wisdom to the simple, gladdens the heart, and gives light to the eyes.

Without the divine word, we are prone to miss the mark; we become disoriented and lost. Charles Schulz's cartoon character Charlie Brown attempts to talk Linus out of his fear of libraries by explaining how irrational it is. All of us, he explains, feel out of place in certain areas. When Linus asks Charlie where he feels out of place, Charlie replies: 'Earth!'[166]

When John Harrison invented the first practical marine chronometer in the C18, he discovered an accurate means of calculating longitude. He solved a problem that had baffled humanity ever since sailors had ventured beyond the sight of land. Without determining longitude, navigators had no means of accurately determining their whereabouts, and countless lives were lost at sea.[167] The Scriptures are our latitude and longitude; they help us find our bearings and establish our whereabouts on life's journey. We read the Scriptures because we are lost and seek a map with which to negotiate the terrain of life. We read the Scriptures because they are spirit and life.

---

[166] Charles Schulz, *The Complete Peanuts, 1959 to 1960*, p.201.
[167] The story is told in Dava Sobel, *Longitude*, Fourth Estate, London, 1995.

FOURTH SUNDAY IN ORDINARY TIME

(YEAR C)

When they heard this everyone in the synagogue was enraged. (Lk 4:28)

I've often wondered what I'd have to say or do to antagonise my parishioners to the point where they'd want to run me out of town, or even worse – do away with me altogether! Jesus returns to his hometown of Nazareth and is invited to preach in the local synagogue. At first, he makes a favourable impression, winning the approval of all. They were astonished, we're told, by the gracious words that came from his lips. But the mood of the congregation changed suddenly, and they hustled him out of the town, intending to throw him down a cliff. What did he do or say that was so offensive?

Jesus mentioned two stories that his audience would have known well, stories set in the middle of the C8BC. The first story involves the prophet Elijah and is to be found in the first book of Kings. On one occasion during a period of severe drought he visited a town called Zarephath. Seeing a widow gathering a few sticks to fuel her stove, Elijah asked her for some water and a scrap of bread. The woman was almost destitute and had only enough food for one more meal for herself and her son. Nevertheless, she made a meal for the prophet, and strangely, the jars in which she kept the ingredients for the meal miraculously replenished themselves, not just on that day, but until the drought ended.

The second story is about the prophet Elisha and comes from the second book of Kings. It tells of an army commander called Naaman who suffered from some kind of virulent skin-disease. Naaman lived in the country of Aram, but through a captive servant girl he hears about a possible cure for his disease through a prophet in faraway Israel. Naaman eventually approaches the prophet Elisha, and he is healed of his affliction after bathing in the river Jordan seven times.

Why did Jesus cause such an uproar when he told those two familiar stories? Jesus reminded the congregation in that synagogue at Nazareth that neither the widow nor the army commander Naaman were Jews. He told them that during a time of drought and famine, Elijah wasn't sent to ease the hardship of anyone in Israel, but rather to a foreigner. Likewise, there were many lepers in Israel, but Elisha wasn't sent to heal any of them.

To a congregation that regarded themselves as members of the chosen people this was an uncomfortable reminder that they were not God's sole concern. In other words, Jesus reminded them that God readily offers his grace *outside* as well as *inside* the borders of Israel – to a pagan Syrian officer and to an *infidel* woman from Zarephath.

What's happening here? Every society is governed by what sociologists call purity laws. A purity system is 'a cultural map which indicates 'a place for everything and everything in its place'.'[168] For example, soil in the garden or even in a pot is in its correct place. But if I were to tip some soil from a pot onto the floor of the church, it is no longer in its correct place. Purity laws establish boundaries around people and indicate permissible degrees of interaction. In some societies those boundaries are rigid and inflexible; in others they are porous.

Until the 1950s the White Australia Policy prevented certain people from migrating to that country simply because they were not 'white'. The apartheid laws of South Africa erected barriers between whites and non-whites, a segregation based solely upon ethnicity. Consider the more benign example of the Amish Mennonite Church. It originated in Europe in the C17 and members of the church began migrating to North America early in the C18, settling first in eastern Pennsylvania. They virtually live in a time warp, geographically segregated from society and having very limited contact with outsiders. The male members of the church wear broad brimmed black hats, beards (but not moustaches), and homemade plain clothes fastened with hooks and eyes instead of buttons. The women wear bonnets, long full dresses with capes over the shoulders, shawls, and black shoes and stockings. No jewellery of any kind is worn. The Amish shun telephones and electric lights, and drive horses and buggies rather than automobiles. They are excellent farmers, but often refuse to use modern farm machinery.

There were rigorous laws regulating purity in first century Palestine. According to Rabbinic tradition reflected in the Mishnah, Jewish society was divided into three groups, based on the purity of their ancestry. The first group consisted of Priests, Levites and full-blooded Israelites. Because their ancestry was unblemished they were considered the true Israel. They were genealogically clean and could freely intermarry. The second group consisted of those people whose ancestry was

---

[168] Jerome Neyrey, *The Social World of Luke-Acts*, Hendrickson, Peabody MA, 1991, p.275.

slightly blemished. It included illegitimate children of priests (i.e. the children of priests who had not married a full-blooded Israelite virgin), proselytes (converts from other religions), and proselyte freedmen. The third group consisted of those with grave blemishes. They were people who could not trace their ancestry, eunuchs made so by men, bastards, temple slaves, the fatherless, and foundlings. Beyond the pale altogether were eunuchs from birth, those with deformed sexual features, hermaphrodites, and finally, Gentiles.[169] By definition, Gentiles were impure and unclean – beyond the pale.

The Temple and the priesthood were at the centre of the purity system. The Mishnah lists the degrees or circles of holiness surrounding the Holy of Holies: 1. The land of Israel; 2. The City of Jerusalem; 3. The Temple Mount; 4. The *hel*, a terrace with lattice work beyond which no Gentile could pass; 5. The Court of women; 6. The Court of the Israelites; 7. The Court of the Priests; 8. The area between the Porch and the Altar; 9. The Sanctuary; 10. The Holy of Holies.[170] There are, therefore, circles or degrees of holiness. The holiest of all, the Holy of Holies, is at the centre and accessible only to the High Priest on the Day of Atonement. Needless to say, Gentile lands were completely off Israel's purity map.

Gentiles were not permitted, under pain of death, to enter the inner courtyards of the Temple. In 1871 archaeologists in Jerusalem discovered an inscription, carved in stone, barring non-Jews from the sanctified area of the Temple. It reads: *No stranger is to enter within the balustrade around the temple and enclosure: whoever is caught will be responsible to himself for his death, which will ensue.* [171]

Jesus confronted his own contemporaries with an unpalatable truth, and they tried to throw him over a cliff. He reminded the narrow-minded folk of Nazareth that God cannot be monopolized by Israel, or indeed by anyone. There is no apartheid in the Kingdom of God. There are no outsiders. All are invited!

---

[169] Joachim Jeremias, *Jerusalem in the Time of Jesus*, SCM Press, London , 1969, pp.153-4.
[170] M. Kel, i. 6-9, cited in Jeremias, op. cit., p.79.
[171] Robert Backhouse, *The Jerusalem Temple*, Candle Books, London , 1996, p.12.

FIFTH SUNDAY IN ORDINARY TIME

(YEAR C)

'Put out into deep water and pay out your nets for a catch.' (Lk 5:4)

Today's readings are about the call to discipleship. What kind of people did Jesus choose to be his disciples? Were only those who were perfect called? Well, that obviously wasn't true. Peter denied three times even knowing Jesus; Judas betrayed him; James and John seemed more intent on positions of honour. In fact, the only person who came close to being perfect turned down Jesus' invitation to follow him. Remember the story of the rich young man. He had kept all the commandments since his youth, and we're told that Jesus looked at him and loved him. 'If you wish to be perfect,' Jesus then said, 'give all you have to the poor and come and follow me.' The young man walked away, for he could not bring himself to give away all his possessions.

Imagine that we are entrusted with the responsibility of electing a world leader. We have three candidates for the position, so let us examine their resumes: Candidate A: Associates with crooked politicians, consults with astrologers, has had two mistresses, is severely disabled, chain smokes and drinks eight to ten martinis a day. Candidate B: Kicked out of office twice, slept until noon, used opium at university, is an undiagnosed manic-depressive and drinks a bottle of whiskey every day. Candidate C: A decorated war hero, vegetarian, doesn't smoke or drink, except for an occasional beer, and has never had an extra-marital affair. Whom shall we choose? Well, Candidate A is Franklin D. Roosevelt; Candidate B is Winston Churchill; Candidate C is Adolph Hitler.

This goes to show that sometimes the candidate who seems to be perfect may be the worst leader in reality. The prophet Jeremiah protested, 'What a wretched state I am in! I am lost, for I am a man of unclean lips ...'. And Peter protested, 'Leave me Lord; I am a sinful man.' But God was not deterred by human sinfulness. Serious sin, monumental failures, weakness, ineptitude and inadequacy are no obstacle to God calling someone to participate in his saving plan for the world.

If – Jesus didn't choose people who were perfect to be his disciples, did he choose people who were well trained and qualified for the job? How did Jesus choose the men who were to be the future leaders of the church? What would have happened if he had requested a management consultancy firm to assess the men he was thinking of calling as the twelve apostles? Their report might have read something like this:

Thank you for inviting us to interview the 12 men that you have chosen for managerial positions in your new organisation. We have given them a number of tests and run the results through a very sophisticated computer program. Each of the 12 men has also been interviewed personally by our psychological and vocational aptitude consultant. We have concluded that most of the nominees are lacking in background, education, and vocational aptitude for such an enterprise. They seem unable to work together as a team, and their work experience in the field is non-existent. Simon Peter is emotionally unstable, and given to fits of temper. Andrew has no leadership qualities. The two brothers, James and John, known as 'sons of Thunder' are a couple of hotheads who will be very disruptive. They place personal interest and positions of honour above company loyalty. Thomas shows a sceptical attitude that would tend to undermine morale. Matthew is a tax collector, an occupation that attracts unscrupulous and dishonest extortionists. Simon, known as the zealot, is little better than a terrorist and will be a source of violent disagreements in the group. One of the 12, however, shows real potential. He is a man of ability and resourcefulness, mixes easily with people, and has contacts in high places. He is highly motivated, ambitious, and responsible. We therefore recommend him as future leader material. Forget Simon Peter, choose instead our candidate. His name is Judas Iscariot.[172]

Once again, the candidate who looks best on paper is the worst leader in reality.

The call of the disciples illustrates a truth that is found elsewhere in the Gospels – it is Jesus who seizes the initiative in calling people to follow him. Jesus issues a decisive call to follow him, a call addressed to people who have not taken the initiative of asking to follow him. But don't think for a moment that the disciples didn't have to agonise over their decision to follow Jesus. What might their own inner voices have whispered to them?

---

[172] Adapted from Jack McArdle, *Stories for Reflection*, The Columba Press, Dublin, 1996, pp.160-1.

Your livelihood is fishing, your family depends upon you; what will become of them?

Who is this wandering healer and exorcist that you would give up everything to follow him? Is he mad? His family certainly thinks he is! You hypocrite! Is a sinful man like you worthy enough? You'll be the laughing stock of every village around the lake. What do you know about preaching?

Making that decision was a courageous step because following Jesus meant much more than simply absorbing and practising his teachings. Jesus called individuals to follow him literally, physically, as he undertook various preaching tours of Galilee, Judea, and surrounding areas. Nor was this a temporary calling. It did not set any time limit on the obligation to follow him. There was no course of studies, the completion of which would release a disciple from constant attendance upon Jesus. This contrasted with the relationship between a rabbinic student and his teacher, the whole point of which was to learn the rabbi's interpretation of the Torah and then leave to undertake one's own career as a rabbi. By contrast, Jesus does not call disciples to learn Torah, but to experience and proclaim the kingdom of God.

Simon Peter and his companions trusted Jesus and put out into the deep, and they netted a huge number of fish. 'Put out into the deep' *Duc in altum!* In the words of Pope John Paul II at the beginning of the new millennium, 'These words ring out for us today, and they invite us to remember the past with gratitude, to live the present with enthusiasm and to look forward to the future with confidence: 'Jesus Christ is the same yesterday and today and for ever' (Heb 13:8).'[173]

---

[173] John Paul II, *Novo Millennio Ineunte*, n.1

SIXTH SUNDAY IN ORDINARY TIME

(YEAR C)

'Happy are you who are poor; yours is the kingdom of God.' (Lk 6:20)

Can we really call the poor and hungry 'happy'? Are those who weep 'happy'? Who in their right mind is 'happy' to be hated, abused and denounced as criminal? This translation of the gospel used in the Lectionary is taken from *The Jerusalem Bible*, published in 1966. That translation was revised in 1985 and published as *The New Jerusalem Bible*. One interesting change in the text of today's gospel is the translators' substitution of 'blessed' for 'happy', and for good reason. The English word 'happy' contains the root *hap*, an archaic word (from Middle English) meaning 'chance' or 'luck'. 'Happy' therefore implies that a person is lucky, that their present state is the result of chance. 'Happy' or 'blessed' is a translation of the Greek *makarios,* a word that has nothing to do with the whim of fate, the vagaries of chance or even luck. It is a word that denotes 'the condition of righteous existence before God,'[174] and there is nothing capricious or arbitrary about that. As William Barclay observes, 'A change in fortune, a collapse in health, the failure of a plan, the disappointment of an ambition, even a change in the weather, can take away the fickle joy the world can give. But the Christian has the serene and untouchable joy which comes from walking for ever in the company and in the presence of Jesus Christ.'[175]

Jesus has proclaimed the rule of God, and they are blessed who 'approach it with the greatest need and capacity for its inexhaustible riches, undistracted by the spurious consolations of the world.'[176] Those consolations – such as wealth, position, prestige and popularity – are a potent brew that often deaden the human spirit. In 1976 the psychoanalyst and social philosopher Erich Fromm wrote *To Have or to Be?*. The title describes two different attitudes to wealth and possessions. The rich and powerful measure success in terms of what they have. The outcast and needy possess the kingdom because their wealth lies in the

---

[174] Luke Timothy Johnson, *The Gospel of Luke*, The Liturgical Press, Collegeville, MN, 1991, p.41.
[175] William Barclay, *Gospel of Matthew*, Volume 1, p.84.
[176] GB Caird, *St Luke,* Penguin Books, Hammondsworth, Middlesex, 1963, p.102.

kind of person they are. Fromm quotes from two poems to illustrate these two different approaches to life. In each of the poems the poet encounters a flower. The C19 English poet Tennyson sees a flower while taking a walk: 'Flower in a crannied wall, / I pluck you out of the crannies, / I hold you here, root and all in my hand.' The C17 Japanese Poet Basho also sees a flower, a nazuna, but his response is quite different: 'When I look carefully / I see the *nazuna* blooming / By the hedge. Ah!'[177]

The difference is striking. Tennyson reacts to the flower by plucking it up, root and all. He wants to have it, to possess it. And, of course, the uprooted flower will soon die. The Japanese poet's reaction to the flower is entirely different. He does not want to pluck it; he doesn't even touch it. He is simply transformed by the flower's beauty in a moment of ecstasy.

Blessed are you who weep now, those in pain and sorrow, and those who are oppressed. Lucy, of Peanuts' fame, approaches firstly Linus, then Schroder, then Marcie, and finally Charlie Brown. She thrusts a pen and paper before each of them asking for a signature. Charlie Brown asks for an explanation, and Lucy replies: 'No matter what happens any place or any time in the world. This absolves me from all blame!' Charlie Brown makes a pertinent observation: 'That must be a nice document to have.'[178] Lucy reflects an attitude diametrically opposed to this beatitude.

One of New York's airports is named after Fiorello La Guardia, the mayor of that city in the 1930s and 1940s. La Guardia was a colourful figure with a flair for the dramatic. On one occasion, he decided to fill in for a sick judge, as he was apparently entitled to do as mayor of the city. A shivering old man was brought before him, charged with stealing a loaf of bread from a baker. The accused pleaded that his family was starving. La Guardia said: 'I have to punish you. The law allows of no exceptions. I hereby fine you ten dollars.' But then he went on: 'I impose on everyone present in this courtroom a fine of fifty cents for living in a town where folk must steal bread in order to live.' And so the accused left the court with $47.50 in his pocket.[179]

Life in the kingdom of God is a complete reversal of the world's values. The 'Alas' – for the rich, for those who have their fill now, for those who laugh now,

---

[177] Erich Fromm, *To Have or To Be?*, Abacus, London, 1976, p.26.
[178] Charles Schulz, *The Complete Peanuts, 1967 to 1968*, Fantagraphics Books, New York, 2008, p.115.
[179] Pierre Lefevre, *One Hundred Stories to Change Your Life*, St Paul Publications, Middlegreen, Slough, 1991, p.19.

and for those of whom the world speaks well – is not a guarantee that 'poverty, hunger, grief, and public resentment were in themselves guarantees of eternal bliss.' It is, though, a recognition that 'the one thing that Jesus requires in his disciples is an emptiness that God can fill, a discontent with the world which will lead them to the wealth, the satisfaction, the consolation, the comradeship of the Kingdom.'[180]

---

[180] GB Caird, op. cit., p.102.

SEVENTH SUNDAY IN ORDINARY TIME

(YEAR C)

Grant pardon, and you will be pardoned. (Lk 6:37)

Sister Helen Prejean's book *Dead Man Walking: An Eyewitness Account of the Death Penalty* was published in 1994 and subsequently developed into a major motion picture starring Susan Sarandon as Sr Helen and Sean Penn as a death row inmate. Interviewed in 2007 on Australian television, Sr Helen revealed that Susan Sarandon was the driving force behind the movie. She persuaded the film director Tim Robbins to read the book, but none of the Hollywood studios was interested in a story about the execution of a convicted killer. He was getting what he deserved. There wasn't even a romantic interest in the story. Perhaps if the nun were to become romantically involved with a prisoner on death row, then they could do something with it!! 'No, no,' Robbins insisted. 'It's a journey about redemption.'[181] And indeed, forgiveness is about redemption, a word that means literally 'to buy back.' Forgiveness buys us back from captivity, from the destructive forces of vengeance and hatred.

Sr Helen began her prison ministry in 1981 when she dedicated her life to the poor of New Orleans. She began writing to Patrick Sonnier, sentenced to die in the electric chair for killing two teenagers, and at Sonnier's request she began to visit him regularly as his spiritual advisor. During the course of these meetings Sr Helen's eyes were opened to the Louisiana execution process, and this experience became the basis for her book. Over the past 20 years she has accompanied five people to death by execution and today educates the public about the death penalty. She is the founder of 'Survive', a victims' advocacy group in New Orleans, and she continues to counsel not only inmates on death row, but the families of murder victims as well.[182]

Sr Helen has witnessed the power of Jesus' words: 'Love your enemies, do

---

[181] ABC Television, *Enough Rope*, 17 September, 2007. An extract of the interview may be viewed at http://www.abc.net.au/tv/enoughrope/video/default_pre_2008.htm?program=enoughrope&pres=20070917&story=1

[182] Information from Sr Helen's website www.prejean.org/

good to those who hate you, bless those who curse you, pray for those who treat you badly.' During an interview by Margaret Throsby on ABC radio, Sr Helen expressed her basic conviction that vengeance doesn't help people move on.[183] She has spent countless hours with the families of the victims of crime. When victims' families have had a loved one murdered they're confused and traumatised; they're in grief and loss, and their whole belief system is shaken. Their first reaction is one of rage, loss and wanting to retaliate. Asked if they want the death penalty, they unequivocally say, 'Yes. I'd like to pull the switch myself; I'd like to kill this person with my bare hands.' The parents of one young girl who was abducted into the woods, raped and stabbed and left to bleed to death were present at the execution of their daughter's murderer. After the execution the media was waiting to interview them. 'How do you feel now, you've waited for five years for this moment?' The father replied, 'He died too quick. I hope he burns in hell.' Sr Helen was also present at the execution and thought to herself:

If these people could watch Robert (the executed murderer) die every week – a thousand, thousand times they could watch him die – when they come home they have to deal with the empty chair, you have to deal with the fact that you've lost your daughter. And even killing the one who killed her still doesn't deal with the basic loss that you have experienced, and that is the spiritual journey that you have to make.

The desire for vengeance is usually the beginning of the journey of every victim's family. But over the years Sr Helen has noticed that almost all of the people that she has met don't stay there. They don't stay there because it begins to be too costly for them. A counterpart of Sr Helen's *Dead Man Walking* is the powerful story of forgiving the unforgivable told by Debbie Morris, author of *Forgiving the Dead Man Walking*. At the age of 16 Debbie and her boyfriend were kidnapped by two men. Over a period of 36 hours they tortured and shot her boyfriend, leaving him for dead, and raped her repeatedly before finally letting her go. For Debbie, there was nothing harder than forgiveness, but nothing more urgent:

The unforgiveness that I was holding on to, the hate, the anger, was destroying my life. I was continuing to let these men have control over me. I was continuing to let myself be victimised because I was hanging on to the hate. I was unwilling to forgive.

She felt that justice would bring healing, and looked forward to certain

---

[183] Interview with Margaret Throsby, ABC Classic FM, 25/07/2003.

milestones – the capture of the two men, then the trial and the sentence that was handed down, and finally the execution of one of the men. But justice is not what healed her:

When I was able to forgive, not only did the hate, anger and pain go away, but the shame did too. ... When I chose to forgive there was a prisoner that was set free, and I realised that that prisoner was myself. [184]

An apt metaphor for the cost of harbouring feelings of vengeance is a jellyfish called Medusa found in the Bay of Naples. The jellyfish sometimes swallows a small snail of the nudibranch variety and draws it into its digestive tract. The snail is protected by its shell and cannot be digested. The snail then slowly begins to eat the jellyfish from the inside out, and by the time the snail is fully grown it has devoured the entire jellyfish.[185] We, too, are devoured when we cannot forgive our enemies or bless those who curse us or pray for those who treat us badly.

---

[184] Interview with Debbie Morris on Philip Yancey's video, *What's So Amazing About Grace?* Zondervan Publishing House.
[185] Cf. Brian Cavanagh, *Sower's Seeds Aplenty,* Paulist Press, New York, 1996, p.35.

EIGHTH SUNDAY IN ORDINARY TIME

(YEAR C)

'How can you say to your brother, 'Brother, let me take out the splinter that is in your eye,' when you cannot see the plank in your own? Hypocrite!'
(Lk 6:42)

A woman brought her granddaughter to Gandhi with a request: 'Tell her to stop eating so much sugar.' Gandhi replied, 'Bring the girl back to me next week.' They went away and returned the following week. But Gandhi put them off again, saying the same thing, 'Bring her back to me next week.' This happened three times. Finally, on the fourth visit, Gandhi said to the girl, 'You should not eat so much sugar. It is not good for you.' The grandmother was a little puzzled. 'We waited four weeks for this simple remark? Why couldn't you have told her that when I first brought her to you?' 'Ah!' Gandhi sighed. 'It's taken me this long to stop eating too much sugar myself.'[186]

The word 'hypocrisy' comes from the Greek *hypokrisis*. In classical and Hellenistic Greek it was the word used to denote an actor on stage. From this use of 'play-acting' or 'acting out' it came to mean a 'dissembler' or 'pretender'.[187] Like actors on stage we pretend to be someone that we are not. We have one set of standards for ourselves and another for others. Jesus makes this point with a verbal cartoon – we become obsessed over a speck of dust in another's eye while oblivious to a plank in our own. This is often called psychological projection – a kind of self-defence mechanism that projects onto others, consciously or otherwise, the very vices that we are struggling to overcome in ourselves.

It is the charge of hypocrisy that undermines the credibility of the church. Robert Blair Kaiser, an American author and journalist, has written a number books on the Catholic Church, but *Cardinal Mahony*, published in 2008, is his first novel.[188] Although Cardinal Mahony is the current archbishop of Los Angeles,

---

[186] Adapted from John Shea, *The Relentless Widow: The Spiritual Wisdom of the Gospels for Christian Preachers and Teachers*, p.53.

[187] Joseph Fitzmyer, *The Gospel According to Luke I-IX,* The Anchor Bible: Doubleday, New York, 1979, p. 64

this is a work of fiction in which the action commences in November, 2008. The (fictional) Cardinal Mahony is kidnapped by a quasi-terrorist organisation, Para los otros (men and women for others), and taken to a secret location in Mexico where he is put on trial. The basic charge is one of hypocrisy. He is a member of a hierarchy that behaves 'like CEOs of General Motors, aloof from the people' and 'very unaccountable for their actions.' He has allowed 'the unwritten rules of his clerical club (to) undermine the rule of the Gospel itself.' He is also accused of robbing 'the patrimony of Christ's poor to enrich crafty lawyers – and keep sodomising priests out of prison.' The spiralling costs of Los Angeles' new cathedral also figure into the equation. The trial proceeds before a jury of retired bishops, and the cardinal is found guilty as charged and sentenced 'to become a Christian.' Well, the fictional Cardinal Mahony undergoes a profound change of heart. Upon returning to Los Angles he sells his private helicopter, resigns membership of the exclusive Jonathan Club, turns the cathedral rectory into a shelter for homeless pregnant women, and takes up residence in the AIDS wing at Queen of Angels hospital.

This novel is about a clash of ecclesiologies or models of church. It is about 'John XXIII Catholics trying to survive in a John Paul II world'; a nonclerical or people's church confronting an institutional church of rule-book Catholics who 'pray, pay and obey' in subservience to the hierarchy; it is a democratic church pitted against church-as-monarchy. At the heart of Kaiser's novel is an indictment: the church is guilty of hypocrisy. One of the cardinal's captors tells him quite bluntly, 'If Jesus visited the Vatican today, he would throw up. What you guys have done to his message!'

Bishop Geoffrey Robinson, retired auxiliary bishop of the Archdiocese of Sydney, has written about the dangers of what he calls institutional hypocrisy. 'As long as the church is made up of human beings, there will always be hypocrisy in it, as in every other institution in the world.'[189] In the popular television series *Yes Minister* and *Yes, Prime Minister* Jim Hacker, minister and then prime minister in the British Government, might cherish the illusion that he is a person of vision and integrity, but in reality he inevitably falls prey to cowardice and desperation, only to be rescued by his scheming and pragmatic cabinet secretary, Sir Humphrey Appleby. In the final episode, 'A Tangled Web', Sir Humphrey informs Jim Hacker that he gave an incorrect answer to the House during question time, or,

---

[188] Robert Blair Kaiser, *Cardinal Mahony: A Novel*, Humble-bee Press, Phoenix, AZ , 2008).

[189] Geoffrey Robinson, *Confronting Power and Sex in the Catholic Church*, John Garrett Publishing, Mulgrave, Victoria, 2007, p.299.

to put it bluntly, he lied to the Parliament. As a result Sir Humphrey, who knows the truth of the matter, is invited to appear before a House of Commons Privileges Committee. Hacker exhorts him to lie. 'Humphrey, you must. Otherwise it will look as though I was lying.' Mounting his high horse, Sir Humphrey tells the prime minister he must be loyal to 'the truth'. 'I'm sorry, Prime Minister, but I cannot become involved in some shabby cover-up.' However, when Hacker is made aware of some embarrassing and indiscreet off-air remarks that Sir Humphrey made during a radio interview, he has a weapon for blackmail. Sir Humphrey is now willing to 'tell an untruth in public ... for you, Prime Minister'. Well, he wouldn't exactly be lying; he'd be making a clarification. And 'the purpose of a clarification is not to make oneself clear, but to put oneself in the clear.'

Bishop Robinson reminds us that 'There has never been a perfect church and there never will be.' And so we 'must work within an imperfect church', never forgetting 'that I am myself an imperfect member of that imperfect church, contributing my problems and failures as well as my assistance.'[190] For that reason, we must not be harsh in judging others, a recurring theme in the writings of the desert fathers and mothers. There was a brother at Scetis who had committed a fault. So they called a meeting and invited Abba Moses. He refused to go. The priest sent someone to say to him, 'They're all waiting for you.' So Moses got up and set off; he took a leaky jug and filled with water and took it with him. The others came out to meet him and said, 'What is this, Father?' The old man said to them, 'My sins run out behind me and I cannot see them, yet here I am coming to sit in judgment on the mistakes of somebody else.' When they heard this, they called off the meeting.[191]

---

[190] Ibid, pp.21-2.
[191] Rowan Williams, *Silence and Honey Cakes*, A Lion Book, Oxford, 2003, p.29.

NINTH SUNDAY IN ORDINARY TIME

(YEAR C)

'I tell you, not even in Israel have I found faith like this.' (Lk 7:9)

Capernaum, an ancient fishing town located on the northern shore of the Sea of Galilee, was the closest to a permanent base that Jesus had during his Galilean ministry. In the gospels of Matthew and Mark it is referred to simply as 'his own city' (Mt 9:1; Mk 2:1). Since 1968 excavations have revealed some remains of the city from the time of Jesus, including the synagogue and the house of St Peter. The Spanish pilgrim Egeria visited Capernaum sometime between 381CE and 384CE and noted that 'In Capernaum the house of the prince of the apostles has been made into a church, with its original walls still standing... There also is the synagogue where the Lord cured a man possessed by the devil. The way in is up many stairs, and it is made of dressed stone.'[192] The remains of the synagogue today's pilgrim sees at Capernaum date from the late C4 to early C5, but it was built on the foundations of the synagogue of the Roman centurion.[193]

Some Jewish elders acting on behalf of a centurion ask Jesus to heal his servant. Who is this centurion? He is a gentile and quite possibly a Roman. His title in Luke's gospel, *hekatontarchos*, translated as centurion, designated an officer at the head of a Roman company of one hundred men. He was not in charge of Roman troops stationed at that time in Capernaum, so he could have been in the service of Herod Antipas leading a company of mercenaries, or he may have been employed in the police or customs service.[194] We're told that his servant is close to death, and he seeks Jesus' help, having heard about his reputation as a miracle worker. Jesus sets out at once, but as he approaches the house the centurion sends word to him, 'Sir, do not put yourself to trouble; because I am not worthy to have you under my roof.' He is obviously aware of the fact that a Jew would be defiled by entering a

---

[192] Quoted in Jerome Murphy-O'Connor, *The Holy Land*, Oxford University Press, Third edition, 1992, p.224

[193] Virgilio C. Corbo, 'Capernaum', in David Noed Freedman (Ed), *The Anchor Bible Dictionary, Volume 1*, Doubleday, New York, 1992, pp.866-869.

[194] Joseph A Fitzmyer, *The Gospel According to Luke I-IX*, p.651.

gentile's house.

Today's gospel is about more than the healing of a servant; it is about the centurion's faith. He would not have been a typical Roman. The average Roman soldier posted in Palestine almost certainly looked down upon the locals as an inferior race, but he didn't. He was respectful of Jewish custom, and from his own funds he had paid for the construction of the local synagogue. And he managed to astonish Jesus; 'I tell you, not even in Israel have I found faith like this.' The centurion's faith:

isn't an abstract belief about God, or the learning of dogmas. It is the simple, clear belief that when Jesus commands that something be done, it will be done. He regards Jesus like a military officer, with authority over sickness and health. If Jesus says that someone is to get well, they will. [195]

We're talking here about a very unfashionable word – obedience! My online dictionary defines it as 'compliance with someone's wishes or orders or acknowledgement of their authority', or as 'unquestioning obedience to the commander in chief.' The centurion tells Jesus that he knows what obedience is: 'I say to one man: Go, and he goes; to another: Come here, and he comes; to my servant: Do this, and he does it.' The etymology of the word 'obedience' is instructive; it comes from two Latin words, *ob* meaning 'in the direction of', and *audire*, meaning 'to hear'. The image is of leaning towards somebody, straining to hear what they are saying. Well, freedom of choice is a core value of modern life. Nobody is going to tell me what to do. Abbot Christopher Jamison says that we might express it in these words: "I want to be free to be me. I express my freedom by exercising my right to choose my clothes, my job and my sexual activity.' But how free are we, really? Our supposedly free choices are so often driven by obedience to a hidden agenda. For example, people today:

are convinced they are choosing their clothes from endless possibilities, ranging from grunge jeans to smart suits. Yet their choices are usually responses to other people's ideas about what they should wear. The fashion houses decide this season's look, the high-street stores mass-produce that look, while photos of fashion icons and advertisements influence us to buy that look.

We use the language of freedom 'but live in thrall to hidden rules'. The danger here is that 'people do not know that they are in thrall to other people's agendas and hence do not see the need to escape from them.' [196]

---

[195] Christopher Jamison, op. cit., pp.72-74.
[196] Tom Wright, *Luke for Everyone*, SPCK, London, 2001, pp.80-1.

The desert fathers and mothers were clear about the centrality of obedience in the authentic spiritual life. Four monks came to see Abba Pambo. Each of them spoke about the virtue of one of the others. The first fasted a great deal; the second was poor; the third had acquired great charity, and they said of the fourth that he had lived for twenty-two years in obedience to an old man. Abba Pambo said to them, 'I tell you, the virtue of this last one is the greatest. Each of the others has obtained the virtue he wished to acquire, but the last one, restraining his own will, does the will of another.'[197]

The virtue of obedience invites people to listen, and then to choose what voices to follow. This involves: *a double exercise of freedom: the freedom of discernment and the freedom of choosing to follow what has been discerned. Obedience that is blind does not exercise discernment and simply follows the most assertive voice or the voice of the one to whom life has been surrendered. ... The fact that we have the phrase 'blind obedience' shows that ordinary obedience is not like this; it is discerning.* [198]

So, when the centurion says to Jesus: 'Give the word and let my servant be cured,' he freely surrenders to the word of Jesus, a word spoken with authority, a word that has the power to effect what it proclaims. This obedient freedom is at the heart of Christian discipleship. It is being at one with Mary, whose response to God's invitation was, 'Let it be done to me according to your word (Lk 1:38).' It is being at one with Jesus who prayed in the garden, 'let your will be done, not mine'(Lk 22:42).

---

[197] Ibid, p.72.
[198] Ibid, pp.76-7.

TENTH SUNDAY IN ORDINARY TIME

(YEAR C)

'Young man, I tell you to get up.' (Lk 7:14)

On October 21, 2008, the British Humanist Association launched the Atheist Bus Campaign. Their modest aim was to raise £5500 in order to sponsor thirty buses across London for four weeks with the slogan: 'There's probably no God. Now stop worrying and enjoy your life.' Within a fortnight the campaign, supported by celebrity atheist Richard Dawkins, had raised considerably more than their modest target.

One of the criticisms that atheists often level against believers is that we are so focused on the next life that we don't enjoy this life. Dawkins tells the story of Cardinal Basil Hume, formerly archbishop of Westminster in London, informing a fellow Benedictine monk that he, Hume, was dying and did not have long to live. The monk replied, 'Congratulations! That's brilliant news. I wish I was coming with you.'[199] The point that Dawkins is making is that all believers should share a similar enthusiasm to die if they really believed that the next life was everything that they claim it is.

On the one hand I think Dawkins is right. All Christians should feel excited about spending eternity in heaven with God. Indeed, St Paul reminds us that the eye has not seen, nor has the ear heard, nor has it entered the human heart what God has prepared for those who love him (1Cor 2:9). On the other hand, I'm not ready to go – just yet! I don't think a belief in the afterlife means that we have to despise our present life on earth. We live with this tension. It was Saint Irenaeus who wrote in the second century that the glory of God is a person fully alive [200] – that is, someone who enjoys life to the full, as Jesus promised (Jn 10:10). But it's hard not to agree with Pope Benedict when he writes, 'Death, admittedly, one would wish to postpone for as long as possible.' But he also recognises that 'to live always, without end – this, all things considered, can only be monotonous and ultimately unbearable.'[201] One of the implicit presuppositions behind the

---
[199] Richard Dawkins, op. cit., p.356.
[200] *Adversus Haereses*, Book IV, Chapter 20, Section 7.
[201] Pope Benedict XVI, *Spe Salvi* (*On Christian Hope*), n.10

atheist slogan, *There's probably no God. Now stop worrying and enjoy life* is that God is somehow responsible for my worries, and as soon as I jettison a belief in God my worries will dissipate. I do not doubt that some people have harboured an image of God that is worrying. As Bishop Geoffrey Robinson points out, 'in the past much of the spiritual life was presented to people in the negative terms of self-denial, self-abasement and rejection of the 'world'.' At its worst 'people were ordered to perform the impossible task of loving a most unlovable god under pain of damnation.'[202] But even if I have a healthy image of God, I still worry over certain things, and I'm sure that atheists aren't immune to worry. To argue that we can deal with our worries single-handedly is to say we can save ourselves by our own efforts, apart from Divine grace. Today's gospel is about raising a young man from physical death, but for a widow whose only son has died, it is raising her from social oblivion. It's about salvation.

We meet Jesus in Nain, a site today identified with the Muslim town of Nein, just over fifteen kilometres from Nazareth as the crow flies and a day's journey from Capernaum. The C4 Spanish pilgrim Egeria mentions visiting a church at Nain that was built from, or upon, the house of the widow whose son was raised.[203] This episode, unique to Luke's gospel, reveals more about the power of Jesus. When he healed the centurion's servant at Capernaum he acted from a distance, and on behalf of a person who was gravely ill; now he raises a person who is dead and about to be buried.

Luke's telling of the story parallels Elijah's raising of the son of the widow of Zarephath, recorded in today's first reading from the first book of the Kings (17:8-24). Jesus came to Nain, just as Elijah came to Zarephath. In each story the mother, a widow, is particularly vulnerable. Not only has she lost her husband; now she has lost her only son, 'her only source of support and her last connection to her husband's family.' In the midst of her grief she is as good as dead in society without a significant male in her life to take care of her.[204] Her plight moved Jesus deeply. In restoring an only son to his mother Jesus reveals God's compassion for the poor and vulnerable. Luke appears to be making a direct allusion to the Elijah story when he tells us that Jesus, like Elijah, 'gave him to his mother' (Lk 7:15; 1Kings 17:23). There is, though, one significant difference between the two stories: 'Jesus raises the widow's son by

---

[202] Geoffrey Robinson, op. cit., pp.26-7.
[203] James F. Strange, 'Nain', in David Noel Freedman (Ed), *The Anchor Bible Dictionary, Volume 4*, Doubleday, New York, 1992, pp.1000-1.
[204] John J Pilch, *The Cultural World of Jesus, Cycle C*, The Liturgical Press, Collegeville, MN, 1997, p.47.

a command of his powerful word, whereas Elijah had to stretch himself over the child three times.'²⁰⁵ The people are astounded and filled with awe when Jesus raises the dead man and gives him to his mother, and they praise God saying, 'A great prophet has appeared among us.' But Luke wants to say more about Jesus through this story, and he does so (beginning at 7:13) by referring to the earthly Jesus as 'the Lord'. The regular use of 'the Lord' for the earthly Jesus in Gospel narrative 'is a trait unique to Luke; no other New Testament Gospel ... employs it.'²⁰⁶ Jesus is more than a great prophet. His miracles 'are not the primary focal point of his ministry. The proclamation of the reign of God is. The miracles merely demonstrate the presence of that reign here and now in the lives of the people who believe.' ²⁰⁷ The note sounded in Luke's overture (the infancy narrative) – 'for he has visited his people' (1:68) – now resonates throughout the gospel. Through the ministry of Jesus, God's sick and sinful people experience the visitation of God 'through physical healing, the raising of the dead, and finally the spiritual equivalent of healing the sick or raising the dead, the forgiveness of sins.' ²⁰⁸ Next Sunday's gospel continues this theme with the story of sinful woman who bathes Jesus' feet in her tears of repentance. Jesus, with a word of power and authority, is with me when I most need him. Now I can stop worrying!

We must also remember that when Jesus healed the centurion's servant, and when he raised up the widow's son, he was reaching out to foreigners. And so, the 'failure to believe on the part of the Jewish leaders, as opposed to the common people, is balanced by the hint that the people God is visiting will no longer be restricted to the Jews.' The time is close at hand 'when the gospel message will reach out to the distant Gentiles, who ... will receive it with faith and so be incorporated into God's people.'²⁰⁹ The power and goodness of God 'disregard national boundaries.'²¹⁰ As Nikos Kazantzakis once wrote, 'The bosom of God is not a ghetto.' In other words, God's heart:

*can embrace everything. It is wide, unpetty, open and antithetical to all that is factional, fundamentalistic and ideological. It is a heart that does not divide things up according to ours and theirs.*²¹¹

---

²⁰⁵ Joseph Fitzmyer, *The Gospel According to Luke*, I-IX, p.656.
²⁰⁶ John P Meier, *A Marginal Jew, Volume Two: Mentor, Message, and Miracles*, p.796.
²⁰⁷ Dianne Bergant, *Preaching the New Lectionary, Year C*, The Liturgical Press, Collegeville, MN, 2000, p.270.
²⁰⁸ John P Meier, *A Marginal Jew, Volume Two: Mentor, Message, and Miracles*, p.789
²⁰⁹ Ibid, p.790.
²¹⁰ Dianne Bergant, Preaching the New Lectionary, Year C, p.266.
²¹¹ Ronald Rolheiser, *Forgotten Among the Lillies*, pp.223-4.

ELEVENTH SUNDAY IN ORDINARY TIME

(YEAR C)

'If this man were a prophet, he would know who this woman is that is touching him and what a bad name she has.' (Lk 7:39)

In *Shame*, a novel about the political turmoil in Pakistan, the author Salman Rushdie reflects upon the message of Georg Büchner's play about the French Revolution, *Danton's Death*. The true dialectic of history, the play tells us, is not a clash between left and right, socialist and capitalist, or black and white, but between 'Virtue versus vice, ascetic versus bawd, God against the Devil: that's the game.'[212] Perhaps this distinction between the epicurean and the puritan lies at the heart of the clash between the West and Islamic fundamentalism. We in the West are the epicures. Freedom of choice is a core value of modern life. 'I don't want to be told what to do. I want to be free to be me.' We live in a culture 'that teaches that freedom means self-assertive and radical autonomy from any external authority.'[213] Abbot Christopher Jamison notes the irony in this, because 'for many people, their supposedly free choices are driven by obedience to a hidden agenda. ... (P)eople use the language of freedom but live in thrall to hidden rules.'[214] The Taliban in Afghanistan are perfect examples of the puritan. After the Russian withdrawal they ruled most of the country from 1996 until 2001, implementing the strictest interpretation of Sharia law ever seen in the Muslim world. A scene from Khaled Hosseini's novel *The Kite Runner* is indicative of their fanaticism. Farzana, accompanied by her husband, goes to the bazaar to buy some potatoes and *naan*. 'She asked the vendor how much the potatoes cost, but he did not hear her, I think he had a deaf ear. So she asked louder and suddenly a young Talib ran over and hit her on the thighs with his wooden stick. He struck her so hard she fell down. He was screaming that the Ministry of Vice and Virtue does not allow women to speak loudly.'[215]

---

[212] Salman Rushdie, *Shame*, Vintage Books, London, 1983, p.240.
[213] George Weigel, op. cit., p.10.
[214] Christopher Jamison, op. cit., pp.72-3.
[215] Khaled Hosseini, *The Kite Runner*, Bloomsbury, London, 2003, p.190.

Welcoming the Outsider

The Taliban in Afghanistan don't hold an exclusive franchise over the Ministry of Vice and Virtue; it also thrives in the West, but packaged more subtly. Religion has never been shy about denouncing vice and praising virtue, as we see in today's gospel. Jesus was invited to dine at the house of a leading Pharisee named Simon, but his host failed to offer the customary hospitality – no slave to wash his feet; no kiss of welcome, no perfumed oil to anoint his head. Instead, 'an unnamed woman, with the reputation of being a public sinner, gatecrashes the party and begins to supply in a most extravagant way the duties of hospitality Simon has ignored.' [216] Simon, the puritan, is aghast at this woman's impudence, and even more shocked that Jesus should allow her to touch him. 'If this man were a prophet, he would know who this woman is that is touching him and what a bad name she has.' There is no place for a woman here at this banquet.

Sadly, Christians can also be guilty of that same lack of compassion for the sinner. Earlier in the year I spoke about Thomas Merton's vocation to the monastic life.[217] On December 10, 1941, he arrived at the Abbey of Our Lady of Gethsemani in Kentucky, USA, a month short of his 27th birthday. For the next 27 years he lived the life of a Cistercian monk until his accidental death in Bangkok on December 10, 1968, at the age of 53. His autobiography, *The Seven Storey Mountain*, was first published on October 4, 1948, and it was a best seller. However, the Trappist vocation was not Merton's first choice. In 1939 he had decided to become a Franciscan, and after a successful interview with the Order's vocation director, Fr Edmund Murphy, he was set to enter the novitiate in August, 1940. But in the months leading up to the date of his reception he became increasingly restless because he hadn't disclosed everything about his past life. He made an appointment to see the vocation director again, and in his own words, 'I told him about my past and all the troubles I had had.'[218] Interestingly, *The Seven Storey Mountain* is not explicit about what in Merton's past would have troubled him so much. In the words of William Shannon, founding president of the International Thomas Merton Society, it emerged some years later 'that, while at Clare College, Cambridge, Merton's sexual drives, unaccompanied by any sense of their true human meaning, led to disaster not only for him but also for an unmarried woman who bore his child.'[219] This disclosure was obviously too much for Fr Murphy, and he advised Merton to

---

[216] Brendan Byrne, *The Hospitality of God*, St Pauls Publications, Strathfield, NSW, 2000, p.74.
[217] Homily for the Second Sunday of Advent.
[218] Thomas Merton, *The Seven Storey Mountain*, Harcourt Brace & Company, Orlando, FL, 1998 edition, p.325.
[219] William H. Shannon, 'A Note to the Reader', in Thomas Merton, *The Seven Storey Mountain*, p.xxii.

write to the provincial and withdraw his application.[220] There was no room in the Franciscans, it would seem, for someone with a background such as his.

Puritans, like Simon the Pharisee, seldom see beyond external appearances, and sadly there is something of Simon in all of us. Fr Ronald Rolheiser once officiated at the funeral of a young man in his early twenties who was killed, while drunk, in a motor accident. 'Death because of irresponsibility and drunkenness! Moreover during the last few years of his life he had been away from the church and the sacraments and had been living with his girl friend. This is hardly what classical spirituality calls "a happy death".' Looking at the faces present at the funeral, it was evident to Rolheiser that there was more than sorrow in them:

Fear was present, real fear that this young man we had all known, loved, understood, and knew to have a good heart, was somehow going to be excluded from heaven and condemned to hell because, for a few brief years of adolescence, he had been mixed up and somewhat irresponsible.

Today's gospel is about repentance and forgiveness, but it is also about compassion. As Karen Armstrong points out, 'The practice of compassion is central to every one of the major world religions – but sometimes you would never know it. Instead, religion is associated with violence, intolerance and seems more preoccupied by dogmatic or sexual orthodoxy.'[221] The God who is revealed to us in and through the ministry of Jesus isn't a strict puritan like Simon the Pharisee, yet sometimes we treat God as if he were. Writing about the death of the same young man, Rolheiser makes this observation:

We, with the fogginess that clouds our understanding, knew that, beneath it all, despite the circumstances of his life and death, he had a good heart, a warm heart, a loving heart that needed just a bit more time and love to burst into charity, chastity and faith. Strange that we should feel that God did not recognise this. We knew how good this young man's heart was. We knew too that his irresponsibility was little more than a combination of adolescent immaturity, laziness, peer pressure and the infectious influence of an amoral culture. Deep down he was not bad, immoral, a candidate for condemnation. He was little more than a child, struggling, feeling his oats, showing off, insecure, merely looking for acceptance and love. On that basis, can we seriously think that he might be excluded from the community of life? How utterly absurd! ... God is a God of infinite compassion. Even more than this young man's parents, God

---

[220] Thomas Merton, *The Seven Storey Mountain*, p.325.
[221] Karen Armstrong, 'Do Unto Others', *The Guardian*, November 14, 2008. http://www.guardian.co.uk/commentisfree/2008/nov/14/religion/print

understood the goodness of this young man's heart. [222]

When addressing the graduating class of Sydney's Campion College in 2008, the bishop of Parramatta, Kevin Manning, made the observation that;

Some Catholics persuade themselves that it is their mission to correct everybody else, other Catholics in particular: to develop a Church of those who are right, rather than a Church of mercy, forgiveness, compassion, justice and love. [223]

---

[222] Ronald Rolheiser, *Forgotten Among the Lilies*, pp.172-3.
[223] Kerry Myers, 'Trained for life, not just for work', in *The Catholic Weekly*, December 14, 2008.

TWELFTH SUNDAY IN ORDINARY TIME

(YEAR C)

'But you', he said, 'who do you say I am?' (Lk 9:20)

Jesus' ministry in Galilee, as Luke tells the story, comes to a climax around questions about his identity. [224] After Jesus had calmed the storm, the disciples, awestruck and astounded, ask 'Who can this be?' (8:25). And Herod the tetrarch is also curious, 'Who is this I hear such reports about?' (9:9). Now, after the miracle of the loaves and fishes, Jesus asks his disciples a fundamental question: 'Who do you say I am?' Peter answers, 'the Christ of God.' Christ is not a surname, it is a title. The Greek word *christos* means 'anointed.' The English word 'Messiah' is an approximate transliteration of the Hebrew meshiah or the Aramaic mashiha, which also means 'anointed.' Thus 'Messiah' and 'Christ' are the same. In the Hebrew Bible three classes of people were anointed: prophets, priests and kings. 'The Christian tradition early fixed on the third of these as giving a clue to Jesus' identity: he was descended from King David and was the Davidic Messiah – David's physical descendant, chosen by God (spiritually 'anointed') to perform a David-like task.'[225]

How would a first century Jewish audience have understood Peter's acknowledgement of Jesus as the anointed one of God? By the time of Jesus the 'expectation of the Messiah embodied one of the principal hopes for Yahweh's intervention to save his people.'[226] The messiah, a king-saviour, would certainly be a political saviour, but his saving acts would never be merely political. The messiahship of Jesus, however, is not going to conform to popular expectations. What the disciples have yet to understand is that Jesus' messiahship 'involves suffering, repudiation, death, even though it may end in resurrection ...'. [227] The idea of a crucified messiah would have been inconceivable to the disciples, an absurd contradiction. How could an executed criminal be the anointed one of God?

---

[224] Brendan Byrne, *The Hospitality of God*, p. 87.
[225] EP Sanders, *The Historical Figure of Jesus*, Penguin Books, London, 1993, p.240.
[226] John L McKenzie, *'Aspects of Old Testament Thought'*; in Raymond E Brown, Joseph A Fitzmyer and Roland E Murphy, *The New Jerome Biblical Commentary*, p.1312.
[227] Joseph A Fitzmyer, *The Gospel According to Luke I-IX*, p.771.

That's not the kind of messiah we want. And herein lies a form of idolatry. Like the Israelites in the desert, we too may be guilty of idolatry, of worshipping a false God. Joseph Ratzinger (Pope Benedict XVI) offers an instructive commentary on that incident recorded in the book of Exodus. After Moses had ascended Mt Sinai the people became restless and prevailed upon Aaron 'to make us a god to go at our head.' (Ex 32:1). Psalm 106 depicts this as an episode of simple idolatry, the worship of false gods: 'They fashioned a calf at Horeb and worshipped an image of metal, exchanging the God who was their glory for the image of a bull that eats grass.' But the idolatry goes beyond worshipping an image. Ratzinger argues that the people of Israel 'remain completely attached to the same God ... who led Israel out of Egypt.' In what sense, then, is this idolatry? Wherein lies Israel's apostasy? Well, first of all in believing that the saving power of the God of Israel can be reduced to the image of a golden calf. 'The people cannot cope with the invisible, remote, and mysterious God. They want to bring him down into their own world, into what they can see and understand.' The Israelites are 'no longer going up to God, but drawing God down into one's own world.'[228] Idolatry is fashioning a god in our own image; it is an attempt to decant the divine into a convenient container.

Tom Wright, the Anglican bishop of Durham, was chaplain at Worcester College, Oxford, for seven years. At the beginning of each academic year he always made time to welcome each of the first-year students individually. He said that most students were happy to meet him, but some admitted, often slightly embarrassed, 'You won't be seeing much of me; you see, I don't believe in God.' Wright had developed a stock response to this admission, 'Oh, that's interesting. Which god is it you don't believe in?' Invariably they stumbled out a few phrases to describe the god they didn't believe in: 'a being who lived up in the sky, looking down disapprovingly at the world, occasionally intervening to do miracles, sending bad people to hell while allowing good people to share his heaven.' Again, Wright had a stock response: 'Well, I'm not surprised you don't believe in that god. I don't believe in that god either. ... I believe in the God I see revealed in Jesus of Nazareth.'[229]

Pilgrims must bend low to enter the Church of the Holy Nativity in Bethlehem, and herein lies a lesson. The present church, built on the site where tradition locates the stable cave in which Jesus was born, once had three entrances. Two have been

---

[228] Quoted in George Weigel, op. cit., pp.62-3.
[229] Marcus J. Borg and N. T. Wright, *The Meaning of Jesus*, HarperSan Francisco, 2000, p.157.

walled up, while the great centre door was reduced in size by the Crusaders, and made even smaller during the Mamluk or Turkish period to prevent looters driving carts into the basilica, and to stop horses from entering.[230] The door was reduced in size for pragmatic reasons, but it also teaches pilgrims an important lesson. We must bow and bend low before the mystery of the incarnation. The anointed one does not reveal a God made in our own image and likeness.

Jesus is, for us as Christians, the decisive revelation of what a life full of God looks like. Radically centred in God and filled with the Spirit, he is the decisive disclosure and epiphany of what can be seen of God embodied in a human life.[231]

Ronald Rolheiser tells of a conversation he had with an elderly colleague who had been one of his mentors and was now a professor emeritus. 'Why does God hide himself?' Rolheiser asked. 'Why doesn't God just appear, physically, beyond doubt, and then we wouldn't have to have faith, we would know God with certainty?' The answer he received took him by surprise:

To ask a question like this is tantamount to looking at the most beautiful day in June, seeing all the trees and flowers in full blossom and asking a friend, 'Where is summer?' To see certain things is to see summer. To see certain things is to see God.[232]

But one sees such things, not with the eyes, but with the heart. In the words of Antoine de Saint-Exupéry's fox, 'You can see things clearly with your heart. What is essential is invisible to the eye.'[233] Truth is known by experience; it is experienced in silence. It is not intellectual; it is existential.[234] Daniel Polish reminds us that every Jewish service ends with a doxology called the Kaddish. As worshippers prepare to leave the synagogue, the liturgy reminds them that God is 'beyond all the praises, songs and adorations that we are able to utter in this world.' This is an acknowledgement that, in the words of Abraham Joshua Heschel:

God cannot be distilled to a well-defined idea. All concepts fade when applied

---

[230] Jerome Murphy-O'Connor, op.cit., pp.210-11; Rivka Gonen, *Biblical Holy Places*, A Palphot Publication, Jerusalem, 1987, p.65; John J. Kolgallen, *A New Testament Guide to the Holy Land*, Loyola University Press, Chicago, IL, 1987, pp.122-3.
[231] Marcus J Borg, *The Heart of Christianity*, HarperSan Francisco, 2003, p.88.
[232] Ronald Rolheiser, *Against an Infinite Horizon*, Hodder & Stoughton, London, 1995, p.140.
[233] Antoine de Saint-Exupéry, *The Little Prince*, Penguin Books, Harmondsworth, Reprinted 2000, p.72.
[234] Ohso, *Zen: Its History and Teachings*, Ixos Press, Lewes, 2004, p.87.

to his essence. To the pious man knowledge of God is not a thought within his grasp.[235] When Peter replied, 'You are the Christ of God', he was making a confession of faith. You are the one anointed to reveal the Father. To see you, to listen to your words, to walk in your company, to be healed by your touch, to be touched by your love, to be embraced by your compassion is to experience the presence of God.

---

[235] Quoted in Daniel F. Polish, *'A little Unbelief is not always a bad thing'*, in America, February 2, 2009.

THIRTEENTH SUNDAY IN ORDINARY TIME

(YEAR C)

Once the hand is laid on the plough, no one who looks back is fit for the kingdom of God. (Lk 9:62)

Today's gospel is about following Jesus, and I would like to draw two lessons from the few verses we have just heard. Firstly, there is always a temptation to say that I will follow Jesus, but there are a few things that I must do first – bury my father, say good-bye to my people at home. But the invitation is now. There never will an ideal time; if we wait for the perfect moment we will miss out. I recall hearing of a newly-opened department store that dealt in a single line of merchandise – husbands. Yes, a department store where women could shop for the perfect husband. There are six floors in the store, and as the shopper ascends from one floor to the next, the attributes of the potential husbands on display also increase. There are, however, a few conditions. The first condition is that a woman can visit the store once only. The second condition is that once you have ascended you can't then change your mind and choose a husband from a lower floor. So, a woman entering the Husband Store was taken by the first floor offerings: Here she finds men who are spiritual and employed in a well-paid job. 'That's great,' the woman thinks, 'but this is only the ground floor and I'm sure I can do better.' On the second floor she finds spiritual men who are employed in a well-paid job and who love children. 'Hmmm. That is tempting, but there are several more floors to go.' On the third floor there are spiritual men employed in well-paid jobs, who love children, and they're extremely good-looking. She's ready to settle for one of the gentlemen on this floor, but maybe, she thinks, I should see what's on offer on the next floor. And she's not disappointed on the fourth floor because here she finds potential husbands who are spiritual, employed in well-paid jobs, love children, extremely good looking, and great with the housework. 'I can't imagine doing much better than this, but I'll take a gamble on the next floor.' On the fifth floor she finds potential husbands who are spiritual, well employed, love children, good looking, help with the housework, and who also have a strong romantic streak. 'What more could I ask for?' she wonders, but having come this far she can't resist seeing what the top floor has to offer. When the elevator doors opens on the sixth floor she is confronted with a sign that reads: 'Welcome. You are the ten millionth visitor to this floor. There are no men on this floor. This floor exists solely as proof that women are impossible to please!'

From one point of view we're all impossible to please. In the face of endless temptations to wait for the right moment, the perfect person, or the ideal conditions, Jesus calls us now. When one of his disciples told Jesus that he had first to organise his father's funeral, the response was a jolt: Let the dead bury the dead. We don't know if the disciple's father was ill or at death's doorstep. He may have been quite healthy, but the disciple wanted to use the obligation to bury his father, however far off that may be, to postpone the invitation to follow Jesus. That's called keeping your options open. Jesus calls for commitment.

The second lesson I would like to draw from today's gospel has to do with the saying 'Once the hand is laid on the plough, no one who looks back is fit for the kingdom of God.' At some stage during our life, most of us make a commitment of one kind or another. More often than not it is a commitment to another person – and for many of you that commitment took the form of marriage vows. When you took those vows, you made a life-long commitment. In theory you acknowledged the shadow side of that commitment. You said that you would take each other for better, but also for worse; for richer, but also for poorer; in health, but also in sickness. 'Until death do us part.'

We're all aware, however, than an increasing number of marriages don't last until 'death do us part.' One factor which has surely affected the increasing rate of marriage breakup is the simple fact that we live much longer than our ancestors. It has been estimated that the average lifespan in ancient Rome was only about 20 years. In Europe during the Middle Ages the average lifespan was about 33 years of age. In 1841 the average life expectation in England was 40 for a man and 42 for a woman. It is only during the last few decades that the bulk of the population has begun to reach the Biblical limit of threescore and ten years. This increased lifespan must surely have some implications for the nature of any commitments that we make. All commitments are tested by time. 'Until death do us part' now means 30 or 40 years longer than it did at the beginning of white settlement in Australia. Relationships are therefore under far greater strains than ever before.

The so-called 'mid-life crisis' often results in profound upheavals in our relationships, in our occupation, and in a whole range of commitments which had given stability to our life. Psychologists locate this 'mid-life crisis' sometime in our forties – at an age by which most of our ancestors would have been dead. And so we experience far more acutely the tension between faithfulness to commitments made when we were young, and the existential tiredness which besets us in middle age.

The American poet Robert Frost expresses this tension in two of his poems. The poem *After Apple Picking* describes the scene at harvest time in an apple orchard. The work is arduous and long, and seemingly never-ending. At one point the persona of the poem says:

For I have had too much
Of apple-picking: I am overtired
Of the great harvest I myself desired.

Apple picking can be a metaphor for any of life's commitments, commitments that we once embraced with such enthusiasm and dedication. But now, that same commitment has left us not just tired, but overtired. Will a good rest revive me, I ask myself, or is this commitment no longer life-giving? Does life now summons me to travel along a different path?

The feelings expressed in *After Apple Picking* must be held in tension with the rather contrary feelings described in another of Frost's poems, *Stopping by Woods on a Snowy Evening*. The poet is travelling by horse and sleigh on his way home, but stops by some enchanted woods. The woods seek to allure the traveller, but he moves on.

The woods are lovely, dark, and deep,
But I have promises to keep,
And miles to go before I sleep, And miles to go before I sleep. [236]

And therein lies a tension which confronts us all at some stage in life's journey. 'Overtired of the great harvest', or 'promises to keep, and miles to go before I sleep.' Today's gospel is about making commitments. 'Follow me', says Jesus. Don't worry about burying your father first; don't even bother about saying good-bye to your family. An unequivocal and very demanding invitation!

But what if we become 'overtired'? The first disciples of Jesus certainly became overtired. Peter, we know, denied even knowing Jesus. At his death they all fled and deserted him. None of them kept his hand on the plough, yet

---

[236] Edward Connery Lathem (ed), *The Poetry of Robert Frost*, Jonathan Cape, Reprinted 1977 London, p.68, p.105

all of them were to go on and do great things for the kingdom of God. And here we find the key to understanding Jesus' words 'Once the hand is laid on the plough, no one who looks back is fit for the kingdom of God.' Once you have taken the plough, keep looking ahead. There is nothing to be gained by looking back on our failures of the past and allowing them to weigh us down. This is a truth symbolically portrayed in the story of Lot's wife, recorded in chapter 19 of the book of Genesis. The Lord destroyed the city of Sodom with sulphurous fire because of the wickedness of those who lived there. Abraham's nephew, Lot, and his family are told to flee the city, and not look behind them. For some reason, Lot's wife looks back on Sodom, the doomed city of sin she has left behind. And the bible records that because of her disobedience she was changed into a pillar of salt. There is a similar message in Greek mythology. Orpheus the musician is grief-stricken at the death of this wife Eurydice. And so Orpheus makes his way to the underworld to plead with Pluto to release his wife from the bonds of death. Pluto is moved by his music and grants the request on the condition that Orpheus does not look back until he has reached earth again. Unfortunately, he looks back at the last moment, thinking that his fortune is too good to be true. Eurydice vanishes from his sight forever.[237]

'Once the hand is laid on the plough, no one who looks back is fit for the kingdom of God.' We have promises to keep, but past failures ought not to weigh us down. Our fidelity lies in the will to be faithful amid all our infidelities, to press ahead, despite the weight of the past.

---

[237] The examples of Lot's wife and Orpheus come from Brian Grenier, *No Turning Back*, St Paul Publications, Homebush, NSW, 1985, p.10.

FOURTEENTH SUNDAY IN ORDINARY TIME

(YEAR C)

'Carry no purse, no haversack, no sandals.' (Lk 10:4)

Assisi is nestled comfortably into the lower reaches of Mount Subasio in Umbria. On the plain below Assisi it's hard to miss a rather large basilica built over a small chapel known as *Sancta Maria degli Angeli*, St Mary of the Angels, or affectionately called the *Portiuncula*, the little portion. The C18 Franciscans missionaries who worked among the indigenous people of what is now the state of California named the city of *Los Angeles* after this small chapel.

On February 24, 1208, the feast day of St Matthias, Francesco (Francis) Bernadone was attending Mass in the small chapel of St Mary of the Angels and the gospel of the day was about how the Lord sent out his disciples to preach. No doubt, like most of us, Francesco had heard this text many times before, but on this particular occasion the gospel spoke to his heart as never before. In the words of an early biographer, 'When he heard that Christ's disciples should not possess gold or silver or money, or carry on their journey a wallet or a sack, nor bread nor a staff, nor to have shoes nor two tunics, but that they should preach the kingdom of God and penance, the holy man, Francis, immediately exulted in the spirit of God.'[238] Francesco – we know him as St Francis of Assisi – heard these words as if they were a direct revelation from God. At the end of Mass he asked the priest to explain the meaning of the text, and he then cried out with great joy: 'This is what I want, this is what I am looking for, this is what I am longing in my inmost heart to do.'

Such a spontaneous and impulsive response to the gospel remained with Francis to the end of his life. In time a small band of followers gathered around him, and he wrote down a short rule of life, little more than a few gospel texts and some practical guidelines. In the spring of 1209 Francis travelled to Rome to seek papal approval for his way of life. He wished to live a simple life based upon the

---

[238] 'The Life of St Francis by Thomas of Celano', Chapter IX, in Regis Armstrong, JA Wayne Hellmann, William J Short (Eds) *Francis of Assisi, Early Documents (Volume 1)*, New City Press, New York, 1999, pp.201-2.

absolute priority of the gospel. Initially the pope, Innocent III, was reluctant to approve such a radical rule of life. Realistically, how could one live in this world with no possessions at all?

What can be said of a person like Francis who wished to take literally the words of today's gospel? The C18 philosopher Voltaire dismissed him in these words: 'A raving lunatic who goes about stark naked, talks to animals, catechises a wolf, and makes himself a snow-wife.'[239] A world view that is restricted to what can be logically proved or empirically verified has little room for a romantic idealist like Francis of Assisi. Now it is true, and it's recorded in the early sources, that Francis on occasion went about stark naked. He began his life of penance by taking off his clothes in public, and he ended his life lying naked on the ground close by the small chapel of St Mary of the Angels. The sources also tells us that he spoke to birds and animals because he recognised them as his brothers and sisters, and he even tamed a ferocious wolf that terrorised the inhabitants of the small town of Gubbio. And he did fashion himself a wife out of snow and rolled naked in the snow to curb the temptations of the flesh, for he was a passionate man.

It was not only Voltaire and the Age of Enlightenment that sneered at Francis. Many of his contemporaries also thought that he was quite mad. But Francis was not opposed to reason. *Ill Poverello,* the little poor man, recognised that human beings are more than just a mind. The C17 physicist, mathematician and theologian Blaise Pascal once observed, 'The heart has its reasons which are unknown to reason.'[240] Francis responded to the gospel not only with his mind, but with his heart and soul as well. Reason always cautions prudence. Don't take any risks, don't detour from the beaten track, hold on to what you have for it may be all there is. So often we fear the promptings of the heart because they beckon us beyond the limits of our known world into realms that are totally new and unexpected.

In sending out his disciples, Jesus told them to leave behind all the supports that might have given them security in their ministry. He asked them to step out in trust. They did, and they returned home rejoicing. And so it was with Francis of Assisi. GK Chesterton's biography of St Francis describes the death of the saint on the evening of October 3, 1226, alongside his beloved chapel of St Mary of the Angels:

---

[239] *Oeujvres Complètes de Voltaire, Tome XXVI: Philosophie Tome I*, Paris 1829, quoted in Eric Doyle, *St Francis and the Song of Brotherhood,* The Seabury Press, New York, 1981, p.1. I am indebted to Fr Doyle for his insights into the life of St Francis.

[240] Martin Turnell, (Tr & Ed), *Pascal's Pensées*, Harper & Row, New York, 1962, p.95.

[Francis] desired even in his death agony to lie bare upon the bare ground, to prove that he had and that he was nothing. And we can say, with almost as deep a certainty, that the stars which passed above that gaunt and wasted corpse stark upon the rocky floor had for once, in all their shining cycles round the world of labouring humanity, looked down upon a happy man.[241]

---

[241] GK Chesterton, *St Francis of Assisi,* Hodder and Stoughton, London, 1924, pp.92-93.

FIFTEENTH SUNDAY IN ORDINARY TIME

(YEAR C)

'And who is my neighbour?' (Lk 10:29)

Travelling through Palestine in the early 1930s, the author HV Morton had made plans to travel down from Jerusalem to Jericho, a steep and winding road that dropped 1200 metres in just 40 kilometres. A friend had warned him to return to Jerusalem by night lest he meet Abu Jildah. 'Who', Morton asked, 'is Abu Jildah?' Abu Jildah was a brigand, he was told, who had shot several policemen. 'There was a price of £250 on his head, and he has a habit of building a wall of stones across the Jericho road, stopping cars, robbing you, and, if you resist, shooting you. He once held up 14 cars in a row on this road, robbed everyone, threatened to cut off a woman's finger because her rings were tight, and was off and away to the hills by the time the police heard about it.' [242]

It was on this same road 'whose serpentine bends and overhanging cliffs might have been designed for highway robbery' [243] that the hapless traveller in today's gospel was attacked by bandits and left for dead. A priest and a Levite passed him by. After preaching a homily on this gospel I was once asked by an elderly parishioner why the priest had passed by the traveller without offering assistance. I offered what I thought were a few plausible explanations, but I could tell they weren't satisfactory. And then I was told, 'Father, the priest passed by without stopping because he knew that the traveller had been robbed already!'

Why did the priest pass by so callously? We're told that he was coming down the road, therefore travelling from Jerusalem to Jericho. He may have just completed his course of service in the Temple and was returning home. Because priests were forbidden to contract corpse impurity, [244] he obviously kept well away from the traveller, just in case the man had already died. Corpse impurity could be contracted merely by overshadowing a corpse, and purification required

---

[242] HV Morton, op. cit., p.85.
[243] Ibid, p.91.
[244] EP Saunders, *Judaism: Practice & Belief 63 BCE – 66 CE*, p.71.

seven days. [245] The book of Numbers, chapter 19, prescribed an elaborate ritual for purification that involved the slaughter and burning of a red heifer. The ashes were kept and mixed with water and sprinkled on impure people on the third and seventh day. After they had washed their clothes and bathed, the impurity was removed.[246] In other words, the priest in this parable faced a dilemma. If this traveller were already dead and he touched him, he became impure. That would entail a return visit to Jerusalem, as well as a costly sacrifice to remove the impurity. How would he explain all of that to an irate wife?

It was a Samaritan who came to the traveller's assistance. If Jesus drove the inhabitants of Nazareth into a frenzy by reminding them of Elijah's act of kindness to a Sidonian widow, and of Elisha healing a Syrian leper, this story must have really riled his audience. Samaritans were the inhabitants of Samaria, sandwiched between Galilee in the north and Judea in the south. Ethnically, Samaritans were 'the presumed descendants of the Israelites tribes of Ephraim and Manasseh (main components of the northern kingdom of Israel), with some admixture over the centuries of non-Israelite groups from Assyrian and Hellenistic empires.' [247] They worshipped Yahweh, but they revered Mt Gerizim instead of Mt Zion in Jerusalem as 'the one valid place to build an altar or temple for the public worship of Yahweh. They also considered that their line of Levitical priests were the legitimate priests of the Mosaic dispensation, as opposed to the priests functioning in the Temple in Jerusalem. Moreover, they accepted only the five books of Moses as authoritative Scripture'. [248]

Jesus reverses the expectations of a complacent audience. The priest or Levite should be the hero of the story and the Samaritan the villain. As Brendan Byrne notes, centuries of holding together the adjective 'good' and the noun 'Samaritan' in the traditional title of this parable, the Good Samaritan, 'have dulled us to the explosive tension of the phrase in the world of Jesus.' [249] The parable refuses to define 'neighbour' in a narrow, ethnic sense. Modern Israel's construction of a vast security barrier is a contemporary symbol of the fear and despair that divides communities along ethnic lines. In the words of the Archbishop of Canterbury, Rowan Williams, the wall is seen as 'one community decisively turning its back on another, despairing of anything that looks like a shared resolution, a shared

---

[245] Ibid, p.72.
[246] Ibid, pp.217-8.
[247] John P Meier, *A Marginal Jew, Volume III: Companions and Competitors*, Doubleday, New York 2001, p.533.
[248] Ibid, p.534.
[249] Brendan Byrne, *The Hospitality of God*, p.100.

future, a truly shared peace.' [250]

One's neighbour 'is not only the fellow member of our own religious or ethnic community but any and every human being in need.' But the parable of the Good Samaritan does more than break open a narrow definition of neighbour. It is 'a call to show mercy and compassion to all the suffering members of our human community, irrespective of religious or ethnic barriers.' Go, and do the same yourself. [251]

---

[250] Quoted in Michael Hirst, 'Dr Williams encouraged by "small gestures" in Middle East', *The Tablet* 7 February 2004, p.38.

[251] John P Meier, *A Marginal Jew, Volume III: Companions and Competitors*, p.547.

SIXTEENTH SUNDAY IN ORDINARY TIME

(YEAR C)

Jesus came to a village, and a woman named Martha welcomed him into her house. She had a sister called Mary, who sat down at the Lord's feet and listened to him speaking. (Lk 10:38-39)

The parable of the Good Samaritan and today's gospel story – Jesus visiting Martha and Mary – are found only in Luke's gospel, and they offer complementary insights into discipleship. Martha welcomed Jesus into her home and began to serve him, yet she is chided for worrying and fretting about so many things. This seems a little strange, especially after the unselfish service of the Samaritan has been presented to us as an example to imitate. But Martha is not chided because she serves. The narrator tells us that she was distracted by all the serving, and Jesus adds that Mary has chosen the better part.

Compassion to one's neighbour is by no means unique to Christianity, and so the parable of the Good Samaritan needs further comment. The story of Martha and Mary provides it. Only to serve, and to become distracted by one's serving, is to lose touch with 'the better part.' It is not enough to be a compassionate person. The disciple of Jesus must also be inspired and nourished by sitting at his feet and listening to him. But let's pause for a moment and be attentive to what is happening in this scene. In first century Palestine male and female roles were strictly demarcated; women were confined to the kitchen and the men to the living room. Mary has crossed a boundary. By sitting at the feet of Jesus she is crossing another boundary because such a posture indicated that someone wished to be a student of a master, his disciple, and this was exclusively a male prerogative. A saying recorded in the Talmud places Mary's impropriety into perspective. The rabbis said: 'It is better to burn the Torah than to teach it to a woman.' Mary ignores this, presents herself as a disciple, and Jesus praises what she has done.[252]
Mary offers Jesus loving attention, a far deeper hospitality than all of Martha's

---

[252] y. Sota 3:4; 19:7. See James Liggett, 'Sermons that Work, Pentecost 7 – Proper 11', http://www.episcopalchurch.org/11735_6991_ENG_HTM.htm. Cf William Bausch, *Once Upon a Gospel*, Twenty-Third Publications, Mystic, CT, 2008, p.213.

frantic activity. Fr William Bausch tells us that he's been to Martha's house.

She's someone I haven't seen in a while and want to do some catch-up time. She has welcomed me with great enthusiasm and has put out the best china and linens and great deserts and every time I look, my coffee cup is miraculously refilled. And she pops up and down to check the stove, the refrigerator, the microwave, talks while moving about until I've had it and finally exclaim, 'For cryin' out loud, will you just sit down and talk with me!' After all, I did come to be with her, not her dishes. [253]

This episode 'makes listening to the 'word' the 'one thing' needed. ... Priority is given to the hearing of the word coming from God's messenger over preoccupation with all other concerns. Martha wanted to honour Jesus with an elaborate meal, but Jesus reminds her that it is more important to listen to what he has to say.'[254] Australian psychologist Peter O'Connor asks how often we've heard the words, 'I feel as though I wasn't heard'? It's one thing to hear at a purely factual level; it is quite another thing to hear the feelings embedded in the words. Take the example of a teenager starting high school. He's embarrassed because he's the only boy in the class wearing unfashionable clothes, and so he tells his parents he wants to wear clothes like his friends. But 'they responded by saying there was nothing wrong with what he had.' What's happening here? The parents have either failed to hear what their son is really concerned about, or they are pretending not to hear what he's really saying. Listening to the hidden subtext, 'sometimes referred to as listening with the third ear, can be difficult and requires that we take time and be receptive. We need to listen to what someone is trying to tell us, rather than just hear their words. [255]

The social commentator Hugh McKay argues that we are reluctant to listen. The first and most important reason why we often fail to listen is that we don't have the courage to do it. And why does listening require courage?

Listening is one of the most psychological courageous things we ever do in our normal personal relationships because listening – real listening – involves seriously entertaining the ideas of the other person. That entails the risk of having to change our minds in response to what we hear. [256]

---

[253] William Bausch, *Once Upon a Gospel*, Twenty-Third Publications, Mystic, CT, 2008, p.212.
[254] Joseph A Fitzmyer, *The Gospel According to Luke X-XXIV*, Doubleday, New York ,1985, p.892.
[255] Peter A O'Connor, *Looking Inwards*, pp.167-8.
[256] Hugh Mackay, *Why Don't People Listen?*, Pan, Sydney, Reprinted 1994, pp.143-4.

The psychotherapist Carl Rogers puts it like this:

If you really understand another person ... if you are willing to enter his private world and see the way life appears to him, without any attempt to make evaluative judgments, you run the risk of being changed yourself. You might see it his way, you might find yourself influenced in your attitudes ... This risk of being changed is one of the most frightening prospects most of us can face.[257]

As one wit observed, the only person who looks forward to a change is a baby with a wet nappy! Few of us relish change, a truth that is illustrated by the story of a serious alcoholic who went to his local doctor for a check up. The doctor was deeply concerned by the amount of alcohol the man consumed each day, but nothing he said seemed to make the slightest impression. The doctor decided to use shock tactics, and so he devised a small test to illustrate the harmful effects of alcohol. He took a live garden worm and dropped it into a glass of drinking water. The worm seemed totally unaffected by the experience, perhaps even enjoying it. So the doctor then took the worm out of the glass of water and dropped it into a glass of pure whisky. The worm coughed and convulsed, contorted and spluttered, twitched and twisted, and finally died in spasms of agony. 'There you are,' said the doctor. 'What does that tell you?' With a sheepish grin the patient replied, 'Well, doctor, 'it just goes to show that if you drink whisky, you'll never get worms.'

There are none so deaf as those who will not hear! Compulsive activity, however commendable and compassionate, runs the risk of being a subterfuge, a 'deceptive distraction from what the Lord really wants.'[258] The Marthas of this world are not attentive to what their Lord truly asks of them. The disciple is one whose service flows from a life that has been transformed by a single-minded attention to the Lord. As Joseph Fitzmyer observes, 'a *diakonia* that bypasses the word is one that will never have lasting character; whereas listening to Jesus' word is the lasting 'good' that will not be taken away from the listener.'[259]

---

[257] Quoted in Hugh Mackay, op. cit., p.144.
[258] Brendan Byrne, *The Hospitality of God*, p.103.
[259] Joseph A Fitzmyer, *The Gospel According to Luke X-XXIV*, p.892.

SEVENTEETH SUNDAY IN ORDINARY TIME

(YEAR C)

'Lord, teach us to pray.' (Lk 11:1)

The disciples ask Jesus to teach them how to pray, just as John had taught his disciples. And so Jesus teaches them the prayer that we know as 'the Lord's Prayer' or the 'Our Father', although the version we traditionally use is based upon the Matthean formulation rather than the more concise form that we have in Luke's gospel. John Meier argues that Luke has kept the basic size and structure of the prayer, while Matthew has preserved the more original wording.[260] If, therefore, we omit what Matthew (or his liturgical tradition) has added, but retain his more laconic and Semitic wording, we end up with a prayer that has three sections: (A) An address ('Father'); (B) Two 'You Petitions' ('hallowed be your name' / 'Your Kingdom come'); (C) Three 'We Petitions' ('Our daily bread give us today' / 'And forgive us our debts as we forgive our debtors' / 'And do not lead us to the test').[261]

Although the New Testament abounds in prayers, hymns and confessional statements, only the 'Our Father' claims to be taught by Jesus to his disciples. If the Our Father is the pattern for all Christian prayer, what does it teach us? Firstly, it is addressed to the Father, almost certainly reflecting Jesus' use of the Aramaic *abbā* – 'my own dear Father' – for God. As John Ashton points out, 'there is no evidence in pre-Christian Palestinian Judaism that God was ever addressed as *abbā* by an individual Jew in prayer.'[262] Moreover, the stark simplicity of this address contrasts with what Rudolf Bultmann called 'the ornate, emotional, often liturgically beautiful, but often overloaded forms of address in Jewish prayers ...'[263]

A number of years ago the author J. B. Phillips wrote a book entitled *Your God*

---

[260] John P Meier, *A Marginal Jew, Volume II: Mentor, Message, and Miracles*, p.291.
[261] Ibid, p.292.
[262] John Ashton, "Abba" in David Noel Freedman (Editor-In-Chief), *The Anchor Bible Dictionary, Volume 1*, Doubleday, New York , 1992, p.7.
[263] R Bultmann, quoted in Joseph A Fitzmyer, The Gospel According to Luke X-XXIV, p.903.

is Too Small. Phillips argued that many people are held back from an intimate relationship with God because of the destructive image of God that has dominated their spiritual horizon, often since childhood.[264] The great C14 theologian and preacher, Meister Eckhart, once wrote: 'The ultimate and highest leave-taking is leaving god for God.'[265] Voltaire once observed 'If God created us in his own image, we have certainly returned the compliment.'[266] We have indeed fashioned a god who is too small, too restrictive, too petty and vindictive, too blurred, and we need to take leave of that god and journey towards God. Jesus invites us to address God as Father, which 'suggests an intimate relationship between the disciples and God that is akin to that of Jesus himself; God is not merely the transcendent lord of the heavens, but is near as a father to his children.'[267] Jesus has introduced the disciples into the family or household of God.[268]

The two 'You Petitions' – 'hallowed be your name' or 'may your name be sanctified' and 'your kingdom come' – must be considered together and help explain each other. The petition to hallow, sanctify or make holy the name of God is not to be found elsewhere in the New Testament, with the exception of a similar expression in John 12:28 where Jesus prays, 'Father, glorify your name.' This petition is asking God 'to manifest himself in all his world-creating and royal power in the near future,' and 'to reveal himself as Father once and for all at the end time.'[269] We then pray, 'your kingdom come.' The kingdom of God 'is simply an abstract way of speaking of God ruling powerfully as king.'[270] And so, the sense of the two 'You Petitions' is: 'Father, reveal yourself in all your power and glory by coming to rule as king.'[271] This prayer yolks two rather diverse images of God – God as *abbā* / Father, and God as king. John Meier argues that such diverse images would not have been as great in a first century Mediterranean society as it is in modern Western societies:

While a first century father might be a symbol of love for his children, he was most certainly a symbol of sovereign power over their lives and fates,

---

[264] JB Phillips, *Your God is Too Small*, Epworth, UK, 1952.
[265] Quoted in Joseph Campbell (with Bill Moyers), *The Power of Myth*, Doubleday, New York, 1988, p.49.
[266] Quoted in M Scott Peck, *Further Along the Road Less Travelled*, Simon & Schuster, New York, 1993, p.230.
[267] Joseph A Fitzmyer, *The Gospel According to Luke X-XXIV*, p.898.
[268] Brendan Byrne, *The Hospitality of God*, p.104.
[269] John P Meier, *A Marginal Jew: Rethinking the Historical Jesus, Volume II: Mentor, Message, and Miracles*, p.297.
[270] Ibid, p.298.
[271] Ibid, p.299.

since within the homes of most first century Mediterranean societies the father was the supreme arbiter of life and death, to say nothing of careers, marriages, and inheritance. The father was a symbol of supreme power in matters domestic; and so he was the object of obedience and reverence, even fear, as well as love. [272]

Three 'We Petitions' follow: 'give us each day our daily bread', 'forgive us our sins, for we ourselves forgive each one who is in debt to us,' and 'do not put us to the test' – petitions for 'sustenance, forgiveness, (and) rescue from overwhelming tribulation.'[273] Bread is a rich and evocative symbol in the Scriptures. The petition for bread conjures up allusions to the eschatological banquet – the use of 'food and a festive meal to signify immortality and the joys of the end time or afterlife.' [274] While this is certainly a prayer for that which is essential for life, one cannot overlook Exodus or Eucharistic overtones, nor Jesus' table fellowship with outsiders such as tax collectors and sinners.

The forgiveness of sins is a major theme in Luke-Acts, and here it is linked with our forgiveness of others. If we do not forgive others, we are in effect asking God not to forgive us. Perhaps the public recitation of the Our Father should be preceded by a warning, just as we have health warnings on cigarette packets: 'Warning! Do not pray this prayer unless you have forgiven your brother or sister from the heart.' The author Robert Louis Stevenson had the custom of daily family worship that included the recitation of the Our Father. On one occasion in the middle of the prayer he rose from his knees and left the room. His wife hurried after him, thinking he may be unwell. 'What is the matter?' she asked. 'Are you ill?' 'No,' he replied, 'but I am not fit to pray the Lord's Prayer today.' [275] James Oglethorpe, English parliamentarian and founder of the colony of Georgia in America, once remarked to John Wesley, 'I never forgive.' To which Wesley replied, 'Then I hope, sir, you never sin.' [276]

Finally, the petition for strength in the face of trial, persecution and temptation reflects a simple and direct faith in God who controls all things. This is a prayer that such trials will 'not prove overwhelming, causing (the community) to fall away from its high vocation.' [277]

---

[272] Ibid, p.300.
[273] Brendan Byrne, *The Hospitality of God*, p.104.
[274] Dennis E. Smith, 'Messianic Banquet', in David Noel Freedman (Editor-in-Chief), *The Anchor Bible Dictionary, Volume 4*, Doubleday, New York ,1992, p.788.
[275] William Barclay, *The Plain Man Looks at the Lord's Prayer*, Collins, London, 1964, p.109.
[276] Ibid, p.110.
[277] Brendan Byrne, *The Hospitality of God*, p.105.

EIGHTEENTH SUNDAY IN ORDINARY TIME

(YEAR C)

'So it is when a man stores up treasure for himself in place of making himself rich in the sight of God.' (Lk 12:21)

When the author Nikos Kazantsakis was a young man he interviewed an elderly monk who lived on Mount Athos. Kazantsakis asked the monk, 'Do you still struggle with the devil?' 'No,' the monk replied. 'I used to, but I've grown old and tired and the devil has grown old and tired with me. Now I leave him alone and he leaves me alone!' Somewhat bemused by the reply, Kazantsakis asked, 'So your life is easy now, no more struggles?' With a wry smile the monk replied, 'Ah no, it's worse. Now I struggle with God!' [278]

Our struggle with the 'devil' is essentially a struggle with the untamed energies of youth – coming to terms with our sexuality and the quest for intimacy; getting married and raising a family; paying off the mortgage; educating the children; and establishing a career. But this struggle can leave us feeling empty and dissatisfied as we journey into the second half of life. The Swiss psychiatrist Carl Jung wrote:

Wholly unprepared, we embark upon the second half of life. Or are there perhaps colleges for 40-year-olds which prepare them for their coming life and its demands as the ordinary colleges introduce our young people to a knowledge of the world? No, thoroughly unprepared we take the step into the afternoon of life; worse still, we take this step with the false assumption that our truths and ideals will serve us as hitherto. But we cannot live the afternoon of life according to the program of life's morning: for what in the morning was true will at evening have become a lie. [279]

Some years ago the Australian psychologist Peter O'Connor wrote an article on the mid-life crisis that explored the feelings of massive uncertainty and confusion that often accompany this stage of life. At the end of the article he placed a small note inviting readers to share some of their experiences. O'Connor received over

---

[278] Slightly adapted from Ronald Rolheiser, *'Spirituality and the second-half of life'*, www.ronrolheiser.com/ (Reflection for August 29, 2003).

[279] CG Jung, *Psychological Reflections: A New Anthology of His Writings*, 1905-1961, ed. J Jacobi Bollingen, Princeton, NJ,1971, pp.137-38.

one hundred replies, all of them expressing the writers' sense of identification with what he had written. A 39-year-old real estate manager described the stress, irritability, fatigue, depression and general dissatisfaction that characterised his life. He wrote that he sought success primarily to improve his family's lot, 'yet in seeking that success I am quite likely to lose them altogether.' Another letter from a man in his early forties expressed the sense of depression that he felt after settling back into work after an extended holiday sailing around the world: 'I find myself back in the same old routine, same old rat-race, competing with the Joneses and being tied hand and foot running the company I formed 18 years ago – there just must be a better way.' Another 52-year-old professional said he was locked into a system that required him 'hail, rain or shine, sick or well.' O'Connor concluded that almost without exception the people who wrote to him were 'successful by ordinary standards, sometimes highly successful, but plagued ... with a sense of purposelessness and futility.' [280] Faustian deals with the devil may result in a bigger paycheck and rapid promotion, but we pay dearly with laborious days, cares of office and restless nights. Vanity of vanities, the Preacher says.

Italy's greatest poet, Dante Alighieri, commenced his epic, *La Commedia*, with the words 'In the middle of our life's way / I found myself in a dark wood / Where the right way was lost.'[281] Also lost is Ivan, the main character in Chekhov's play Ivanov:

I've worn myself out. At 35 I feel like a man after a drunken bout, I'm old already. I've put on an old man's dressing gown. I go about with a heavy head, with a lazy soul, tired and broken, without faith, without love, without aim; I wander about among my friends like a shadow and I don't know who I am, or why I live, or what I want.[282]

Having wrestled with the 'devil' and stored up treasure, we are often puzzled to discover that we are not happy. Erich Fromm observes that we live in a society in which the supreme goal is to have – and to have more and more, a society in which 'the very essence of being is having; that if one *has* nothing, one *is* nothing.' [283] But even though that leaves us tired and broken, depressed and dissatisfied, we are afraid to let go of what we have. Sigmund Freud discovered that his patients 'did not want to be free men but successful bourgeois and did not want

---

[280] Peter O'Connor, *Understanding the Mid-life Crisis Sun Books*, Melbourne, Reprinted 1982, pp.7-8.
[281] Quoted in Alan Jones, *The Soul's Journey Cowley Publications*, Boston, 2001, p.34.
[282] Quoted in O'Connor, *Understanding the Mid-life Crisis*, p.14.
[283] Erich Fromm, *To Have or To Be*, p.25.

to pay the radical price that the change from the predominance of having over that of being would have required.'[284] There can, however, be a rude awakening. The American journalist Gail Sheehy, author of *Passages*, had a life-altering experience in Northern Ireland when she was on assignment for a magazine. 'I was talking to a young boy ... when a bullet blew his face off.'[285] She suddenly experienced what she calls 'the arithmetic of life.' In a moment of awakening she realised that 'No-one is with me. No-keeps me safe. There is no one who won't ever leave me alone.'[286] At the age of 35 this tragic shooting was a wake up call. 'Take stock! Half your life has been spent. ... What about the part of you that wants to contribute to the world? ... You have been a performer, not a full participant.' To be confronted for the first time with what she calls 'the arithmetic of life' was 'quite simply, terrifying.'[287]

Confronted by the same 'arithmetic of life' and considerably older than Sheehy, Malcolm Muggeridge was less fearful:

I am old, and in at most a decade or so will be dead. ... The prospect of death overshadows all others. I am like a man on a sea voyage nearing his destination. When I embarked I worried about having a cabin with a porthole, whether I should be asked to sit at the Captain's table, who were the more attractive and important passengers. All such considerations become pointless when I shall so soon be disembarking. As I do not believe that earthly life can bring any lasting satisfaction, the prospect of death holds no terrors. Those saints who pronounced themselves in live with death displayed, I consider, the best of sense. [288]

When we are lost in a dark wood the gospel assures us that the way ahead lies in the daunting prospect of wrestling with God, not in building bigger barns. In 1967 Muggeridge spent three weeks at the Cistercian abbey of Nunraw in Scotland to make a television documentary about life in an enclosed religious order. He reflected:

By all the laws of Freud and the psycho-prophets, the monks are depriving themselves of the sensual satisfactions which alone make a whole life possible; they ought to be up the wall and screaming. Actually, I found in Nunraw a quite exceptional peace; it is the children of affluence, not deprived monks, who howl and fret in psychiatric wards. [289]

---

[284] Erich Fromm, *Greatness and Limitation of Freud's Thought*, Farrar, Straus and Giroux, New York, 1969, p.49.
[285] Gail Sheehy, *Passages*, Bantam Books, New York, 1977, p.2.
[286] Ibid, p.5.
[287] Ibid.
[288] Malcolm Muggeridge, *Jesus Rediscovered*, Fontana Books, Bungay, Suffolk, 1969, pp.57-8.
[289] Ibid, p.65.

NINETEETH SUNDAY IN ORDINARY TIME

(YEAR C)

'Get yourselves purses that do not wear out, treasure that will not fail you, in heaven where no thief can reach it and no moth destroy it.' (Lk 12:33)

Last week's gospel told the story of the man with the bumper wheat crop, and warned us against storing up riches rather than making ourselves rich in the sight of God. This Sunday's gospel continues the same theme. 'Get yourselves purses that do not wear out, treasure that will not fail you. ... where your treasure is, there will your heart be also.' And the chilling reminder, 'You too must stand ready, because the Son of Man is coming at an hour you do not expect.'

But the Son of Man doesn't always come unexpected and unannounced, and we must therefore be prepared. Fr Paul Nevill, a renowned headmaster of the English Benedictine College Ampleforth, was attending the annual September meeting of the Headmasters' Conference some time in the 1930s. One of Fr Nevill's independent school colleagues was burbling away about all that he sought to achieve for the pupils at his school. 'What we try to do,' he explained, 'is to equip our boys for life.' Sotto voce, Fr Nevill was heard to murmur, 'How fascinating! You see, at Ampleforth we always seek to prepare our boys for death.'[290] That isn't as morbid as it might first sound. In preparing students for death, you are in reality giving them the best possible preparation for life, for you are inviting them to reflect upon what is truly important and life-giving.

In saying that I have in mind one of the most inspiring books that I've read recently, *Tuesdays With Morrie*, written by Mitch Albom. *Tuesdays With Morrie* is the moving story of Mitch Albom's weekly meetings with his old professor Morrie Schwartz who is dying of motor neurone disease. Morrie describes the disease as being 'like a lit candle: it melts your nerves and leaves your body a pile of wax.' Morrie knows how he will die:

I'm going to suffocate. Yes. My lungs, because of my asthma, can't handle the disease. It's moving up my body ... It's already got my legs. Pretty soon it'll

---

[290] Anthony Howard, *Basil Hume: The Monk Cardinal*, Headline Book Publishing, London, 2005, p.293.

get my arms and hands. And when it hits my lungs .... [291]

In the final stages of motor neurone disease a person has a totally alert mind that is imprisoned in a totally unresponsive body. They are frozen inside their own flesh. When Morrie was diagnosed with the disease in 1994 his doctors guessed that he had about two years to live. Morrie knew it was less. The Son of Man was not going to knock at Morrie's door and find him unprepared.

Mitch Albom had been profoundly influenced by Morrie during his years at college. In thinking of Morrie, Mitch was reminded of the words of Henry Adams, 'A teacher affects eternity; he can never tell where his influence stops.'[292] When Mitch finally graduated from college he hugged his dear and wise professor and promised to keep in touch. But, of course, he didn't. It was purely by chance, some 16 years later, while watching television that Mitch found out that his much-loved professor was dying. He decided to make the 700 km journey to visit him. It was a Tuesday, and those visits continued over 14 Tuesdays until Morrie's death.

And who was Mitch Albom? Mitch was a sports writer for the *Detroit Free Press*. The city of Detroit had a voracious appetite for sport. In Mitch's own words:

They had professional teams in football, basketball, baseball, and hockey – and it matched my ambition. In a few years, I was not only penning columns, I was writing sports books, doing radio shows, and appearing regularly on television, sprouting my opinions ... I was part of the media thunderstorm that now soaks our country. I was in demand.

Mitch had married after a seven-year courtship, and he was back to work a week after the wedding. He told his wife, Janine, that they would one day start a family, something that she wanted very much. But that day never came. Instead, Mitch buried himself in work. In his own words, 'I traded lots of dreams for a bigger pay check, and I never even realised I was doing it.'[293]

Morrie gradually lost control of his leg and thigh muscles and was confined to a wheelchair. He knew that he would die within the year, but death was not a subject that he shied away from. When one of his academic colleagues at College died of a heart attack, Morrie went to the funeral. He came home depressed – not because he was reminded of his own imminent death, but because of all the wasted words. 'What a waste,' he said. 'All those people saying all those wonderful things, and

[291] Mitch Albom, Tuesdays *With Morrie,* Hodder, Sydney, 1997,pp.9-10.
[292] Ibid, p.79.
[293] Interview with Margaret Throsby, ABC Classic FM, 4/9/2001.

(he) never got to hear any of it.'[294] Morrie had a better idea. He made some calls; he chose a date and arranged a 'living funeral' with a small group of friends and family. As each of them spoke and paid tribute to him, Morrie cried and laughed with them. And that was important, because all the heartfelt things we never get to say to those we love, Morrie said that day.

What did Morrie and Mitch talk about during their Tuesday meetings? The subject of what they jokingly referred to as 'classes' was the Meaning of Life, and it was taught from experience. On one Tuesday Morrie asked the question, 'What if today were my last day on earth?' But of course, our culture doesn't encourage us to ask such questions. Morrie explains:

We're so wrapped up with egotistical things, career, family, having enough money, meeting the mortgage, getting a new car, fixing the radiator when it breaks – we're involved in trillions of little acts just to keep going. So we don't get into the habit of standing back and looking at our lives and saying 'Is this all? Is this all I want? Is something missing?' [295]

Morrie's strong conviction is, 'Once you learn how to die, you learn how to live.' He explains, 'Everyone knows they're going to die, but nobody believes it. If we did, we would do things differently.' And what advice does he offer? 'Do what the Buddhists do. Every day, have a little bird on your shoulder that asks, 'Is today the day? Am I ready? Am I doing all I need to do? Am I being the person I want to be?"'[296]

On their second-last Tuesday together, Mitch asks Morrie the question, 'What if you had one day perfectly healthy ... What would you do?'

'*Twenty-four hours?*'

'*Twenty-four hours.*'

'*Let's see ... I'd get up in the morning, do my exercises, have a lovely breakfast of sweet rolls and tea, go for a swim, then have my friends come over for a nice lunch. I'd have them come one or two at a time so we could talk about their families, their issues, talk about how much we mean to each other. Then I'd go for a walk, in a garden with some trees, watch their colours, watch the birds, take in the nature that I haven't seen in so long now. In the evening, we'd all go together to a restaurant with some great pasta, maybe some duck – I love duck – and then we'd dance the rest of the night. I'd dance with all the wonderful dance partners out there, until I was exhausted. And then I'd go home and have a deep,*

---

[294] Mitch Albom, op. cit., p.12.
[295] Ibid, pp. 64-65.
[296] Ibid, p.81.

wonderful sleep.'
  'That's it?'
  'That's it.'
  It was so simple. So average. I was actually a little disappointed. I figured he'd fly to Italy or have lunch with the President or romp on the seashore or try every exotic thing he could think of. After all these months, lying there, unable to move a leg or a foot – how could he find perfection in such an average day? Then I realised this was the whole point. [297]

Morrie had indeed learned the lesson of today's gospel. He stood ready, at least metaphorically, for the coming of the Son of Man. It did not find him unprepared, for he had indeed stored up treasure where no thief could reach it and no moth destroy it. Once you learn how to die, you learn how to live.

---

[297] Ibid, pp.175-176.

TWENTIETH SUNDAY IN ORDINARY TIME

(YEAR C)

*'I have come to bring fire to the earth, and how
I wish it were blazing already!'*
(Lk 12:49)

In a nutshell, what is the basic teaching of Jesus? I guess most of us would answer: 'Love God with all your heart, and love your neighbour as yourself.' That, after all, was the answer that Jesus himself gave when asked the question, 'Which is the first of all the commandments?' (cf. Mk 12:29-31). We might also recall that Jesus promised to bring us peace: 'Peace I bequeath to you, my own peace I give you (Jn 14:27).' Admittedly, he added that his was a peace that the world could not give, but it was peace nevertheless. And at the birth of Jesus, did not the angels praise God with the words, 'Glory to God in the highest heaven, and on earth peace for those he favours' (Lk 2:14)? Today's gospel, with its promise of division, is such a sharp contrast to the stereotypical image we have of Jesus. How do we make sense of his threat to bring division, even within the family itself?

The effect of these words of Jesus remind me of a trick that the great composer Ludwig van Beethoven sometimes played on polite salon audiences, particularly when he suspected that they weren't really interested in serious music. He would perform one of his own slow movements on the piano, a piece of music so gentle and beautiful that everyone would be lulled into thinking the world was a soft, cosy place. Then, as the final notes were dying away, Beethoven brought his whole forearm down with a crash upon the keyboard, laughing at the shock he gave to the assembled company. Perhaps that wasn't the most subtle way of telling his hearers that the world was full of pain was as well as of beauty, but the shock of that crash of notes arousing his audience from beautiful thoughts and semi-slumber is a good image for what Jesus has said in today's gospel. [298]

Jesus is talking about the cost of commitment, a theme foreshadowed at the

---

[298] Cf. Tom Wright, *Luke for Everyone*, pp.158-9.

very beginning of Luke's gospel. When Mary and Joseph bring the baby Jesus to the temple in Jerusalem, the prophet Simeon tells them that this child 'is destined for the fall and for the rise of many in Israel, destined to be a sign that is opposed' (Lk 2:34). In other words, the mission of Jesus will not bring 'the sort of peace by which domestic tranquillity is undisturbed.' He will divide households and create a division among the people.[299]

During the course of our lives all of us have made commitments of one kind or another, and we're aware of the demands they make upon us. To marry and raise a family, for example, is a profound commitment that radically alters the course of our lives. Our primary allegiance is to our husband or wife, and that commitment must take precedence over every other relationship in our lives. In today's gospel Jesus tells his disciples that the demands of God's kingdom are so important that they must take precedence over every other commitment and allegiance in their lives; they are even more important than the sacred bonds of family unity. Today's first reading from the prophet Jeremiah is also about the cost of commitment. The background to this reading is the growing military threat posed by Babylon. Zedekiah, king of Judah, hopes to stave off a possible invasion by entering into an alliance with Egypt. Jeremiah counsels otherwise, but his words are unwelcome and he is thrown down a well in an attempt to silence him. Jeremiah could have taken the soft option and told people what they wanted to hear, but he chose to be a person of integrity. The alternative is summed up in the accusation levelled against Charlie Brown on more than one occasion: 'The whole trouble with you is that you're wishy-washy.'[300]

Christopher Booker's *The Seven Basic Plots* is based on the premise that 'various basic themes and situations seem to recur through human storytelling', that there are a 'small number of plots which are so fundamental to the way we tell stories that it is virtually impossible for any storyteller ever entirely to break away from them.'[301] In other words, there are seven basic coat hangers on which storytellers hang their narrative. Booker's seven basic plots are these: Overcoming the Monster; Rags to Riches; The Quest; Voyage and Return; Comedy, Tragedy, and Rebirth.

If I could focus briefly on two of these plots, the Quest and Overcoming the Monster. We're familiar with all manner of monsters – creatures that seek to

---

[299] Luke Timothy Johnson, op. cit., p.209.
[300] Charles Schulz, *The Complete Peanuts, 1965 to 1966*, Fantagraphics Books, New York, 2007, p.309
[301] Christopher Booker, op. cit., p.6.

oppress or destroy the hero – the giant in Jack and the Beanstalk, Cinderella's step-sisters, the witch in Snow White, the shark in Jaws, the list is endless The monster is invariably a threatening force 'out there', a creature that seeks to block the hero or heroine. According to Booker, though, the essence of the monster is that 'dressed up in symbolic form, it is a hugely magnified personification of the human capacity for egotism, which is invariably shown as immensely powerful, unfeeling for others but also in some crucial respect blind, lacking in understanding.'[302]

No type of story is more instantly recognizable to us than a Quest. There might be a variety of goals – buried treasure, the golden fleece, the holy grail, the ark of the covenant, a new homeland or the secret of immortality. There are invariably temptations and monsters that seek to block the hero in his quest, but ultimately he achieves his goal. And what is that goal? The Quest is not about seeking treasure 'out there.' The Quest is about 'human life as a journey towards the ultimate goal of wholeness and self-realisation.' [303] It presents 'an idealised pattern of how any human being can travel on the long, tortuous journey of inner growth, finally emerging to a state of complete self-realisation.'[304]

Today's gospel is about a quest. Jesus has come to bring fire to the earth, and he wishes it were blazing already. That fire is the fire of the Holy Spirit, and in time the disciples will receive that same Holy Spirit, manifested as 'tongues as if of fire' (Acts 2:3). And here is a fundamental truth: we will achieve our ultimate goal of wholeness and self-realisation when this fire burns within our hearts. Such was the experience of the two disciples on the road to Emmaus when joined by a mysterious stranger. 'Did not our hearts burn within us,' they said, 'as he talked to us on the road and explained the scriptures to us?' (Lk 24:32). But, like all quests, there are obstacles – monsters that seek to block the hero's path. The 'monster' that seeks to deflect us from the quest may be the people who are closest to us, members of our own family. The 'monster' may also be the human capacity for egotism, the self that rebels against the invitation to discipleship, or just sheer inertia or wishy-washiness.

Dietrich Bonhoeffer, the German Lutheran theologian who was executed by the Gestapo days before the close of World War II, wrote a book that he called *The Cost of Discipleship*, a title that in fact embodies the theme of today's gospel. In *The Cost of Discipleship* he asked this question: 'And if we answer the call to

[302] Ibid, p.219.
[303] Ibid, p.221.
[304] Ibid, p.222.

discipleship, where will it lead us? What decisions and partings will it demand?'[305] The cost of discipleship is about making choices that are authentic, liberating and life-giving; choices based upon love and integrity. We make a radical and deeply challenging choice to follow Jesus and turn away from selfishness and self-centredness; we resolve to leave behind our compulsions, addictions, fears and insecurity, to move out of the prison of the ego.

Bonhoeffer talks about cheap and costly grace. Cheap grace seeks the consolations of religion without conversion. Costly grace:

is the treasure hidden in the field; for the sake of it a man will gladly go and sell all that he has. It is the pearl of great price to buy which the merchant will sell all his goods. It is the kingly rule of Christ, for whose sake a man will pluck out the eye which causes him to stumble, it is the call of Jesus Christ at which the disciple leaves his nets and follows him. [306]

Costly grace is prepared to pay the price of discipleship; it is dearer than any other commitment or relationship in life.

---

[305] Dietrich Bonhoeffer, *The Cost of Discipleship*, SCM Press, London, Third Impression, 2004, p.xxxiv.
[306] Ibid, p.4.

TWENTY-FIRST SUNDAY IN ORDINARY TIME

(YEAR C)

'We once ate and drank in your company; you taught in our streets.'
(Lk 13: 26)

There were two monks walking beside a river. The younger monk kept on pestering the older monk with endless questions about the river. 'Where does it come from? Where is it going? How fast is it flowing? How deep is it? What's it like? What's the temperature of the water?' The further they walked the more elaborate, the more searching, became the young monk's questions about the river. The elder monk became increasingly exasperated and finally turned to the young monk and pushed him into the river: 'There! There you are! Now you know!' [307]

We can spend a lot of time looking at the river, asking questions about the river, but there comes a moment when we have to jump in. It is a moment of commitment, of awakening, a moment of enlightenment, a moment of conversion. Our journey of faith is like that. It's not enough to say 'Lord, we once ate and drank in your company; you taught in our streets.' In other words, 'Lord, I went to a Catholic school; I attended Mass fairly regularly; I put money on the collection plate; I've read the gospels.'

Jesus seems to be opposed to the kind of religion that has similarities with vaccination. Up until fairly recently, smallpox was one of the world's most dreaded diseases. Some outbreaks of the disease killed millions of people. In 1967, for example, over two million people died from smallpox. If it didn't kill a person it left awful scabs and scars. It was only as recently as 1977 that the World Health Organisation declared that smallpox had been eradicated.

The English surgeon Edward Jenner (1749 – 1823) discovered how to combat smallpox. He noticed that people who had suffered an attack of cowpox were immune to smallpox. Cowpox was a relatively harmless disease that people

---

[307] This story is told by Laurence Freeman on his audio tape, *Christian Meditation*, released by Pauline Books and Media, Sydney.

caught from cattle. So Jenner decided to inject people with a dose of cowpox, and that made them immune to smallpox. That's why we call the process 'vaccination' - the Latin word for 'cow' is *vacca*.[308]

Spiritual vaccination works like this: we are inoculated with the equivalent of cowpox – a tiny, harmless dose of religion, and from then on we are rendered immune to any serious outbreaks of religion in our lives. Jesus constantly spoke out against people who outwardly appeared to be pious and devout people, but inwardly their hearts were far from God.

We can faithfully observe the externals of religion, but ignore the weightier demands of our faith. An American priest was once accosted late at night by a robber demanding money, not far from a large church on 51st Street. It was cold, so the priest was rugged up in an overcoat and scarf. As he reached for his wallet the scarf fell loose, and the would-be robber suddenly noticed that his victim was wearing a clerical collar. 'Oh, sorry Father', the robber said. 'I would never rob a priest.' And so the two men began talking. The priest, who was a heavy smoker, offered the man a cigarette. The would-be robber shook his head. 'No thanks Father, I've given up cigarettes for Lent!'

And, of course, we can be very devout Catholics, as long as it doesn't cause any inconvenience to our way of life. We want the warmth of the womb, but not the pain and travail of a new birth. Consider the example of the woman who listened avidly to all of her parish priest's sermons. She regarded him as the fountain of all wisdom, until one day he preached on the evils of alcohol. She immediately arose from her pew and stormed out of the church. A friend asked what had upset her. 'Well, Father's marvellous when he's preaching', she said, 'but now he's started meddling!'

In other words, religion can be relegated to life's periphery – little more than an optional extra, certainly nothing to disturb a good night's sleep. The great Church of Scotland minister George MacLeod had fought courageously in the First World War and was awarded the Military Cross for valour. In later years, he became a pacifist, at a time when pacifism was not a popular cause. Nevertheless, he espoused this cause with great passion at every convention of the General Assembly of the Church of Scotland. But he soon realised he was not being taken seriously; in fact his interventions were regarded with a degree of amusement.

MacLeod was a perceptive man and likened his situation to a missionary who was sent to preach the gospel among a primitive tribe in Africa. In due course,

---

[308] *Encyclopaedia Britannica*, CD 97, under the headings 'Edward Jenner' and 'Smallpox'.

the missionary learnt their language and was accepted among them. Before long he was invited by the tribal elders to participate in their annual festival – a festival which the missionary found abhorrent and obscene. And so, in powerful words, he fiercely denounced this evil ritual as a filthy abomination. The natives didn't appreciate his intervention, and violently set upon him, beating him almost to death. The missionary limped back to the village, and continued with his missionary work as if nothing had happened. On the same occasion the following year, he again denounced the obscene rituals of their festival, and again he was severely beaten. For nine consecutive years, he repeated his denunciation at festival time, with the inevitable outcome on each occasion. Eventually, he died a natural death. On the year following the missionary's death, as the time for the annual festival drew near, the chief of the tribe sent a request for another missionary – because by now the missionary's denunciation of their festival had become part of the show![309]

When the gospel message becomes no more than an amusing and harmless 'part of the show', the blazing fire of the gospel is all but extinguished. Alas for us if the call to conversion is deemed to be no more than 'meddling'. Alas for us if the rituals of our faith vaccinate us against a change of heart. Alas for us if we spend our life talking about the river, fearful of ever taking the plunge.

---

[309] An adapted version of MacLeod's story. See Ronald Ferguson, op. cit., p.365

TWENTY-SECOND SUNDAY IN ORDINARY TIME

(YEAR C)

'When you have a party, invite the poor, the crippled, the lame, the blind.'
(Lk 14: 13)

On a Sabbath day Jesus had been invited to dine at the house of one of the leading Pharisees. We are told that he was under close scrutiny, which suggests that there were hostile motives behind the invitation. The lectionary omits the story that follows, the healing of a man with dropsy, and passes on to the parable about places of honour. On the face of it, this story about taking the lowest place at a banquet may seem like a lesson in etiquette that echoes advice given in the book of Proverbs (25:6-7): 'In the presence of the king do not give yourself airs, do not take a place among the great; better to be invited, 'Come up here', than be humiliated in the presence of the prince.' The selection of today's first reading from the book of Ecclesiasticus also suggests a lesson in humility. The first century Mediterranean world was a society in which people were highly conscious of honour and shame; life was about gaining honour and avoiding shame. However, this parable is not a lesson on 'deft manoeuvres on how to be first.' Playing the role of the prophetic comic, Jesus challenges the underlying cultural assumptions that lead people to even entertain the idea of jockeying for positions of honour.[310]

Consuming Passions is the title of a book written on the anthropology of eating by Peter Farb and George Armelagos. They conclude that in both simple and complex societies, 'eating is the primary way of initiating and maintaining human relationships ...'.[311] Anthropologists argue that you can learn a lot about a society by looking closely at who eats together. They argue that the table is a miniature of society at large. The term they've coined is 'commensality'. It comes from the Latin word mensa, meaning 'table'. It therefore means literally, whom do you sit with at the dining table? Commensality examines what we would call table

---

[310] John Shea, *The Relentless Widow: The Spiritual Wisdom of the Gospels for Christian Preachers and Teachers*, p.247, p.250.

[311] Peter Farb and George Armelagos, *Consuming Passions: The Anthropology of Eating*, (Houghton Mifflin, 1980), p.4 , p.211. Cited in John Dominic Crossan, *Jesus: A Revolutionary Biography*, HarperSan Francisco, 1994, p.68.

fellowship. Who eats with whom? [312]

Consider this hypothetical situation. Imagine that a rather unkempt stranger came unannounced to your front door around lunch time asking for some food, a person we might euphemistically call a 'knight of the road.' How would you respond? You could order him to leave immediately, or you'll call the police. Or you could ask him to wait at the front door while you go into the kitchen and prepare him a sandwich, making sure that the security door is firmly locked. Or perhaps you could take a risk and invite this total stranger into your house to join you for a snack around the kitchen table. Or, going one step further, why not invite this stranger to join your family around the dining table for the evening meal? Or, perhaps even more implausibly, you might invite this stranger to return later that evening as your guest at an intimate dinner party with some of your closest and dearest friends.

Let me confess how I have responded when such 'knights of the road' turn up at the presbytery door. I invariably ask them to wait at the front door while I rush off to the kitchen to prepare them a sandwich. Occasionally when the same person returns day after day on a regular basis I confess that I've told them I'm busy at the moment and asked them to come back in half an hour – knowing that I'd be out then! That's why the sting in the tail of today's gospel passage makes me feel uncomfortable.

Well, some of those scenarios are highly improbable and totally inappropriate in our society. We just wouldn't invite an unkempt stranger into our house, let alone to an intimate dinner party with our closest friends. And yet, that is the contemporary equivalent of what Jesus is asking of his Pharisee host. Jesus exhorts his host to invite the poor, the crippled, the lame and the blind. This would have been cultural suicide in the Mediterranean world of Jesus' day where reciprocity and the practice of inviting people of equal status were the twin pillars of ancient dining customs. Guests who are crippled, lame or blind are quite obviously people of a lower social status than the host. 'To associate with such is to dishonour one's own status.' [313] What, where, how, when, and with whom we eat tells us a great deal about the social hierarchy within a given society. The table mirrors society, and in the gospels Jesus so often uses the table to mirror the Kingdom of God.

On March 12, 1931, Mahatma Gandhi, then aged 60, and 79 of his disciples

---

[312] The discussion on commensality comes from John Dominic Crossan, op. cit., pp.68-69.
[313] John J Pilch, op. cit., p.132.

set out to walk 380 kilometres to the sea. They were defying a government ban that prevented people taking salt from the sea. The march received wide press coverage, not only in India, but throughout the world. The walk soon became a triumphant march. Villagers welcomed Gandhi and his followers by casting flower petals before them and sprinkling water on the road to keep the dust down. In every village hundreds of people abandoned their work and joined them, at least for part of the way.

Gandhi was a staunch opponent of the iniquitous caste system, and he abhorred the way in which the untouchables were treated. He described it as a 'blot on the soul of India.' Towards evening, Gandhi and his followers arrived at a large and prosperous village. He was graciously welcomed, and the head of the village invited him to stay in his house to bathe, eat and rest the night. Gandhi thanked the leader but refused his offer of hospitality. 'Where are your untouchables?' he asked. 'I will stay with them.' And so he spent the night among the untouchables in their hovels on the outskirts of the village. There he ate with them.

One of the criticisms levelled against Jesus by the Pharisees was that he welcomed sinners and ate with them. When Jesus and Gandhi ate with the outcasts of their own quite different societies they were offering a radically challenging vision of the Kingdom of God. Jesus constantly moved beyond ingrained prejudices and welcomed the outcast. The community that bears his name is likewise called to move beyond the prejudice born of ethnic and racial background, sexual orientation, gender, occupation, religious affiliation; marital status – the list is long indeed. Jesus summons us not to division, but to a fresh discovery of all people as our brothers and sisters in the human family, a family in which there are no outsiders.

TWENTY-THIRD SUNDAY IN ORDINARY TIME

(YEAR C)

'Anyone who does not carry his cross and come after me
cannot be my disciple.'
(Lk 14:27)

Today's gospel contains some of Jesus' most challenging sayings. First of all, let's consider one of the most startling of these statements. What does Jesus mean when he says that we can't come to him without hating our father, mother, wife, children, brothers, sisters, and even our own life? We have idioms in English that are never interpreted literally. For example, 'It's raining cats and dogs', or 'I'm so hungry that I could eat a horse.' Jesus' own language (he spoke in Aramaic) also had its own idioms.

Semitic languages, by and large, do not have a word for 'prefer'. When a person prefers one thing over another, he or she is said to 'love' one (the thing 'preferred') and 'hate' the other. 'Hate', then, is simply an expression of rejecting something (possibly something quite good in itself) in favour of something considered more desirable. While it would be wrong to water down the strength of Jesus' prophetic utterance, what he is saying, then, is that family allegiances – so strong in the Palestinian culture of Jesus – have to take second place as far as following him is concerned. Those who adopt his mission, his commitments and way of life will inevitably cause some pain and sacrifice to those who hold them dear and who perhaps have other plans for them. [314]

Jesus then tells us that 'Anyone who does not carry his cross and come after me cannot be my disciple.' A cross is made up of two intersecting beams. It is therefore a symbol of decision; standing at the crossroads you can go one way or the other. We are at a point of crisis, a word that comes from the Greek *krinein*, meaning to judge or decide. So, 'take up your cross and follow me' is talking about making choices that are authentic, liberating and life-giving; choices based upon love and integrity. At the crossroads we make a radical and deeply challenging

---

[314] Brendan Byrne, 'Commentary on the Twenty-Third Sunday in Ordinary Time, Year C', in LiturgyHelp.com.au

choice to follow Jesus and turn away from selfishness and self-centredness; we resolve to leave behind our compulsions, addictions, fears and insecurity, to move out of the prison of the ego.

Let us look at the lives of two people, one a fictional character, and the other a saintly woman who died on September 5, 1997. Let us see what happens to them at the crossroads. The fictional character is Billy, from the movie *Billy Elliott*. He's an eleven-year-old lad growing up in the village of Easington in England's industrial northeast during the 1984 miners' strike. Billy's mother had died the previous year, so he lives at home with his father, elder brother and senile grandmother. Both his father and brother are on strike, and the family budget is very tight.

Sent to learn boxing, Billy is introduced to ballet when a local class, all girls, is forced to share the village hall with his boxing club. Billy is entranced and he readily exchanges his boxing gloves for a pair of ballet shoes, although he, too, has to confront within himself the local perception that male dancers are 'poofs' or 'sissies'. Billy's father explodes when he discovers that his son is participating in ballet classes: 'Lads do football, or boxing, or wrestling.' In terms of the imagery of today's gospel, Billy has to 'hate' his father and brother to follow his dream and realise the unique gift that is his.

The story does have a happy ending. Billy's father finally acknowledges his son's talent, and at some considerable sacrifice accompanies him to London for an audition with the Royal Ballet School. The audition doesn't go well. Billy mumbles inarticulately when asked a few basic questions, and the board members are less than impressed with his violent conduct towards another auditioning student in the locker room. As Billy and his father leave the room, one of the board members, almost as an afterthought, asks Billy a final question: 'What does it feel like when you're dancing?' Slowly, Billy comes to life:

Don't know. Sort of feels good. It's sort of safe and that ... but once I get going ... then I, like, forget everything ... and ... sort of disappear. I sort of disappear. Like I feel a change in me whole body. Like there's a fire in my body. I'm just there ... flying ... like a bird. Like electricity. Yeah ... like electricity.

And yes, after an agonising wait, Billy receives a letter of acceptance to the Royal Ballet School – only because he was prepared to stand up to his father and elder brother, only because he was prepared to pay the price that his calling demanded.

Blessed Teresa of Calcutta (Mother Teresa), founder of the Missionaries of Charity, died on September 5, 1997. This remarkable woman also had an experience at the crossroads. Born in Macedonia on August 27, 1910, Agnes Gonxha Bojaxhiu's family was of Albanian descent. From the age of 12 she felt God calling her to become a missionary, and at the age of 17 she left home to follow this vocation. Agnes joined an Irish order, the Institute of the Blessed Virgin (known as the Loreto Sisters), and was given the name Teresa after St Therese of Lisieux. After initial training in Dublin Teresa was sent to India, and from 1931 until 1948 she taught at St Mary's High School in Calcutta, and from 1944 she was appointed the school's principal. In September 1946 while on a train journey from Calcutta to Darjeeling to make her annual retreat she received what she called a 'call within a call.' She had been deeply disturbed by the degrading poverty in Calcutta's slums and felt called to work amongst the poorest of the poor. She was at the crossroads. Do I continue to teach at St Mary's, or do I leave this good work behind and launch out into the unknown, without any resources? After a lengthy period of discernment she received permission to leave the school and devote herself to working among the poor in the slums of Calcutta. Here Teresa started an open-air school, and she also learned basic medicine so that she could visit the sick in their homes. In 1950 Teresa received permission from the Holy See to start her own order, the Missionaries of Charity. Did an inner voice try to dissuade her: How can one person alleviate the poverty of Calcutta? Her reply: 'We ourselves feel that what we are doing is just a drop in the ocean. But the ocean would be less because of that missing drop.' In all that she did Mother Teresa was guided by the gospel. In her own words:

At the end of our lives, we will not be judged by how many diplomas we have received, how much money we have made or how many great things we have done. We will be judged by 'I was hungry and you gave me to eat. I was naked and you clothed me. I was homeless and you took me in.'

Taking up a cross demands that we make decisions that are life giving. It involves counting the cost, and, sadly, that cost may at times involve disappointing those whom we love the most.

TWENTY-FOURTH SUNDAY IN ORDINARY TIME

(YEAR C)

'He was lost and is found.' (Lk 32)

The story in today's gospel is best known as the parable of the prodigal son. Sometimes it is called the parable of the merciful father; the *Jerusalem Bible* calls this parable 'the lost son (the 'prodigal') and the dutiful son'. One wit observed that the most appropriate title should be the parable of the absent mother, arguing that none of this drama would have taken in the first place if there had been a mother present in the home!

Which title captures the essence of this parable's message? As with all parables, the context offers a significant clue, and the immediate context of this parable is a complaint by the Pharisees and scribes. Every society is governed by purity laws. Purity laws are a way of saying that 'there is a place for everything, and everything should be in its proper place.' Purity laws are about establishing and maintaining boundaries. Jesus lived in a society that had rigid boundaries, and he was constantly accused of violating those boundaries. 'This man welcomes sinners and eats with them,' the Pharisees complain.

Pharisees were *perushim*, the separate ones, although they did not geographically separate themselves like the Essene community at Qumran by the shores of the Dead Sea. The Pharisees arose around the middle of the second century BC as one response to the radical Hellenisation unleashed by Antiochus IV and his Jewish supporters. According to John P. Meier:

[the Pharisees] emphasised the zealous and detailed study and practice of the Mosaic Law, the careful observance of legal obligations in concrete areas of life such as tithing, purity laws (especially concerning food, sexual activity, and the proper treatment of the dead), the keeping of the Sabbath, marriage and divorce, and temple ritual. As they developed their characteristic legal observances, they correspondingly developed a theory that justified these observances: they possessed a normative body of traditions – the traditions of the fathers (or the elders) – which went beyond the written Mosaic Law but which was (or at least should be) incumbent on the whole people of Israel. [315]

In response to the Pharisees' complaint, Jesus tells the story of the father and his two sons. I'd like to focus on the three main characters in the story. Firstly, there is the father. He divides his estate openly, so that before he dies his sons know exactly what's coming to them. Some time ago I met a priest who was about to lead a pilgrimage to the Holy Land. He told me that the pilgrimage would be the third overseas trip this year for one of the ladies accompanying him. The woman explained that now she'd retired she intended to enjoy herself. She didn't want to leave her son and daughter with the terrible responsibility of deciding how to spend their inheritance! The father in this parable is not so cynical, but he realises that his son wants to be free. 'That freedom includes the possibility of his leaving home, going to a 'distant country,' and losing everything. The Father's heart knows all the pain that will come from that choice, but his love makes him powerless to prevent it.'[316]

The younger son takes advantage of his father's generosity: 'Give me my inheritance now. I can't wait around for you to die.' And so he leaves his father's house. In the course of the story he squanders his inheritance and ends up feeding pigs. You have to remember that this is a Jewish boy. Pork is unclean, forbidden. To tend pigs is equivalent to becoming alienated from his tradition, his religion, his family values. So now he's alienated not only from his father's house, but also from his people. It is therefore all the more poignant that when he returns home his father accepts him. He places a ring on his finger and sandals on his feet – symbols of belonging, once again, to the family. The past has been forgotten. He is welcomed back, not as a servant, but as a son.

The elder son in this parable refuses to enter the house. He is resentful at the love and forgiveness his father has lavished upon his brother. One day the devil was crossing the African desert when he came across a group of small devils who were tempting a holy hermit. They tempted the hermit with images of beautiful women, but to no avail. Then they began to sow doubts about the faith in his mind, but the holy man stood firm. As a last resort they surrounded him with all the comforts imaginable, and told him that his austerities were a waste of time. But the hermit would not be moved. Then the devil stepped forward and drew his assistants aside. He told them their methods would never succeed. 'Let me show you how it is done', he said, as he went up to the hermit and whispered in his ear: 'Have you heard the news? Your brother has just been made Bishop of

---

[315] John P Meier, *A Marginal Jew, Volume III: Companions and Competitors*, p.330.
[316] Henri Nouwen, *The Return of the Prodigal Son*, Darton, Longman and Todd, London, 1992, p.90.

Constantinople.' And at those words a scowl of malignant jealousy clouded the serene face of the holy man.[317] It was this same malignant jealously that clouded the elder brother's judgment.

Let's turn the parable around another way. What in essence was each of the two sons really saying?[318] The younger son does not want a father. The older son does not want a brother. There are people who want no father, no one to answer to, no limits, no constraints, no responsibility, no-one to stand in judgment over them. They wish to be free to do whatever they want. The social commentator Hugh Mackay has labelled the generation of Australians who passed through adolescence and early adulthood during the 1960s as the 'Me Generation'. The Me Generation was a label that reflected their aggressive obsession with personal gratification, personal freedom and personal power. Mackay argues that the Me Generation saw itself as idealistic but, in the end, generally settled for only one ideal: self-fulfillment.[319]

How easily 'do your own thing' transmuted into 'greed is good'. And where does that leave a person? Looking after swine, and eating their leftovers, as the younger son found out. Then there are those like the elder brother who say: 'I have no brother'. In other words, I have no concern for the plight of others. I am not responsible for the misfortunes of others. A rabbi once asked his disciples, 'How can we determine when the night has ended and the new day begun?' One disciple replied, 'When you can see the form of an animal in the distance and recognise whether it is a sheep or a dog.' Another disciple responded, 'When there is enough light to tell the difference between a black thread and a white thread, then the new day has dawned.' But the rabbi answered: 'The new day has dawned when you can look into the face of every man and woman and recognise the face of your brother or sister. It you cannot do that, it is still night.'[320] That was a lesson the Pharisees and scribes had yet to learn.

---

[317] James A Feehan, *Story Power*, Resource Publications, San Jose, CA,1994, p.50.
[318] A perspective on the story inspired by William Bausch, *Telling Stories, Compelling Stories*, Twenty-Third Publications, Mystic, CT, Third Printing, 1992, p.17.
[319] Hugh Mackay, *Generations: Baby Boomers, their parents & their children*, Pan Macmillan, Sydney, 1997).
[320] Mark Link, *Vision 2000*, Tabor Publishing, Allen, TX , 1992, p.228.

TWENTY-FIFTH SUNDAY IN ORDINARY TIME

(YEAR C)

'The children of this world are more astute in dealing with their own kind than are the children of light.' (Lk 16:8)

Reading through an anthology of Jewish stories I was amused at how self-deprecating Jewish humour can be, often turning stereotypes on their head. Against the background of anti-Semitic jokes that portray Jews as greedy and materialistic, Solomon Reuben tells the story about two Jews who are walking down a street in Brooklyn when they pass a Catholic church. They are astonished to see a large sign on the gate that reads 'Convert to Catholicism, get $5000.' One friend says to the other, 'What do you think that means, 'Convert to Catholicism, get $5000?' It sounds interesting.' His friend says, 'You can't be serious.' The other says, 'Five thousand dollars is five thousand dollars, I'm going in.' The man goes in, his friend waits. And waits. And waits. When he comes out, his friend asks, 'Well, did you get the five thousand dollars'? The man just looks at him and says, 'Can't you people think about anything else but money?' [321]

Well, today's gospel invites us to think about money. The English word 'money' has an interesting history. In Roman mythology Juno was the chief goddess – the wife of Jupiter and the mother of Mars. Among her many titles was 'Moneta', which means the 'Warner', presumably because she warned of imminent danger. Just as Catholics are accustomed to naming churches after Our Lady using one of her many titles, the ancient Romans named temples after Juno using one or other of her titles. The temple dedicated to Juno Moneta was located on the Capitoline Hill from 344BC. It later housed the Roman mint. The product of the mint – money – derives from the title of the goddess, Moneta, the Warner. Some Roman coins carried the image of Juno, together with the word 'Moneta'. Maybe our currency – like cigarette packets – should carry a warning: 'Money may be a hazard to our spiritual health.'

---

[321] Steve Zeitlin (Ed), *Because God Loves Stories: An Anthology of Jewish Storytelling*, Simon & Schuster, New York, 1997, p.270.

Today's gospel tells the story of the dishonest steward. We're told that a steward is dismissed because he has squandered his employer's resources. But what precisely did the steward do that was dishonest? There are two explanations. The first and obvious explanation is that the steward shrewdly embarked upon an opportunistic and fraudulent course of action to save himself from personal and financial ruin. When he significantly discounted the amount that various creditors owed his master, the steward sought to feather his own nest, perhaps by ingratiating himself with potential employers, but more likely by setting up the possibility of blackmailing them in the future. [322] But this reading of the parable strains our credulity. Would any employer who has been swindled out of a great deal of money turn around and applaud the ingenuity of the perpetrator?

If that scenario seems improbable there is an alternative explanation. The rich man dismissed the steward because of accusations that he had been 'wasteful with his property.' In other words, he was guilty of some form of mismanagement, either through fraud or incompetence. Since the steward neither denied nor defended himself against the accusations he may indeed be guilty as charged. In other words, he was dishonest for what he had done, not for what he was about to do. A number of commentators suggest that the steward may not have acted dishonestly when he substantially reduced a number of debts. Such a steward was in fact an estate manager (*oikonomos* in the Greek text), a person who was 'not merely a head-servant placed in charge of the household staff, but a trained, trusted, and duly empowered agent of the master.'[323] It was not uncommon for an estate manager to enjoy considerable autonomy in overseeing his master's affairs, and to receive a substantial commission for his efforts. According to this scenario, once the steward was dismissed he settled a number of outstanding debts, but forfeited his own commission to ingratiate himself with his master's creditors. A short term loss for a long term gain! The steward is therefore held up to us as an example of someone who has resorted to extreme and shrewd measures to ensure a comfortable future for himself.

And how do we use our money? Jesus wasn't an economist, and the gospel doesn't offer fiscal advice that is readily applicable to the C21. But Jesus, the wisdom teacher, offers 'wise principles that can direct our thoughts and actions about money and possessions.'[324] This parable is 'not a warning against the destructive nature of riches,' but a lesson in 'the prudent use of material

---

[322] Daniel J Harrington, 'Money and Spirituality', *America*, September 17, 2007, p.39.
[323] Joseph A Fitzmyer, *The Gospel According to Luke, X-XXIV*, p.1097.
[324] Ibid.

possessions.'[325] The disciples are to be as astute in their use of money as the unjust steward was in furthering his own interests. The truth is that:

many people in our world display enormous intelligence and energy in financial matters in comparison with the little attention that they pay to the state of their souls. The industry, creativity and tenacity that go into making money and securing one's financial well-being often far outweigh the time and effort given to life's ultimate questions: Who am I? What is my goal? How do I get there? [326]

Today's gospel also asks, 'Whom do we befriend with our wealth?' In a nutshell, the gospel 'warns' us to convert money into heavenly capital by sharing it with others, particularly the needy. 'If the worldly manager is prepared to take violent action against himself, how much more – in view of the higher stakes operative – should the hearers of Jesus ('children of light') be prepared to do so. They should be ready to give away their wealth now in the form of alms so that when the great reversal comes and the poor have their privileged places in the kingdom, these same poor will welcome them into 'eternal dwellings', offer them the hospitality of God.'[327] The Jewish rabbis had a saying, 'The rich help the poor in this world, but the poor help the rich in the world to come.'[328] Our true wealth is not in what we keep, but in what we give away.

---

[325] Ibid, p.1098.
[326] Daniel J. Harrington, 'Money and Spirituality', p.39
[327] Brendan Byrne, *The Hospitality of God*, p.134.
[328] William Barclay, *The Gospel of Luke*, p.216.

TWENTY-SIXTH SUNDAY IN ORDINARY TIME

(YEAR C)

'If they will not listen either to Moses or to the prophets, they will not be convinced even if someone should rise from the dead.' (Lk 16:31)

So, you're not financially well off? Well, here's a sobering exercise. Next time you're on the internet, go to the global rich list site[329], type in your annual income, and see where you're placed on the world rich list. My stipend of less than $15000 per annum makes me the 805 250 903 richest person in the world. I'm not exactly in the same league as Bill Gates, but surprisingly I'm still in the top 14 percent of the richest people in the world. And while you're on the internet, check out the miniature earth site. If hypothetically, we could turn the population of the earth into a small community of 100 people, keeping the same proportions we have today, this site shows us what our scaled down earth would look like. Sixty-one people would be Asians, 12 would be Europeans, eight would be North Americans, and five would come from South America and the Caribbean; 13 would be African, and one person would come from Oceania. Of our miniature earth of 100 people, 47 percent would live in an urban area; nine are disabled; 43 live without basic sanitation; and 18 live without an improved water source. Six of the hundred people in our hypothetical village own 59 percent of the entire wealth of the village. Thirteen are hungry or malnourished; 14 can't read, and only seven are educated to secondary level. Twelve own a computer, but only three have an internet connection. The village spends $US1.2 trillion on military expenditure, but only $100 billion on development aid. Eighteen of our villagers struggle to live on US$1 or less per day; 53 struggle to live on US$2 or less per day. If you keep your food in a refrigerator, your clothes in a closet, and if you have a bed to sleep in and a roof over your head, then you are richer than 75 percent of the world population.[330]

We live in a world of extremes – extreme poverty and extreme wealth. When Leona Helmsley, a billionaire New York City hotel operator, died on August 20,

[329] www.globalrichlist.com
[330] http://www.miniature-earth.com/me_english.htm

2007, she was entombed next to her husband Harry in a mausoleum constructed for $1.4 million. Helmsley, nicknamed the 'Queen of Mean', also left her dog, Trouble, a $12 million trust fund – a sum that was reduced to $2 million a year later by a judge of the Manhattan Surrogate Court. Trouble must have been devastated! According to Reuters UK, Trouble's caretaker, Carl Lekic, said that $2 million would be 'enough money to pay for the dog's maintenance and welfare at the highest standards of care for more than 10 years,' according to an affidavit. Lekic said the money would cover annual costs of $100 000 for full-time security, $8000 for grooming and $1200 for food. Lekic is paid a $60 000 annual guardian fee out of the inheritance.[231]

The miniature earth website is a sobering backdrop for today's readings. The prophet Amos, writing in the sixth century BC offers a graphic description of the indulgence of the wealthy in his day. That they are wealthy is not the point; that would have been deemed a blessing from God. However, their compassion has been smothered by luxury and they spare no thought for others. They are exactly like the rich man in today's gospel. The rich man of the parable is unnamed – he is often called Dives – but that is simply the Latin word for 'rich person.' He is neither wicked nor evil; he is simply self-centred and insensitive. The parable opens with a powerful contrast between the extravagant luxury of the rich man and the destitution of Lazarus. The rich man has all that he could ever need: clothed in purple and fine linen, and feasting sumptuously ever day. Lazarus (the only person to be given a name in a gospel parable) is in a state of total poverty: full of sores, waiting for the scraps that fall from the table as the dogs lick his wounds. Since dogs were considered unclean animals, this detail adds to the indignity of Lazarus' situation.[232] The rich man has closed his mind, his heart, and even his eyes as he sits back, bloated.

But the setting changes and their fortunes are dramatically reversed after death. He who was outside is now inside, and he who was inside has been cast outside. The great gulf in life between luxury and destitution now becomes a chasm, impossible to cross, between Lazarus in the bosom of Abraham and the rich man in the flames of Hades. If no attempt had been made to cross the gulf during life, it is impossible to do so in death.

The Australian biblical scholar Fr Brendan Byrne has entitled his commentary on the gospel of St Luke *The Hospitality of God*. He explains that the word

---

[231] http://uk.reuters.com/article/oddlyEnoughNews/idUKN1634773920080617?sp=true
[232] Brendan Byrne, *The Hospitality of God*, p.136.

hospitality :

conjures up the context of guests, visitors, putting on meals for them, providing board and lodging, making the stranger feel 'at home' in our home – enlarging our home to make that wider 'at homeness' possible... Hospitality, in a variety of expressions, forms a notable frame of reference for the ministry of Jesus.[333]

Today's readings confront us with a brazen lack of hospitality and the human reluctance to welcome the outsider.

In the light of today's gospel this Sunday is designated as Social Justice Sunday in many dioceses. In 2007 the Australian Catholic Bishops released a statement entitled *Who is My Neighbour? Australia's Role as a Global Citizen.*[334] The title of the Bishops' Statement comes from the Gospel of St Luke. Responding to the question, 'Who is my neighbour?' Jesus told the story of the Good Samaritan. It was a despised outsider who proved to be the true neighbour to the man who had been left for dead by the roadside. The Statement is a call for us 'to act more in the interests of our neighbours who do not share our prosperity and security.' In other words, it is a call to heed the Lazarus at our door.

There are all manner of ways in which we can do this. In the lead up to Christmas I was pleasantly surprised when a friend told me about the rather unusual presents she had bought her family. She visited the World Vision website, clicked on 'Smiles' and began shopping from the online catalogue. She bought six chickens on behalf of her daughter ($36), a goat ($39) for one son, and a piglet ($47) for the other; her husband is getting the Vegie Pack ($44). Each member of the family receives a card informing them of the gift that has been given in their name to help poor children, families or communities. This innovative scheme means that each gift a person buys represents the type of activities that World Vision will carry out on behalf of the donor. So, if you buy a chicken or a vegie pack, for example, your contribution will go towards World Vision's agriculture and environment work to help communities grow nutritious food, generate income and protect and revive their environments. If you buy a mosquito net or a toilet, you'll be contributing to their work in helping communities gain access to basic healthcare, water and sanitation.[335] In 2008 this one program raised just under four million dollars worth of aid. The Australian Catholic Bishops' Statement states that first world countries need to increase their

---

[333] Ibid, p.4.
[334] The text of the Statement may be found at http://www.socialjustice.catholic.org.au/
[335] http://www.worldvision.com.au/Smiles/GiftCatalogue/Default.aspx

commitment to overseas aid. The amount spent on armaments far outweighs the amount spent on development aid.

When we look at the state of the world today we can easily respond by saying 'What can I do that will make the slightest bit of difference?' When Mother Teresa took the step of leaving the Loreto Sisters to found a new congregation dedicated to serving the poorest of the poor in Calcutta, she must surely have wondered what difference her efforts would make. Her response is heartening: 'We ourselves feel that what we are doing is just a drop in the ocean. But the ocean would be less because of that missing drop.'

TWENTY-SEVENTH SUNDAY IN ORDINARY TIME

(YEAR C)

'The apostles said to the Lord, 'Increase our faith.'' (Lk 17:5)

'I believe that.' This statement contains both the subjective and objective dimensions of faith. 'I' refers to the individual who believes – the subjective dimension of faith. 'That' refers to the content of our faith, what it is that we believe. This is the objective dimension of faith, sometimes referred to as the 'deposit of faith.'[336] When the apostles asked the Lord to increase their faith they were most likely asking not for a primitive version of the Apostles' Creed (objective faith) but rather for a deeper trust in God and in Jesus their teacher (subjective faith).[337] The prophet Habakkuk, writing on the eve of the Babylonian invasion of Jerusalem, is reassured that 'the just (person), because of his faith, shall live.' Undoubtedly the prophet and his audience understood those words in the subjective sense, as a promise that those who remained faithful to God would survive the devastation that lay ahead. [338]

Marcus Borg notes that faith is 'utterly central to the Christian life', and all but two of the 27 books of the New Testament use the noun 'faith' or the verb 'believe.' He identifies four primary meanings of the word 'faith' in the history of Christianity: Faith as assensus; faith as *fiducia*; faith as *fidelitas*; and faith as *visio*.[339] Faith as assensus refers to what we might call the content of faith or objective faith. A pious young Jew who had devoted his life to studying the sacred texts of his religious tradition, suddenly closed the copy of the Talmud that he had been reading and, without any apparent reason, ran out of the house into the middle of the town square, crying out, 'What is the meaning of life? I cannot go any further; I cannot study one additional verse of Torah without knowing the meaning of life.' Some fellow students ran to his aid and tried to calm him down, but to no avail. They could not convince him to return to his studies,

---

[336] Cf 1Tim 6:20; 2Tim 1:12-14. The deposit (*parathēkēn*) of faith is an important theme of the Pastoral Letters.
[337] Daniel J Harrington, 'Two Dimensions of Faith', *America,* October 1, 2007, 47.
[338] Ibid
[339] Marcus J Borg, *The Heart of Christianity*, HarperSan Francisco, 2003, pp.27-42.

so they recommended that he visit a learned and saintly rabbi who lived in a nearby village. The pious young lad set out immediately to visit the rabbi, and no sooner had he entered his house than he whispered nervously, 'Rabbi, what is the meaning of life? I must know, I cannot go on any longer, I cannot study another page, until I know: What is the meaning of life?' The rabbi walked over to the young man, looked into his eyes, and suddenly slapped him. 'Why, rabbi? Why did you slap me? What have I done? All I did was ask, 'What is the meaning of life?'' To which the rabbi replied, 'You fool. You have such a good question. Why exchange it for an answer?'[340]

The Austrian poet Rainer Maria Rilke (1875 – 1926) had something similar in mind when he wrote to a young poet:

Don't search for answers, which could not be given to you now, because you would not be able to live them. And the point is, to live everything. Live the questions now. Perhaps then, someday far in the future, you will gradually, without even noticing it, live your way into the answer. [341]

The year before he died Thomas Merton (1915 – 1968) had this to say:

Can I tell you that I have found answers to the questions that torment the people of our time? I do not know if I have found answers. When I first became a monk, yes, I was surer of 'answers.' But as I grow old in the monastic life and advance further into solitude, I become aware that I have only begun to seek the questions.[342]

What the pious young student had yet to learn was stated succinctly by the Christian French philosopher Gabriel Marcel: 'Life is not a problem to be solved but a mystery to be lived.'[343] The Australian cartoonist Michael Leunig has one of his characters admit, 'I really can't see the point of life.' His female companion, comfortably ensconced with a book and a glass of red wine, replies, 'It's not pointy. It's round and soft.'[344]

Faith as fiducia is best understood as trust. Trust does not mean that we are immune from doubt. *Mother Teresa: Come Be My Light* is a recently-published collection of letters written by Mother Teresa,[345] and these letters reveal the inner turmoil of this saintly woman. She endured relentless aridity (spiritual dryness)

---

[340] Adapted from Steve Zeitlin (Ed), *Because God Loves Stories: An Anthology of Jewish Storytelling*, op. cit., p.273.
[341] Quoted in Jonathan Montaldo & Robert G. Toth (eds), *Bridges to Contemplative Living with Thomas Merton, One: Entering the School of Your Experience,* Ave Maria Press, Notre Dame, IN, 2006, p.25.
[342] Ibid, p.24.
[343] Ibid, p.14.
[344] *The Sydney Morning Herald* 2009 Calendar, September.

for over fifty years, with one brief respite, until her death in September 1997. 'In my soul I feel just that terrible pain of loss – of God not wanting me – of God not being God – of God not really existing,' she wrote to a confessor in 1959.[346]

Fr John Kavanaugh, professor of philosophy at St Louis University (USA), tells of meeting Mother Teresa in Calcutta during December 1975 and for a few days in the following March. During that time he celebrated Mass at the Missionaries of Charity motherhouse and worked at the House of the Dying, but he also had a number of conversations with Mother Teresa. Shortly before he left Calcutta he asked her to pray for him. Mother Teresa asked, 'For what?' He replied 'For clarity.' She immediately said no, she would not pray for that. Fr Kavanaugh complained that she seemed always to have clarity and certitude. 'I've never had clarity and certitude,' she said. 'I only have trust. I'll pray that you trust.'[347] Faith as *fiducia* is a radical trust in God.

Faith as *fidelitas* is being faithful, not to statements about God, but to the God who is revealed, however imperfectly, in biblical, creedal or doctrinal statements. In the words of Fr Roland Rolheiser, 'Ultimately faith is not in the head or the heart but in the action of a sustained commitment. Faith is fidelity, nothing more but nothing less.'[348] The opposite to *fidelitas* is not doubt or disbelief, but infidelity or idolatry. The central meaning of idolatry is 'giving one's ultimate loyalty or allegiance to something other than God. (It is) centring in something finite rather than the sacred, who is infinite and beyond all images.' *Fiducia* is 'being loyal to God and not to the many would-be gods that present themselves to us.'[349]

Faith as *visio* is about a way of seeing, and this is the essential meaning of *metanoia*, repentance. Faith does not filter out pain and suffering and all the absurdities of human existence. They are as much a part of our life as they are of anyone's. It is *not* what we see that faith transforms; it is rather *how* we see. A Zen saying puts it this way: 'Before enlightenment, chopping wood and fetching water; after enlightenment, chopping wood and fetching water.' In his book *The Structure of Scientific Revolutions*, the American physicist Thomas Kuhn showed how almost every significant breakthrough in science has involved a break with the old ways of seeing the world.[350] He coined the term paradigm shift to describe

---

[345] Brian Kolodiejchuk, *Mother Teresa: Come Be My Light*, Doubleday, New York , 2007.

[346] James Martin, ' "In my soul." The long dark night of Mother Teresa.' (*America*, September 24, 2007, p.14

[347] John F Kavanaugh, 'Godforsakenness: "Finding one's heart's desire",' *America*, October 1, 2007.

[348] Ronald Rolheiser, '*Fidelity – Our Greatest Gift to Others*',Column for 9-02-2009, http://www.ronrolheiser.com/

[349] Marcus Borg, op. cit., pp.32-33.

a new way of seeing. One of the most famous examples of a paradigm shift is associated with the name of the Polish astronomer Nicolaus Copernicus. In the sixteenth century the prevailing view of the universe was geocentric, or earth-centred. The prevailing paradigm had the Earth at the centre of the universe, with the sun, planets and stars rotating around the Earth. But Copernicus proposed a heliocentric, or sun-centred, theory of the universe. What ensued has been called the 'Copernican Revolution'. The dethronement of the Earth from the centre of the universe caused a profound shock to C16 sensibilities. Many people resisted and rejected the notion that the Earth was not at the centre of the universe. But what had really changed? Certainly nothing 'out there' had changed. The universe was as it had always been. What had changed was our way of seeing, our way of interpreting and understanding the universe. Faith as *visio* involves a similar transformation. Writing to the Christians of Rome, St Paul exhorted them, 'Do not model your behaviour on the contemporary world, but let the renewing of your minds transform you.' (12: 2). The faith that enables a radical trust in God, the faith that claims the total allegiance of our heart, and the faith that transforms our vision of life will indeed uproot a mulberry tree and plant it in the ocean.

---

[350] Thomas S Kuhn, *The Structure of Scientific Revolutions,* The University of Chicago Press, Third Edition, 1996.

TWENTY-EIGHTH SUNDAY IN ORDINARY TIME

(YEAR C)

'Stand up and go on your way. Your faith has saved you.' (Lk 19)

In last Sunday's gospel the disciples asked the Lord to increase their faith. Jesus replied, 'Were your faith the size of a mustard seed you could say to this mulberry tree, 'Be uprooted and planted in the sea,' and it would obey you.' In today's gospel we see such a faith in action. Ten lepers called out: 'Jesus! Master! Take pity on us.' His response to their plea was an abrupt command, 'Go and show yourselves to the priests.' Jesus would have failed Pastoral Care 101 with a response as uncaring as that. Surely he should have said something like, 'It must be difficult being a leper ....'.[351] Luke's telling of the story, however, puts the spotlight on Jesus – he who speaks the word of God with power and authority. At the command of Jesus the lepers set out in faith, and here faith is obedience to the word of Jesus. It was only after they had set out on the journey – the Jewish lepers to Jerusalem and the Samaritan leper presumably to Mt Gerizim – that they were healed.

What is Luke telling us in this story? We are told that only one of the lepers – the Samaritan – returned to give thanks. Why does Jesus rebuke the other nine lepers who continued on their way? They were, after all, fulfilling the prescriptions laid down in the book of Leviticus as he had commanded them to do. They were being obedient to the Law.

Jesus sent the Samaritan on his way with the words, 'Your faith has saved you.' Those words could also be translated as 'Your faith has made you whole.' How is the Samaritan's faith different from that of the other nine? What, apart from a physical healing, has made the Samaritan whole? Naaman, the leper healed by Elisha, holds the key to that question. 'Having been healed of his leprosy, the gentile Naaman recognises that the God of Israel was at work through Elisha the prophet. Naaman makes a public profession of his conviction ('Now I know that there is no God in all the earth, except in Israel') and promises to offer sacrifice

---

[351] David Buttrick, *Homiletic*, Fortress Press, Philadelphia, 1987, p.338.

only to Yahweh.'[352] In other words, he offers praise and worship. The Samaritan also offers praise and thanksgiving (*doxazōn* and *eucharistōn* in the Greek text), both of which are Lukan words for worship. Luke is telling us that the Christian life is more than an obedient faith. It is also worship. The wholeness of a Christian life will include both obedience and worship. Obedience by itself can degenerate into moralism, a list of 'dos' and 'don'ts', relating more to law than to God. On the other hand, worship without obedience can turn into an insipid Pietism.[353] Salvation or 'wholeness' means an obedient faith, but it also means coming together in the Christian assembly to praise and give thanks to God who has set us free.

Today's gospel is yet another example of one of St Luke's perennial themes: Jesus welcomes the outsider. Let us pause for a moment to consider lepers and Samaritans. The medical name for leprosy is Hansen's disease, and biblical scholars and medical scientists agree that Hansen's disease was not to be found in first century Palestine. No trace of the disease has been found in any of the ancient bones excavated in Israel. The leprosy mentioned in the gospels covers a variety of skin ailments, many of which were not contagious. For the most part the leprosy we read of in the bible was curable and its symptoms were those of a number of relatively superficial skin diseases. Nevertheless, the Book of Leviticus (13:29-37) makes it clear that when a priest diagnosed such a disease the person was rendered ritually unclean. That meant that they had to move to a safe distance from town until they were cured. The story is set in the borderland between Samaria and Galilee, a no man's land – an appropriate place to dump contagious people.[354]

It was the role of the priest to determine if a person had been cured and to perform the rite of purification. Leprosy was devastating because it exiled a person from home, family and friends. It was as if they were dead. It is highly probable that a number of people present at Mass today are suffering from skin conditions, such as psoriasis, that would have been diagnosed as leprosy in biblical times.

From the Jewish standpoint the leper who returned to give thanks was doubly cursed. Not only was he a leper, but he was also a Samaritan. The origin of the Samaritans that we read about in the gospel goes back to the eighth century before Christ. Assyria had conquered the northern kingdom of Israel in 722 BC

---

[352] Daniel J Harrington, 'Thanksgiving as public witness to God's action', *America*, October 8, 2007.
[353] David Buttrick, p.338, p.339
[354] David Buttrick, p.336

and resettled the territory with pagans from other parts of their empire. In time these resettled pagans intermarried with the Jews who had survived the conquest. Samaritans were therefore regarded as half-breed schismatics, and a deep-seated animosity developed between Jews and Samaritans. It's interesting that the two gospel stories that present a Samaritan favourably are found in Luke's gospel – the parable of the Good Samaritan, and today's story.

The Jesus whom we encounter in the gospel of Luke constantly challenges existing boundaries. As disciples of Jesus we must never exclude today's lepers and Samaritans. In the Christian community there must never be people considered beyond the pale.

St Francis of Assisi is one of the best-loved saints of the Christian church. The story of his conversion includes an extraordinary change in his attitude towards lepers – the most miserable and wretched outcasts of medieval society. That change of attitude reflected one of the greatest victories of grace in his entire life. Francis was an exceedingly fastidious young man who keenly abhorred lepers. Shortly before his death in October 1226, Francis wrote in his *Testament:*

The Lord granted me, Brother Francis, to begin to do penance in this way: While I was in sin, it seemed very bitter to me to see lepers. And the Lord Himself led me among them and I had mercy upon them. And when I left them that which seemed bitter to me was changed into sweetness of soul and body... [355]

Despite a natural loathing for lepers, Francis visited leper-houses around Assisi, washing lepers' ulcerated flesh and serving them in whatever way he could. A delightful story about Francis and a leper tells how he overcame his natural repugnance. One day, when he was riding near Assisi he came across a leper lying on the road. Francis dismounted, took the leper into his arms and kissed him. He then rode off, but as he turned to wish the leper farewell, the leper was nowhere to be seen.[356] The moral of the story is clear. The leper was Christ, and Francis learnt at first hand that what is done to the least, the outcast, the most despised, is done also to Christ. When we learn to embrace the leper, whomever the leper might be in our own lives, that which seems bitter will be changed into sweetness of soul and body.[357]

---

[355] Regis J. Armstrong and Ignatius C. Brady, *Francis and Clare: The Complete Works*, Paulist Press, New York, 1982, p.154.

[356] St Bonaventure, Major Life I, 5, in Marion A Habig (ed), *St Francis of Assisi: Writings and Early Biographies*, Franciscan Herald Press, Chicago, 1983, p.638; 1 Celano 17, in Habig, p.243; 2 Celano 9, in Habig, pp.370-371; *Legend of the Three Companions* 11, in Habig, pp.900-901.

[357] Adapted from Eric Doyle, *St Francis and the Song of Brotherhood*, op. cit., pp.10-11.

TWENTY-NINTH SUNDAY IN ORDINARY TIME

(YEAR C)

'Jesus told his disciples a parable about the need to pray continually and never lose heart.' (Lk 18:1)

The story of the persistent widow and the unjust judge offers a lesson in prayer. If an unjust judge finally succumbs to a widow's entreaties, how much more will God respond to our persistent prayer? If an unjust and self-centred judge is moved to action, surely God will readily answer our prayers without delay. But is it that simple? I am sure that most of us can cite examples of fervent, heartfelt and persistent prayers that remained unanswered, sometimes leading to disillusionment and discouragement. If God intervenes in human affairs to change the course of events, why is that intervention so selective? Why is one person healed while the prayers of others remain unanswered? Unanswered? Perhaps we can sympathise with the cynic who observed that God always answered his prayers: 'God usually says 'No!'' Is that because we simply lack the persistent and aggressive faith of the widow, as suggested by the ominous note that concludes today's gospel: 'But when the Son of Man comes, will he find any faith on earth?'

One response to the dilemma posed by intercessory prayer is to reject the notion that God intervenes at all in human affairs. Marcus Borg, a member of the Jesus Seminar and a well-known biblical scholar says 'I do not and cannot believe that God is an interventionist.'[358] John Shelby Spong, the retired Episcopal bishop of Newark, USA, is adamant that we live in a world 'that has no reason to believe that any danger has ever subsided, any sickness been cured, any natural disaster averted, or any war won in response to the prayers of human beings.' To believe otherwise, he argues, is 'naïve at best and unbelievable at worst.'[359] Well, there must be a high percentage of naïve people around. A Gallup opinion survey published in 1989 found that about 82 percent of Americans polled believed that 'even today, miracles are performed by the power of God.' Only six percent

---

[358] Marcus J Borg, *The Heart of Christianity*, p.196.
[359] John Shelby Spong, *Why Christianity Must Change or Die*, HarperSan Francisco, 1998,p.140.

completely disagreed with the proposition.[360]

At the other extreme, some approach intercessory prayer as if God were a vending machine. Insert the correct prayer formula, fulfill a few basic requirements, and your request will be answered without fail. Consider the novenas to St Jude or St Martha that are left behind in the pews of Catholic churches. The novena to St Jude is to be said on nine consecutive days and a copy of the prayer is to be left behind daily in the church. The novena comes with an assurance that 'this prayer has never been known to fail. Your request will be granted on or before the ninth day.' The novena to St Martha is a little more demanding. It must be recited for nine consecutive Tuesdays. On each Tuesday a candle must be lit, and a copy of the prayer must also be left in the church 'in order to help another soul in distress and to help support devotion to St Martha.' One must also recite the *Our Father*, the *Hail Mary* and the *Glory Be* three times, but the novena comes with an iron-clad guarantee: 'This miraculous St Martha grants anything, no matter how difficult, before the termination of the ninth Tuesday.'

There are certainly gospel passages that encourage us to petition God. Jesus told his disciples that everything they asked for in prayer they will receive, if they have faith. But faith is a radical trust in God. It is a faith that claims the total allegiance of our heart; a faith that transforms our vision of life. It is a faith that prays 'your kingdom come, your will be done.' On the night before he died, Jesus prayed on the Mount of Olives, asking the Father 'if you are willing, take this cup away from me.' But he added, 'Nevertheless, let your will be done, not mine.'

Reflecting on his experience in the healing ministry, the Australian Jesuit Frank Wallace writes that it has led him more deeply into the mystery of expectant faith. Once he used to pray, 'Lord if it is your will, heal this person here.' But he became increasingly uneasy with the 'if it is your will' bit, because it seemed like a cop-out:

I have come to see that God always answers prayers for healing, but I have also accepted that how he heals and when he heals must be left to him. ... God is more concerned with being present to us in suffering, and that he seems to prefer changing us and our attitudes, and giving us strength, hope and patience, to changing situations. When we meet this God ever present in time of trouble, and stop looking for the God with the magic wand, we are allowing ourselves to

---

[360] George Gallup, Jr, and Sarah Jones, *100 Questions and Answers: Religion in America*, Princeton Religion Research Center, 1989, quoted in John P Meier, *A Marginal Jew, Volume Two: Mentor, Message*, and *Miracles*, pp.520-1.

be drawn into the paschal mystery and to meet God who is love. [361]

The English rabbi Lionel Blue writes about his pious Russian grandmother who had assured him that if he prayed for something unselfish with all his heart God would make it happen. But then he 'thought of all the prayers that must have been said in those cattle wagons making their night journeys to the concentration camps with their cargoes of human misery. Their prayers must have been among the sincerest ever but they weren't answered in any way that I could understand.' His return to religion and prayer grew out of a realisation that religion wasn't magic. Rabbi Blue offers us an important insight when he tells us that prayer is 'not a way to change the cosmos to suit my convenience, but a way to start changing myself. Prayer didn't make my problems vanish but it did give me enough courage to face them.' [362]

---

[361] Frank Wallace, *Encounter Not Performance*, EJ Dwyer, Newtown, NSW, 1991, p.32.
[362] Lionel Blue, 'Finding my religion', *The Tablet,* 12 May 2001, p.679.

THIRTIETH SUNDAY IN ORDINARY TIME

(YEAR C)

'For everyone who exalts himself will be humbled, but the man who humbles himself will be exalted.' (Lk 18: 14)

Today's readings offer a further lesson in prayer. The prayer of the humble 'pierces the clouds', the book of Ecclesiasticus tells us, and the parable of the Pharisee and the tax collector is a lesson directed to 'some people who prided themselves on being virtuous and despised everyone else.' The Pharisee is intent on parading his good deeds and religious observance before others. His prayer is 'a catalogue of negative virtues and minor pieties,' and there are enough examples from rabbinic literature to conclude that this parable is not a caricature. The Talmud tells us that Rabbi Nehunia ben Hakaneh used to pray daily on leaving the rabbinical school:

I give thanks to thee, O Lord my God, that thou has set my portion with those who sit in the house of instruction, and thou has not set my portion with those who sit in street corners, for I rise early and they rise early, but I rise early for words of Torah and they rise early for frivolous talk; I labour and they labour, but I labour and receive a reward and they labour and do not receive a reward; I run and they run, but I run to the life of the world to come and they run to the pit of destruction.[363]

Israel ben Eliezer (1700-1760), known as the *Baal Shem* Tov, was the charismatic founder of Hasidism in Eastern Europe. On one occasion the *Baal Shem* Tov stopped at the threshold of a House of Prayer and refused to enter. When those around him asked why he explained, 'I cannot go in. It is crowded with teachings and prayers from wall to wall and from floor to ceiling. How could there be room for me?' Onlookers were puzzled by what he had said, so he explained: 'The words from the lips of those whose teaching and praying does not come from the hearts lifted to heaven, cannot rise, but fill the house from wall to wall and from floor to ceiling.'[364]

---

[363] GB Caird, *Saint Luke*, p.202.
[364] Slightly adapted from Martin Buber, *Tales of the Hasidim*, Schocken Books, New York, 1975, p. 73.

Rabbi Lionel Blue tells a story about the Jewish Day of Atonement, the most solemn and serious fast in the Jewish year. As the service was about to begin, a hush came over the assembled congregation. The venerable rabbi held out his hand for silence. Instead of going to his pulpit, he approached the Holy Ark with tears in his eyes. With theatrical flair he flung open the doors of the Ark and prostrated himself before the scrolls. 'Lord,' he said in a strained voice, 'have mercy on me, for I am only dust and ashes.' After his confession the congregation watched him as he arose and took his place at the reading desk. He opened his prayer book, and was about to commence the solemn service. But before he could do so, the cantor of the synagogue said gently, 'Wait!' He too approached the Holy Ark, and following his venerable rabbi in all things, gently opened the doors of the Ark, and prostrated himself humbly before the scrolls. 'Lord,' he said. 'I too seek mercy, for I too am just dust and ashes.' In the silence, he took his place at the reading desk, and signed to the rabbi that the service could begin. But there was one more confession to be heard, from the humblest servant of the synagogue. The janitor moved forward from the back of the synagogue with tears in his eyes. And while the congregation watched, moved and astonished, he too climbed the steps to the Ark with bowed head. He opened its door lovingly, and also prostrated himself, and spoke piously and gently. 'Lord,' he said, 'have mercy on me, a sinner, who is but dust and ashes.' Eying the janitor with utter disdain the rabbi breathed deeply, turned to the cantor and said 'Look who presumes to think he is only dust and ashes!' [365]

The Swiss psychiatrist and psychoanalyst Carl Jung tells a story about being visited by an uncommonly saintly man who seemed to be without a flaw. After a few days in this man's presence Jung felt completely unworthy and uncomfortable. It was only after meeting the man's unhappy wife that he realized the great cost she paid for his 'saintliness.'[366] The prayer of the rabbi and cantor, like that of the Pharisee, is filled with pompous self-importance, a posturing before God. The prayer of the janitor, like that of the tax collector, is one of heartfelt simplicity. Such prayers come from hearts lifted to heaven. The prayers of the rabbi, cantor and Pharisee cannot rise, but fill the house from wall to wall and from floor to ceiling. Perhaps they should pray for what spiritual writers refer to as the grace of insecurity – the insecurity that enabled St Paul to acknowledge that 'when I am weak, then I am strong' (2 Cor 12: 10).

---

[365] Slightly adapted from Lionel Blue, *Bright Blue: Rabbi Lionel Blue's Thoughts for the Day*, British Broadcasting Commission, London, 1985, pp.52-3.

[366] Alan Jones, *Soul Making*, p.37.

THIRTY-FIRST SUNDAY IN ORDINARY TIME

(YEAR C)

'For the Son of Man has come to seek out and save what was lost.' (Lk 19:10)

A friend of mine who speaks several languages fluently once told me that reading anything in translation was like kissing a woman through a veil! There is an Italian saying: *traduttore traditore* – which is a play on words. It means the translator is a traitor. In other words, when we translate from one language to another we often betray the meaning of the original text. I believe that this has happened in the translation we've just heard of today's gospel, and it affects the way in which we interpret the story.

The focus is on Zacchaeus. Zacchaeus was a tax collector – in fact we're told that he was a senior tax collector – and obviously a wealthy man. Who were these tax collectors, and why do the synoptic gospels generally lump them together with 'sinners', 'Gentiles' or 'prostitutes'? What is the significance of Jesus accepting the hospitality of a tax collector? Palestine had paid taxes to Rome ever since Pompey's conquest in 63BC. Today's gospel story is set in the affluent and important town of Jericho, which is in Judaea. After 6BC Judaea came directly under the Roman prefect and taxes were collected by officials directly employed by the Romans. The Romans were foreign conquerors, and their taxes were regarded as robbery and extortion. Talmudic literature provides ample evidence of the severity of taxation under Roman domination,[367] and tax collectors were hated and dreaded, especially as the burden of taxation became increasingly intolerable. They were known to resort to torture and excessive force to exact payment.[368] Rabbinic texts, although not committed to writing before the C3AD, incorporate earlier oral traditions that lump both tax and toll collectors together with robbers, murderers and sinners, and they are included in

---

[367] Cecil Roth, 'Taxation', *Encyclopaedia Judaica*, CD Rom.
[368] Daniel Sperber, 'Tax Gatherers', *Encyclopaedia Judaica*, CD Rom.

the lists of 'despised trades' that no observant Jew would enter.[369] Zacchaeus, a despised, hated and socially ostracised tax collector, displayed a certain degree of courage in mingling with the crowds to catch a glimpse of Jesus, especially since he was a short man:

One can only imagine the reaction of neighbours and even of friends and relatives, as Zacchaeus's house became more lavishly decorated, as more slaves ran about at his bidding, as his clothes became finer and his food richer. Everyone knew that this was their money and that he had no right to it; everyone knew that there was nothing they could do about it. [370]

Let's come back to the question of mistranslation. After Jesus tells Zacchaeus that he must stay at his house today the translation from the Greek text that we've just heard reads: 'Look, sir, I am going to give half my property to the poor, and if I have cheated anybody I will pay him back four times the amount.' The point I'm taking issue with is this: this translation (from the *Jerusalem Bible*) has Zacchaeus using the future tense: 'I am going to give' and 'I will pay him back.' However the Greek text uses the present tense, which should be translated as 'I give away half of what I own to the poor. If I have extorted anything from anyone, I pay it back four times over.' The significance of the present tense means that Zacchaeus is talking about what he normally does, his customary behaviour, rather than a single spontaneous act of generosity.[371] In other words, 'he is not such a bad tax collector after all!'[372] And, by the way, the name Zacchaeus is the Greek form of the Hebrew name Zakkai, meaning clean or innocent.[373]

What is the effect of this mistranslation? Quite simply, the use of the future tense places the spotlight on Zacchaeus and his 'conversion' and almost ignores the reaction of the bystanders. They are the people in this story who truly need conversion. 'They all complained,' the gospel tells us, 'when they saw what was happening.' Notice the word 'all' (*pantes* in the Greek) – which would include

---

[369] John R. Donahue, 'Tax Collector' in David Noel Freeedman (Ed), *The Anchor Bible Dictionary*, Volume 6, Doubleday, New York , 1992, pp.337-8.

[370] Tom Wright, *Luke for Everyone*, pp.222-3.

[371] Luke Timothy Johnson, op. cit., pp.285-6; Joseph A Fitzmyer, *The Gospel According to Luke X-XXIV*, p.1225. The tense of the verbs is classed as the iterative or customary present. The Latin Vulgate uses the present tense, but the future tense is retained in a number of recent translations, including the *New Jerusalem Bible* and the *New American Bible*. The *New King James Bible* uses the present tense.

[372] Brendan Byrne, *The Hospitality of God*, p.151. Byrne notes that 'This interpretation, long suppressed in the Christian interpretive tradition, has been forcefully and effectively revived by Fitzmyer'.

[373] Joseph A Fitzmyer, *The Gospel According to Luke X-XXIV*, p.1223.

'the disciples and the crowd and the opponents whom Luke always pictures accompanying Jesus on the way to Jerusalem.'[374] Like the elder brother in the parable of the prodigal son, or like Simon the Pharisee, they are indignant at the gracious treatment of someone whom they deem to be a sinner. Such contempt and righteous indignation sees only the splinter in another's eye while oblivious to the log in one's own. Salvation comes to Zacchaeus' house not because of anything he has done; it comes rather because of what Jesus has done. Jesus has accepted Zacchaeus and brought him in from the margins to the centre. Fr Brendan Byrne finds in this story a reminder of the practice of the L'Arche communities founded by Jean Vanier. The mentally or physically challenged persons for whom they care are always given a central place in the community.[375]

Philip Yancey tells a story about one of his friends who was approached for help by a prostitute who was in wretched straits – homeless, sick and unable to buy food for her young daughter. The woman disclosed that she had been offering her daughter for sex to support a drug habit. She explained that she made more money out of her daughter for an hour than she could earn on her own in a night. Yancey's friend asked the woman if she had ever thought of going to a church for help. A look of pure, naïve shock crossed the woman's face: 'Church!' she cried. 'Why would I ever go there?' I was already feeling terrible about myself. They'd just make me feel worse.'[376] What struck Yancey about his friend's story is that people like this prostitute sought out the company of Jesus. The worse people felt about themselves, the more they saw Jesus as a refuge. 'Has the church lost that gift?' Yancey asks. 'Evidently the down-and-out, who flocked to Jesus when he lived on earth, no longer feel welcome among his followers. What has happened?'[377]

With this in mind it was heartening to read that the Catholic parish of Corinda-Graceville in the Archdiocese of Brisbane (Queensland) has offered to fly the parents of a convicted Australian drug smuggler to Bali so that they can be with their son.[378] Twenty-one year old Scott Rush is one of six Australians on death row over the failed Bali Nine heroin smuggling ring. Scott's mother has told the parish priest of Corinda-Graceville, Fr Tim Harris, that the family were not doing too badly considering the circumstances. Their hearts had been broken, but they

---

[374] Luke Timothy Johnson, op. cit., p.285.
[375] Brendan Byrne, p.151.
[376] Philip Yancey, *What's So Amazing About Grace*, Zondervan, Grand Rapids, MI, 1997, p.11
[377] Ibid.
[378] Reported in *CathNews*, 2 November, 2007.

were determined to do everything they could to make sure Scott knew they would always love him and be there for him.[379] Hopefully, the Church can also manifest that same love and compassion, however abhorrent we may regard the crime! A congregation might be tempted to adopt the same mentality as the people present in Jericho and argue, 'Why should we spend our money on a drug smuggler; surely there are more deserving people in the parish?'

The people present in Jericho that day resented the way that Jesus treated Zacchaeus because of who he was and what he did. Perhaps we could take to heart these words by an unknown poet:

I dreamed death came the other night
And heaven's gate swung wide.
With kindly grace an angel
Ushered me inside.
And there to my astonishment
Stood folks I'd known on earth,
Some I'd judged and labelled
Unfit, of little worth.
Indignant words rose to my lips
But never were set free –
For every face showed stunned surprise;
Not one expected me.[380]

---

[379] Reported in *CathNews*, 17 February, 2006.
[380] Mark Link, *Vision 2000, A Cycle,* Tabor Publishing, Allen, TX , 1992, p.246.

THIRTY-SECOND SUNDAY IN ORDINARY TIME

(YEAR C)

'Now he is God, not of the dead, but of the living; for to him all men are in fact alive.' (Lk 20:38)

A rabbi in a small Russian town at the turn of the century was walking across the village square on his way to the synagogue. The local policeman didn't have much time for Jews, and he was in a foul mood that morning. He thought he'd take it out on the rabbi. He yelled out, 'Hey, rabbi, where do you think you're going?' The rabbi answered, 'I don't know.' That answer infuriated the policeman. 'What do you mean, you don't know where you're going? Every morning at eleven o'clock, for as long as anyone can remember, you've crossed this village square on your way to the synagogue. Here it is, eleven o'clock and you're walking across the village square in the direction of the synagogue. Don't tell me you don't know where you're going. Are you trying to make a fool out of me? Let me teach you a lesson.' So the policeman grabbed the rabbi, forcibly marched him across the road to the local jail, and threw him into a cell. The rabbi then looked at the policeman and said: 'You see, officer, I was quite right when I told you that I didn't know where I was going!'[381]

Where are you going? That is a question some of us spend our whole lives avoiding. What awaits us beyond the grave? Nothing, according to the Sadducees, neither reward nor punishment. They refused to believe in any kind of resurrection from the dead. Their bizarre story about a woman who outlived each of her seven husbands was directed against what they believed to be the Pharisees' absurd belief in the resurrection of the dead. The Sadducees were essentially conservative, and belief in the resurrection was a relatively late development within Judaism; from their point of view it was a modern heresy. The Sadducees also realised that any belief in life beyond the grave might encourage a bolder resistance to the Roman occupation, in the same way that today's suicide bombers are motivated by the prospect of a martyr's

---

[381] Adapted from M Scott Peck, *Further Along the Road Less Travelled*, pp.69-70.

reward in heaven. Since the Sadducees were among the aristocracy of Judaism, it was to their advantage to maintain the status quo by cooperating with the Romans.

Today's second reading from the second book of Maccabees reflects a firm and unequivocal belief in the resurrection of the dead. The story about seven brothers who were martyred during the reign of Antiochus IV Epiphanes (175-164 BC) comes from the end of the C2BC. Antiochus attempted to impose Hellenistic culture as a means of unifying the diverse Seleucid empire. He prohibited all Jewish rites, dedicated the Temple in Jerusalem to Zeus, and executed anyone who possessed a copy of the Torah or a child who had been circumcised. His decrees met with passive resistance at first, but later with open defiance. The seven brothers were ordered to eat pig's flesh, but they choose to die rather than disobey the Law, relying on God's promise that they will be raised up.[382]

Death and the inevitability of our own death is not a subject that many people can talk about comfortably. The psychiatrist M. Scott Peck, author of *The Road Less Travelled*, says that he has had to push at least half of his patients to face the reality of their death. He argues that their reluctance to face the reality of death seems to be a part of their illness. He believes that we live in a cowardly, death-denying culture.[383] A psychiatrist colleague once told Peck that in her town, after one high school student had died of leukemia and another died in an automobile crash, the students petitioned the principal to introduce an elective course on death and dying. A minister of religion even stepped forward and offered to organize the course and find the teachers for it, free of charge. But any new course had to be approved by the school board. The board immediately voted nine to one against such a course on the grounds that it was morbid.[384] It is normal to be afraid of dying. Dying is going into the unknown, and to a degree it is healthy to be fearful of entering the unknown. What is not healthy is to try to ignore it.

Elisabeth Kubler-Ross, formerly the professor of psychiatry at the University of Chicago, has written extensively on the subject of death and dying. In fact, the title of her best-known book is *On Death and Dying*.[385] She found that people invariably go through various stages when they are told they're dying. The first

---

[382] George W.E. Nickelsburg, 'Resurrection: Early Judaism and Christianity' in David Noel Freedman (Ed) *The Anchor Bible Dictionary*, Volume 5, Doubleday, New York, 1992, pp.684-691; John Whitehorne, 'Antiochus', in David Noel Freedman (Ed), *The Anchor Bible Dictionary*, Volume 1, Doubleday, New York, 1992, pp.269-272.

[383] Ibid, p.50.

[384] Ibid, p.52.

[385] Elisabeth Kubler-Ross, *On Death and Dying*, The Macmillan Company, New York, 1969.

stage is denial. People deny they're dying. 'It can't be happening to me; it's a wrong diagnosis; there must be a mistake.' And when they finally accept the fact of their approaching death they get angry - angry at the doctors, angry at the nurses, angry at the hospital, angry at their relatives, angry at God. When anger doesn't get them anywhere, they start to bargain. 'Take away my cancer and I'll go back to church again. Maybe if I start being nicer to family things will improve.' And when bargaining doesn't seem to get any results, they become depressed. Those people who work through the stage of depression enter the fifth stage, that of acceptance. This is a stage of great spiritual calm and tranquillity, and even light, but sadly, not everyone reaches this final stage.

Many of you at Mass today are familiar with what we call the 'migrant experience.' With great courage you left behind your homeland and launched out into the unknown to make a new life in Australia. This entailed learning a new language and plunging into an alien culture. With the passing of years you've begun to call Australia home – and many of you have lived more than half of your lives in this country – but perhaps you've never really felt as though you're a 'fair dinkum' Aussie. Strangely, though, when you've returned to visit the land of your birth you find that things aren't as you remembered them, and you no longer belong there either. Sadly, there is nowhere on the face of the earth that you feel fully at home: You can never really say I'm a native to this place!

The New Testament writers tell us that this world, beautiful as it is, is not our ultimate home. We are all migrants; we are not native to this place. The American Carmelite poet Jessica Powers expresses this truth beautifully in a poem entitled *The Homecoming*:

The spirit, newly freed from earth,
Is all amazed at the surprise
Of her belonging: suddenly
As native to eternity
To see herself, to realize
The heritage that lets her be
At home where all this glory lies.

By naught foretold could she have guessed
Such welcome home: the robe, the ring,
Music and endless banqueting,
These people hers; this place of rest
Known, as of long remembering
Herself a child of God and pressed
With warm endearments to His breast. [386]

In the C19 a tourist from the United States of America visited the famous Polish rabbi Hafez Hayyim. The tourist was astonished to see that the rabbi's house was only a simple room filled with books. The only furniture was a table and a bench. 'Rabbi, where is your furniture?' asked the tourist. 'Where is yours?' replied Hafez. 'Mine? But I'm only a visitor here, I'm just passing through.' To which the rabbi replied, 'So am I.' [387]

---

[386] Regina Siegfried and Robert F Morneau (Eds), *Selected Poetry of Jessica Powers*, Sheed & Ward, Kansas City, MO, 1989, p.53.
[387] Christina Feldman and Jack Kornfield (Eds), *Stories of the Spirit, Stories of the Heart*, HarperSan Francisco, 1991, p.347.

THIRTY-THIRD SUNDAY IN ORDINARY TIME

(YEAR C)

'Your endurance will win you your lives.' (Lk21:19)

Despite the fact that nursery rhymes are traditional songs or poems taught to young children (in the nursery, presumably!), many of them are satirical commentaries on people or events of the time. We're all familiar with Jack and Jill who went up the hill to fetch a pail of water, and Georgie Porgie who kissed the girls and made them cry. Jack and Jill were not two individuals, but liquid measures. The jack was half a pint, and the jill (actually 'gill') was a quarter pint. When in the C17 King Charles I tried to reform taxes on liquid measures he met stiff opposition from parliament. In an attempt to circumvent this opposition the king decreed that the volume of a jack be reduced, but the tax was to remain the same. When the jack 'came tumbling down' the jill followed suit. Jack's 'breaking his crown' was an allusion to the fact that drinking glasses had a line to indicate the quantity of a jack. Above that line there was often a crown. Even today in Britain many pint glasses have a line marking the half pint level with a crown above it. So 'breaking the crown' refers to reducing the volume of the jack. And Georgie Porgie who kissed the girls and made them cry was the ever-so-naughty George Villiers (1592 – 1628), the first Duke of Buckingham and reputedly the 'handsomest-bodied man in all of England.' The nursery rhyme is a thinly veiled allusion to his sexual exploits.

All of this illustrates a simple point: There is no text without context. In other words, if we hope to understand any piece of writing, we have to appreciate the historical, social and cultural context in which it was written. Week after week we listen to readings from the Scriptures because we believe that these texts are maps for our own journey of faith. Sometimes the readings are clear and easy to understand; at other times they are difficult and obscure. In reading the Scriptures we are confronted with a fundamental difficulty. We are reading documents that are at least 2,000 years old, translated from other languages, and written in a culture that is fundamentally different from our own.

Keeping that in mind, consider the imagery of today's readings: 'The day is coming now, burning like a furnace,' the prophet Malachi tells us. And Jesus speaks of wars and revolutions, nation fighting against nation. 'There will be great earthquakes and plagues and famines here and there; there will be fearful sights and great signs from heaven.' Not an optimistic outlook! What is the message behind the doom and gloom?

This is an example of what is called apocalyptic writing. If we want to understand apocalyptic writing we need to study its context. Apocalyptic means literally 'to remove the veil' or 'to reveal.' It is as if the future is veiled from our sight, and apocalyptic writing seeks to reveal what lies ahead. Apocalyptic is not a literary form we are familiar with in contemporary English, but it flourished within Judaism in the two hundred years before Christ, and it was popular within the Christian church during the first one hundred years of the Christian era.

Apocalyptic literature is invariably addressed to communities in a state of crisis or persecution, and it seeks to offer hope and reassurance that all will be well. It also has its own distinctive features, its own set of symbols and images. It uses graphic imagery to engage the imagination. Its stock in trade imagery includes upheavals and calamities on a cosmic scale – wars, earthquakes, stars falling from heaven, darkness over the earth, and the moon turning to blood. It would be a mistake to interpret such imagery literally, and in this respect it has a good deal in common with the kind of art we know as surrealism. When we look at a painting by Salvador Dali, for example, one thing is very clear. This is not photo-realism. The artist is not presenting reality as the human eye sees it. The artist is painting reality as seen by an inner eye, as perceived by the imagination. One of his best known paintings is called *The Persistence of Memory*. The soft or melting clocks that are such a striking feature of this painting are challenging the assumption that time is rigid or deterministic.

What, then, is Luke's message in this gospel passage? Luke is warning his own community that they must endure opposition and persecution. But, he adds, stand firm; your endurance will win you your lives. You will be victorious. And how, we might ask, would that give a community hope and encouragement in the midst of persecution? Imagine a time during the Second World War when London was being bombed relentlessly night after night, and Hitler seemed invincible. If at such a moment someone were able to gaze into the future and show the citizens of London a vision of themselves after the war – a vision of themselves emerging victorious and the enemy defeated – that surely would give them hope and strengthen their determination to endure the present moment when things seem darkest. That's how apocalyptic writing functions. It offers hope when the present moment seems hopeless. To the persecuted community it says: In the face of aggression and seemingly invincible odds, when powerful forces are marshalled against you, victory is yours. Stand firm!

On a Saturday in 1884 Matt Talbot stood on one of the many Dublin bridges that cross the River Liffey. He was 28 years of age, and as he stared into the waters of the river he made a decision that changed his life forever. An alcoholic since he was twelve, Matt decided to stand up to the powerful force of his addiction. That bridge, linking Customs House quay on the north bank to City quay on the south bank is today called Talbot Memorial Bridge, and a statue of Matthew Talbot stands at the south end. On that day in 1884 he stood on the bridge in a state of despair. He was penniless and in a desperate state because he hadn't been able to find work that week. He waited outside his favourite pub in the hope of scrounging a drink from his friends, but all he met was refusal after refusal. His friends recall: 'Matthew lived for one thing only; to drink. He would have done any work at all to get money to drink.' [388] When he returned home that day he was sober, and after supper that evening he told his mother that he was going to take a vow that he would never drink again. But that led to a bitter interior struggle. 'He was hounded by a cruel craving produced by 16 years of an uncontrolled dominance of his body by wine, beer and port.' Matt Talbot's life is an eloquent witness to the message of apocalyptic writing. When powerful forces are marshalled against you, victory is yours through the power of God working powerfully within you. 'Your endurance will win you your lives.' [389]

---

[388] St Vincent de Paul Society, *The Venerable Matthew Talbot*, Petersham, Victoria 2007, p8.
[389] Ibid, p.12.

OUR LORD JESUS CHRIST, UNIVERSAL KING

(YEAR C)

'Today you will be with me in paradise.' (Lk 23:43)

When the Roman emperor Hadrian (76-138 AD) visited Athens he summoned into his presence the philosopher known as Secundus the Silent, for he wished to test the man to see whether or not he was really committed to silence. The emperor, himself a philosopher, greeted Secundus, but he maintained his customary silence. Then Hadrian said to him, 'Speak, philosopher, so we may come to know you. It is not possible to observe the wisdom in you when you say nothing.' Secundus remained silent. The emperor spoke again, 'Secundus, before I came to you it was a good thing for you to maintain silence, since you had no listener more distinguished than yourself, nor one who could converse with you on equal terms. But now I am here before you, and I demand it of you; speak out, bring forth your eloquence.' Secundus, unafraid of the emperor, said nothing. In frustration the emperor summoned the executioner. 'I do not want any man to live who refuses to speak to the emperor Hadrian.' But the emperor called the executioner aside privately and said to him, 'When you are leading the philosopher away, talk to him along the road and encourage him to speak. If you persuade him to make an answer, cut off his head; but if he does not answer, bring him back here unharmed.' Secundus remained silent and his life was spared. How he lived was how he was willing to die.[390]

'Today you will be with me in paradise.' Yet another outcast is welcomed into the Kingdom. How Jesus lived was how he died, welcoming the outsider. Throughout the entire ministry of Jesus, especially as it is recorded in the gospel of Luke, Jesus invites the outcast, the rejected, and the ostracised into the Kingdom of God. The lost sheep, the lost son, the ten lepers, Zacchaeus the tax collector, the despised Samaritans. Sunday after Sunday the gospel readings during this year

---

[390] I am indebted to John Shea (*The Relentless Widow: The Spiritual Wisdom of the Gospels for Christian Preachers and Teachers*, p.325) for the reference to Secundus the Silent, but my account of his interrogation comes from Ben Edwin Perry (Tr) *Life of Secundus the Philosopher,* http://www.mountainman.com.au/essenes/Life_of_Secundus_the_Philosopher.htm

have reminded us of Jesus' ministry to those who are lost. Now that Jesus has been lifted up on the cross, yet another lost one is welcomed into the Kingdom.

During the years between 1953 and 1962 Monsignor Loris Capovilla was personal secretary to Angelo Roncalli, then Cardinal Archbishop or Patriarch of Venice. In 1958 Angelo Roncalli was elected pope, taking the name John XXIII. Some years ago Mgr Capovilla was interviewed by *The Tablet*, and during the course of that interview he was asked if he recalled any incidents that revealed the character and spirituality of Angelo Roncalli.[391] There was one particular incident Capovilla singled out, and it occurred while the future pope was Patriarch of Venice.

When Roncalli was first appointed to Venice he expressed a wish to visit all the priests of his diocese. One particular priest whose name was Don Giovanni had become bitter and twisted. He lived in a retirement home, no longer celebrating Mass, nor reciting the Divine Office and he was often drunk. Roncalli was warned against visiting Don Giovanni. He was told that he would be met with savage abuse and caustic criticism. But Roncalli insisted, and went to visit the retirement home where Don Giovanni lived.

The old priest raged against bishops in general, against Roncalli's predecessor in particular, about the church at large, and about other priests. He was a bitter and disaffected man. Don Giovanni spoke vehemently about the injustices he believed he had suffered from those in authority. Roncalli let him go on and on without interruption. Finally, he put his arm around the old man's shoulder and said, 'Don Giovanni, we are both old men. And soon we will have to stand before the tribunal of God. What use is it to dwell on all these things? What use?'

Roncalli encouraged the man to make a new beginning, to start praying and celebrating Mass again. He then turned to Capovilla and said: 'Don Giovanni has lost his breviary. I want you to find another one and send it to him. And then I want you to arrange for a tailor to come here to measure him for a new cassock.' Roncalli then gave Don Giovanni 400 000 lire, the equivalent of about $400. Roncalli then left quite content. That evening Don Giovanni was playing cards with his friends in the retirement villa. 'This new cardinal is quite a good fellow,' he told them. And together they spent the entire gift of 400 000 lire drinking to Cardinal Roncalli's good health. Word spread quickly, and all the priests of Venice were greatly amused at Roncalli's naivety. How foolish Roncalli was, they said, to think he could visit Don Giovanni, slap him on the back, pay him a

---

[391] Louis Capovilla, 'Pope John and his Council', *The Tablet*, 7 November 1992, p.1391.

compliment, give him some money, and expect that to change his life.

Capovilla was upset by the whole incident and spoke his mind to Roncalli. The future Pope John XXIII responded quite simply:

Do you really think that I believed one visit would be enough to change that man's life? It wasn't to change his life that I went to see him, but to begin to take away the bitterness. If you can take away the bitterness, then maybe, later, his life will begin to change. But if you don't take away the bitterness, nothing else you do is of any worth.

Even from the cross Jesus reached out to the lost one, just as he had throughout his entire ministry. He sought to heal the bitterness of those rejected and ostracised by the orthodox religious establishment of his own day. The kingship of Jesus does not manifest itself in absolute power and authority. It is a kingship that lovingly searches for those who are lost.

BIBLIOGRAPHY

William Barclay, *The Gospel of Luke*, The Saint Andrew Press, Edinburgh, Reprinted 1971.
William J Bausch, *Storytelling: Imagination and Faith*, Twenty-Third Publications, Mystic, CT, 1984.
William J Bausch, *Telling Stories, Compelling Stories*, Twenty-Third Publications, Mystic, CT, 1991.
William J Bausch, *A World of Stories,* Twenty-third publications, Mystic, CT, 1998.
William J Bausch, *Touching the Heart*, Twenty-Third Publications, Mystic, CT, 2007.
William J Bausch, *Once Upon a Gospel*, Twenty-Third Publications, Mystic, CT, 2008.
Dianne Bergant, *Preaching the New Lectionary*, Year C, The Liturgical Press, Collegeville, MN, 2000.
Dietrich Bonhoeffer, *Life Together,* SCM Press, London, Seventh Impression, 1968.
Dietrich Bonhoeffer, *The Cost of Discipleship*, SCM Press, London, Third Impression, 2004.
Christopher Booker, *The Seven Basic Plots*, Continuum, London, 2004.
Marcus J Borg, *The Heart of Christianity*, HarperSan Francisco, 2003.
Raymond E Brown, Joseph A Fitzmyer, & Roland E Murphy (Eds) *The New Jerome Biblical Commentary*, Geoffrey Chapman, London, 1989.
Raymond E Brown, *The Birth of the Messiah*, Doubleday, New York, 1979.
Raymond E Brown, *The Death of the Messiah*, Volume 1, Doubleday, New York, 1993.
Brendan Byrne, *The Hospitality of God*, St Pauls Publications, Strathfield, NSW, 2000.
GB Caird, *St Luke*, Penguin Books, Harmondsworth, Middlesex, 1963.
FL Cross and EA Livingstone, *The Oxford Dictionary of the Christian Church*, Oxford University Press, Reprinted 1997.
Christina Feldman and Jack Kornfield (Eds), *Stories of the Spirit, Stories of the Heart,* HarperSan Francisco, 1991.
Joseph A Fitzmyer, *The Gospel According to Luke I-IX*, Doubleday, New York, 1979.
Joseph A Fitzmyer, *The Gospel According to Luke X-XXIV*, Doubleday, New York, 1985.
Christopher Jamison, *Finding Sanctuary*, Phoenix, London, 2007.
Luke Timothy Johnson, *The Gospel of Luke,* The Liturgical Press, Collegeville, MN, 1991.

Alan Jones, *Soul Making*, HarperSan Francisco, 1985.
Alan Jones, *Passion for Pilgrimage*, Morehouse Publishing, Harrisburg, PA, 1989.
Alan Jones, *Living the Truth*, Cowley Publications, Boston, MA, 2000.
Alan Jones, *The Soul's Journey*, Cowley Publications, Boston, MA, 2001.
John P Meier, *A Marginal Jew, Volume II: Mentor, Message, and Miracles*, Doubleday, New York, 1994.
John P Meier, *A Marginal Jew, Volume III: Companions and Competitors*, Doubleday, New York, 2001.
Thomas Merton, *The Silent Life*, Farrar Straus & Giroux, New York, 1957/1991.
Thomas Merton, *Disputed Questions*, A Harvest Book, San Diego, 1960.
Thomas Merton, *New Seeds of Contemplation*, Burns & Oates, London, Reprinted 2003.
Thomas Merton, *The Wisdom of the Desert*, Sheldon Press, London, 1974.
Thomas Merton, *Thoughts in Solitude*, Burns and Oates, London, Sixth Impression, 1991.
John Moses, *The Desert, An Anthology for Lent*, Canterbury Press, Norwich, 1997.
John J Pilch, *The Cultural world of Jesus: Sunday by Sunday, Cycle C*, The Liturgical Press, Collegeville, MN, 1997.
Ronald Rolheiser, *The Restless Heart*, Hodder & Stoughton, London, 1979.
Ronald Rolheiser, *Against an Infinite Horizon*, Hodder & Stoughton, London, 1995.
Ronald Rolheiser, *Seeking Spirituality*, Hodder & Stoughton, London, 1998.
Ronald Rolheiser, *Forgotten Among the Lilies*, Doubleday, New York, 2005.
John Shea, *Eating With the Bridegroom*, Liturgical Press, Collegeville, MN, 2005.
John Shea, *The Relentless Widow*, Liturgical Press, Collegeville, MN, 2006.
Tom Wright, *Luke for Everyone*, SPCK, London, 2001.
Philip Yancey, *Finding God in Unexpected Places*, Hodder & Stoughton, London, 1995.
Philip Yancey, *What's So Amazing About Grace*, Zondervan, Grand Rapids, MI, 1997.

www.ingramcontent.com/pod-product-compliance
Lightning Source LLC
Chambersburg PA
CBHW050903160426
43194CB00011B/2264